A Gathering of Angels

A Gathering

of

Angels

✝

by

Larry Dean Hamilton

Sigma Σ Logo™

Books e•books

A Gathering of Angels

Inquiries should be addressed to

Sigma$\sum$Logo™ Books
Sigma Logo Books, LLC
1801 7th Street, Suite 260
Bay City, Texas, USA 77414-5118
www.sigmalogobooks.com

First Edition

Cataloging-in-Publication Data

Hamilton, Larry Dean

A Gathering of Angels

p.   cm.

1. Homosexuality—History—20th Century. 2. Homosexuality—Discrimination.

3. Homosexuality—Civil rights. 4. Homosexuality—Religion. 5. Gays—Public Opinion.

6. Gay rights.

I. Title. II. Author.

ISBN 0-9754321-0-9 Hdk

ISBN 0-9754321-1-7 Ebook

HQ 76.8 U5   306.766 H 187

On the cover: Pencil sketch of the author by Jim Cozby, October 19, 1970. Used by permission of Larry Dean Hamilton.

Sigma, eighteenth letter of the Greek alphabet, is used symbolically to denote *standard deviation*. In notation, it represents *the sum of*.

Printed in the United States of America
at Morgan Printing in Austin, Texas.

About the author

Larry Dean Hamilton holds a Bachelor of Arts in English Literature from The University of Texas at Austin. Previously on the editorial staff of Time-Life Books, Larry was a key organizer and participant in Houston Gay Conference 1982. He led the way in establishing and organizing Matagorda County AIDS Awareness. Larry, a sometime poet, treks along a sandy shore, mindful of accumulated litter and debris—mindful of earlier footsteps.

Other books by the author

Poetry

Hotel Chelsea and The Sound

Late Autumn Debris:
The Vesey Street Poetry and
Twenty-third Street Poems

Love Is Orange

About the book

The events recounted in this book are true, and all characters are real persons. Names in some cases have been altered for privacy and other reasons obvious; time sequence, where appropriate, condensed to allow for more precise telling.

The Pink Triangle

Gay males in Nazi Germany were described as bent, slang for homosexual. Nazis, intolerant of homosexuals, incarcerated them in concentration camps. Gay males were made to wear a Pink Triangle on their prison stripes to identify their undesirable trait. The Pink Triangle, adopted following the Stonewall Riots as a symbol of Gay Liberation, recognizes our common humanity through brotherhood and our continuing shared struggle to overcome discrimination. It also signifies pride. We remember and pay homage to the many men who suffered atrocities of the Holocaust, the many who perished in forced labor and death camps. Few of their stories survive.

The triangle is used symbolically to represent the Trinity in Christian art. In primitive art, the triangle represents life.

Acknowledgments

Joan Dickerson showed that mere sexual preference is no cause for alarm; Gene H. LePere persevered throughout evolution and revision of this work; Joe C. Colvin kept me going through belief and continued support; Cheryl Stahle assisted with the manuscript; Gayle 'Birdie' Morris researched and critiqued; Hugh B. Jones gives reason to hope a kinder community can arise.

Jim, this book is for you.
We shared much, not enough,
finally too little.
I only wish, together,
we could share it now.

In Loving Memory —
JDH — 1944 – 1985
— LDH, October 19, 2003

Be not forgetful to entertain strangers:
for thereby some have entertained angels unawares.

—Hebrews 13:2

Contents

—————— Σ ——————

Foreword

The light shines in the darkness, but the darkness has not understood it.

–John 1:5.

What does it mean to be gay? I cannot answer that question. I cannot give the sense of meaning to a life's struggle for acceptance and belonging. I cannot describe feelings of rejection and hatred. I cannot tell of fear. I cannot speak of denial and discrimination. I cannot talk of loneliness and despair. I cannot relate the emptiness of being pushed outside the community of man, of being barred from God's loving embrace within the house that bears God's name. I am not gay. I am only a man, human, with all of the frailty, the shortcomings, the warts and the scars of my humanity.

What does it mean to be gay? Dean describes his journey of more than half a century, a journey that tells of his search for acceptance, for belonging—a search for love. His life is not a life I can easily understand. He takes me to places beyond my familiarity, a life that moves through the night while I and others are sleeping comfortably at home in our beds. His search introduces me to desires and situations outside the sphere of my knowledge.

Dean's experience *becomes* my experience—his experience is the human condition. We all search for those same things that have driven Dean's journey. Dean's story is the shared story of humanity, the need for inclusion, not exclusion; the need for acceptance, not rejection; the need for being embraced, not denied.

Dean searches for love, not lust, as he clearly distinguishes, "Love [is] the only thing I've found that seems worthwhile." Do we not all seek that human warmth discovered in an embrace? The level of intimacy of which Dean relates goes well beyond the sexual needs of the physical body. Dean's sense of love moves into the realm of the spiritual. It encompasses an intensity of passion usually associated with divine celebration. Dean's story reveals great personal sacrifice.

—————— Σ ——————

——————— Σ ———————

A Gathering of Angels finds its beginning in a park on a bright, sunny afternoon, awaiting the beginning of a march to protest lack of concern for gay men ravaged by the HIV virus. The men go about a routine familiar to all, talk of friends, recovery, loss, death—those same matters I weave through a daily schedule. I found myself mingling in the park, except the men Dean presents are ill, death a foregone conclusion. Is that any different from all of mankind? We are all dead at birth. The men Dean shows us are simply on a faster ticking clock. "It is deadly serious. People are dying." Dean relates, "I got a sense of oneness and brotherhood...feelings of deep joy...this is my community." I am shown a profound sense of community and purpose, a shared experience of pain, suffering and death within the gay community that cannot be understood by the rest of us.

Carried with Dean and men I do not know on a march of several miles under the hot Texas sun, I march with them into the night where they are funneled into a dark place. The rejected, the hated, the feared and despised suddenly take on human face as I watch savage bludgeoning conducted without mercy on a grassy lawn. Can this be Nazi Germany? I find I must remind myself these are gays in Houston. I find I must examine my own heart—is this the way *I* feel about *them?* How can I step back into my safe, comfortable world and sleep peacefully at night—my own young son, sweet child of my heart, could one day be found on that grassy lawn.

Dean tells of a young gay man he met. The two of them participate in a rally at the Free Speech Area three days later, culmination of the protest begun by the march. The two of them hold hands, look into one another's face. They are at a moment of choice—turn back and save themselves, or take a step forward, from which there is no turning back. "We may not this day walk beyond this field." How many of us find such a moment in our safe, comfortable lives? This is not Nazi Germany. These are gays in Houston. I think of my own home, where I double-check the door locks each evening to ensure safety for my family so that we may sleep peacefully and without fear. I do not know the feeling of having no place to call home, no place of safety and security. I do not know the feeling of being hunted by my own kind.

"What is there for me, one shunned as different? I am lost—totally, forever lost. Where can I find hope? How can I be loved?" I cannot miss the anguish of these words, the utter and complete longing for comfort. The search for love is a fundamental motivation shared by all. How crushing a

——————— Σ ———————

disappointment to recognize one is abandoned by the institution called to embody compassion—"robed in a guise of love." The Church did not invent love or compassion—these precious values of heaven drown in an earthly sea of fear. I reflect on the preaching of intolerance. The pulpit is built by men. It supports the weighty Word, but cannot endure the weighty mouth.

A Gathering of Angels is told plainly and simply, many of the stories simple and lovely. Dean displays candor and honesty in the telling of his journey through a long night on the ferry. "Still, it is a long night...we are each alone." The pages of Dean's life sparkle with light, images of hope he carries with him. His sense of love seems to have a brilliance of its own, a sense of love that is buoyed by innate faith in the eternal goodness of love and sustained by a vision of the profound nature of love. Jesus said, "I am the light of the world. Whoever follows me will never walk in darkness, but will have the light of life"–John 8:12. The search for intimacy, for life shared is the light we are drawn to, a moth on a summer night.

"I hurt more deeply than I ever imagined possible; my hurt, one of love. I couldn't conceive anything more human." There is *nothing* more human than the need for love. We must be careful how we read our Bibles, explore what scripture really says. Being gay is being a sinner–judgment by many. To the larger world, gays are all the same. What would Jesus do? In asking the question, we must be prepared to hear the answer. Jesus said, "This is my command: Love each other"–John 15:17. Jesus did not qualify the command; neither should we.

"Touching another's body I touch deeper need....The complete giving of oneself I've discovered tantamount to love. I've come to think giving is more significant than getting. That seems to me the path of intimacy." Dean's search is a healthy search. The goal is intimacy, not sex. To give more than to get is the antithesis of narcissism—it is the heart's desire. "More than all I want are three words, I love you." Surely this single statement eloquently expresses the longing of mankind!

"I like to think we could have made it had there been a scrap of paper other than [a] notebook kept day-to-day, his thoughts about us read to me on Friday nights...a scrap of paper we couldn't get in Hallmark." Marriage between same-sex partners is centerpiece on the political and social table at this time. Although attitudes seem to be changing in a difficult and gut-wrenching way for many, that scrap of paper was hardly possible

—————— Σ ——————

forty years ago. For most, it is still not possible. Desire for permanence is a commendable goal. Commitment within a relationship benefits from support within the community at large. Dean gives pause for reflection in his statement, "my gay self is denied celebration on the same altar at which non-gay celebrate." His meaning goes beyond need for acceptance and inclusion. To be denied the finest sacraments of society's most revered house dramatically underscores the prejudice which gays face.

Same-sex marriage is under debate in the Church arena as well, a key question being whether gay is an innate characteristic or an acquired one. Dean's story leaves little doubt for speculation. He did not choose to be "different." He struggled and longed to be "non-different." The need tears at the heart—it was not to be met within the larger community. The "question" should not be a question for debate. How can we, as a society professing to embody God's love, deny what isn't ours to give? How can we, as a society professing to embody the basic tenet *all men are created equal,* deny that most basic of Creation's gifts?

Dean in the telling of his story expresses a depth of love, a capacity for giving love and sharing love, reflective of the fullness of love expressed two thousand years ago, that of Jesus—poignantly related by John in his Gospel. In matters of the heart, there is only one dependable authority.

What does it mean to be gay? I cannot answer that question. I am not gay. Dean gives me a heartbreaking glimpse into what it has meant for him being gay. Many times in his story he relates of his tears falling. My own heart can vouch for that—my own heart is not set in cement. Dean gives me a courageous view of what it means to be human. Reading *A Gathering of Angels,* I feel more confident answering the question, what does it mean to be human. We must always remember—Jesus wept.

The Rev. Dr. Hugh B. Jones, Jr.
April 6, 2004

—————— Σ ——————

To the reader—

> We travel all night on the ferry,
> strangers on a journey—
> may your heart be opened.
>
> *— LDH*

We are dying

Meet the boys and girls from out of town tonight at Red Square. I was intrigued. Invitation to meet guys from out of town is invitation to adventure —chance to explore the unknown sets my foot on the path. I asked JC about Red Square. "Probably a bar," he shrugged. "Chasing whims is what gets you in trouble—it *keeps* you there, Baby Dean!"

JC did not share my eagerness—we have a history. He has to be cajoled. Later, he relishes the experience—telling and retelling for years. Today, he is given to abandon, carefree as a breeze—giddy. It is true, what he said of me, my whimsical nature—I keep spontaneity in my hip pocket.

ACT-UP hosted the hospitality event at Red Square—safe environment following the AIDS march, set to begin shortly. JC and I strolled along Fannin Street in Houston's Hermann Park, awaiting signal. We arrived early—JC needed no additional nudge. His enthusiasm mounted for days. He was effervescent—a holiday rocket exploding.

"This is my first," he kept reminding me. "I had a *real* job—I *had* to be discreet. You traipsed about—Baby Dean, the militant queer!" He mused, grinning. "Have you *ever* had a real job—Baby Dean, the interviewer's nightmare. *Previous Experience—Fantastic Faggot! Career Queer!*"

JC delighted himself—I said he was giddy. Envious of my free spirit, he takes great care to introduce me, his "friend who dropped out of college and ran away to New York to become a hippie!" I usually play back to him, except today my attention is focused on activity building in the park.

The Republican National Convention convening in Houston is poised to set George Bush campaigning for a second term in the White House—gays have no place at *his* table. JC keeps himself informed on matters of public policy. My dislike stems from the Bush stance on homosexuality—debate, no debate. To what esteem I am held is long a sore spot—I determine not to sit at the back of the bus.

——————— Σ ———————

The face of God shone brightly, the air hot and humid under a clear sky—typical of a summer afternoon in Houston. The park bustles, people streaming into the area, more coming. I want to cruise the crowd, especially on the prowl for a guy I met the previous afternoon at an Episcopal Church. The boy—tall and slender with mellow brown eyes—was young and good-looking. He seemed a little self-conscious—somewhat reserved. A spark *somewhat* leaped between us. A little *self-conscious* picking him up at a church social, I invited him to the upcoming march. It was a social thing I did, one of civility—less cleric, more lay. He *somewhat* accepted my invitation—others from the Church planning to march as well. "Great!" I said, not at all *self-consciously,* "I'll see you there, okay?"

JC attends the Church. He has a house in Montrose, Houston's gay mecca near downtown. The burgeoning gay ghetto centers on the intersection of Montrose Boulevard and Westheimer. My first encounter with Westheimer came during the mid-sixties when it was a mecca for coffeehouses. I occasionally found my way there for guitar ballads and local folk singers. The mystique of Montrose wafted even then—perfume of promise.

JC's Church is not exactly Montrose, being in a nearby area adjacent Rice University—academia blends well with Montrose. The Church Rector, a caring woman herself non-gay, opens the rectory Sunday afternoons to members of her parish—a setting somewhat social within shadow of the Christian chapel. "It's upbeat, a good place to meet nice people," JC insisted, "better than the alternative—a gay bar."

Nice people did meet that afternoon, gay and lesbian, of various ages. I was easily welcome, the group warm and friendly. I sensed in them—including the guy I met—a feeling of stiffness. He seemed ill at ease with his sexuality within religious confines—standing outside the door of church doctrine, a thief in the master's house. I did not feel entirely comfortable, having nothing to do with either my sexuality or God. My unease drew from knowing homosexuality is not sanctioned by the Episcopal Church—not officially. Episcopal is no different than other mainstream denominations—my gay self is denied celebration on the same altar at which non-gay celebrate. I get a hollow feeling being fed at the back door.

I drove to Houston from Bay Prairie where I was living—resigned to living. JC invited me for the week. Keen on politics, he was eager to protest the Bush White House, eager to join the AIDS march. Democratically

———————— Σ ————————

engaged, JC wanted the Bush Republicans disengaged. He had never picked up a sword to draw a line in the sand, gay territory having been gained scrap by scrap. Partly, he wanted to own the experience, a sixties-type march, feeling he could now do so without fear of recrimination—protest demonstrations by longevity having achieved legitimacy. I alerted him to reality. "JC, this is not for fun, it's serious stuff. People are suffering, they're hurting. In the process speaking out, they sometimes get hurt." JC was giddy.

"Dizzy," Carl said of him a previous evening. "JC, you're as dizzy as ever." Carl and his longtime lover, Mark, share a home in Montrose. JC and I stopped for a visit, inviting them to join us for dinner. They declined, preferring quality time at home together, Mark with a diagnosis of HIV-positive. Mark recently converted a potting shed back of the house to install a hot-tub, doing most of the work himself. He led me out back for a look, beaming to show off the result—a cozy, intimate escape. He set about adjusting valves and gauges, inviting me to share the hot-tub.

Let me set this straight. There was nothing about the situation sexual. Sharing a hot-tub is much like sharing a warm, secure friendship—intimacy is shared nakedness. Carl and Mark, each what I call a sweetheart of a guy, are real angels. Some years previous, a time when I was young, my life going nowhere but down the tubes, Carl was a real angel for me. Despite that, my old-fashioned, prim and proper morals don't rear themselves between lovers—especially lovers also friends. Carl may have known my nature. He wasn't disturbed Mark took me to the potting shed alone. The reason likely has to do with what Carl and Mark share within their relationship—trust. I wanted to share Mark's tub that night—JC and I had dinner plans. I promised Mark to return—I had the whole week in town. I didn't foresee a larger pool into which I'd plunge.

Hermann Park is a sprawling expanse of green south of downtown, some of it preserving a vestige of natural. The greenbelt partially surrounds Houston's Medical Center, through which Fannin—a major thoroughfare leading from downtown—cuts a swath. The march will also cut through this glass-and-chrome miracle of modern science, a vast complex on the cutting edge of medical technology—itself head-to-head on the cutting edge with a tiny but deadly, ancient and all-but-unknown foe, the HIV virus.

Orchestrated by a national coalition ACT-UP, the march aims to keep public attention focused. The holocaust set loose first on gay men still

———— Σ ————

devastates, unchecked, our ranks; genocidal policies set in place by the Bush White House, unchecked, still denies desperately needed help. The President's attitude, reflective of his party, resurrected a well-beaten dog—queers are dispensable. Lack of commitment in the Bush White House extends to lack of care, lack of concern, lack of compassion. Commitment is not lacking within the gay community—death hovers, anxiety broods, fear grips, grief anguishes, frustration weeps. *We are dying!*

Crazed with a taste for victory, the nation's Republicans are converged on Houston to launch a whitewashed White House bid to grab four more years. Tension is high, disease ravages—George Bush does not want in-your-face confrontation to mar his supreme moment. *We are dying!*

The march is set to begin mid-afternoon and arrive at Houston's Astrodome early in the evening—timed to coincide with opening ceremony calling the convention to order. The march is long, extending some miles, ending—I think—on public access grounds. Across Kirby opposite the Dome, a grassy meadow designated Free Speech area is set aside for groups and individuals opting to do just that—exercise constitutional right of free speech. This, the only place for curious onlooker and passive bystander and any other wayward to stand and gawk or wave and cheer, the only place open to a general public—only proper credentials gain entry into the convention. Security is tight—this is no afternoon church social.

Gay organizers at the last minute obtained the required parade permit, granted by the city—with little doubt it first met White House approval. Protestors are in Houston, demonstrations certain—uncertainty merely a question *legally* or *illegally*. Early on, application for a permit was approved. In sudden about-face, approval was withdrawn, the application denied. At the eleventh hour, the permit was issued—reason for the turnaround, something I never knew. It is hardly a puzzle. The Bush White House could ill afford to ignore public pressure demanding the march; a campaigning George Bush could ill afford to suppress the march; were permit to march denied, all hell would break loose on the streets of Houston.

Many people gather in the park, still more coming—gays and lesbians, queers and dykes, young and old and everywhere in-between. The park is a sea of beautiful humanity, men and women as vividly diverse as the rainbow colors worn by some and the acronyms worn by many. ACT-UP, NOW, Queer Nation, Radical Faeries—we are a people well represented.

——————— Σ ———————

Today is no celebration. It is deadly serious, people in diverse places dying. Many men gathered in the park are extremely sick, some barely able to stand unaided. All share bodies ravaged in one way or another by the disease—share the burden of failing flesh, share the task of holding fast. I glimpse in them strength I'm not sure my body holds.

Signal to begin the march had yet to be called when HPD mounted officers appeared on Fannin, coming from the vicinity of the Medical Center. Two dozen or so strong, the troop eased single-file up the street, halting opposite the park. They sat patiently atop steeds. Expressions I glimpsed, leers and grins, a face turned from view to laugh, gave me a sense we in the park are little more than amusement at their whim.

I mentioned to JC presence of mounted officers. "Strictly routine," he assured me. "Houston's come a long way, Baby Dean, very liberal. Gays have tolerance and acceptance—no one worries about such nonsense. It's history, very sixties—like you!" I doubt I looked convinced. "Besides," he added, "Houston is not going to let anything ugly happen. The city is in the spotlight, media attention all week—the entire country, the whole world watching. Houston has come a long way, Baby Dean!"

It isn't what I wanted to hear. JC is often given to exaggeration, as times he extolls my supposed history of marches and demonstrations. True, I participated in some living in New York. Later, from Bay Prairie, I made a point of driving to Houston in 1978 to march in Houston's first Gay Pride Parade. We began at the Exile, a cruise-bar on Bell Street downtown. Gays and lesbians took to the street hand-in-hand—we marched gaily forward. We may have had no permit—we had fear. We may have had no right—we had each other. We may have had no glitter—we had pride, dignity. I still hear my heart pounding wildly. That day, I *felt* the meaning of gay. I consider myself a Gay Libber, proud to wear a Pink Triangle. I may be classified local agitator, never classed with a larger league, activist. JC portrays me larger than life. This march set to begin is the largest of which I've been part.

I had yet to meet the gay Christian. JC encountered a couple of guys from the Church. They aren't staying for the march, only came to the park for a firsthand look. They made no excuse. Word spread throughout Montrose warned Houston gays to stay away—there would be trouble.

"Word from who?" I demanded to know. "Trouble from where?" JC didn't bother to ask those questions—a Republican scare tactic, he assured

———————— Σ ————————

me, aimed at keeping Houston's gay population away from the march, preventing their numbers from swelling the ranks. "All eyes are on Houston this week," he reminded me, "Houston is putting her best foot forward!"

I should not have listened to JC. He was giddy, flushed with excitement. I too was lightheaded. I got a feeling of belonging, rekindling in me a sense of oneness and brotherhood. I experienced feelings of deep joy I'd not for sometime felt, not felt since the sixties. These are my boys, bodies broken, spirits not crushed. I belong to them. I belong here, among them. This is my community. Sense of that fills me with pride and awe. I will go with my boys down the street wherever it leads, however far. I will go with them any distance, to any end, even the edge of darkness. I can do no other; without them, there is no place for me to go.

JC began to fret, disappointed his Church abandoned him and disappointed his city turned away—such abstractions he personalizes. "No one came today," he bemoaned, "not one—not a single face. Who can Houston queers expect ever again to stand up for them? Oh, Baby Dean, this is a sad day—a sad, sad day for Houston!"

A mood altogether mellow can describe the scene, mounted officers facing the park, sometimes calming a fretful steed; a sprawling mass of humanity lounging in the park, some sitting, others prone on the grass—a scene Matisse may have painted. There is anticipation, no agitation. Men discuss daily affairs, reacquainting old friendships, meeting new; inquiring of others left behind; bringing up-to-date the history of relationships, new formed and old broken; the comings and goings of daily life, of rally and recovery, of loss, of death. Our record descends from ancient time, a history passed word of mouth—the myths and the legends of our conquests and our disasters, of our exploits and our deeds; the memory of our faces, the knowledge of our names; the victories of our love, heartaches of our pain; kept alive, set to history on the tongues of traveling poets and bards.

Organizers of the march make continued sweeps, warning protestors, "keep off the street, stay in the park, do not step off the curb, do not go into the street, stay in the park." The march is to be peaceable, guided not by guerrilla warfare tactic. Protestors seek to have their voice heard through accepted means. A tense political climate is explosive, a tinderbox needing but a spark. Concern for bodily safety of protestors, concern for their safety on city streets and in public places, especially gay places, comes not from

———————— Σ ————————

law enforcement but from gay leadership. Sickness from the disease intolerance spread, a pandemic outbreak of fear—protestors can find themselves in peril from their own brothers.

ACLU volunteers meet in small groups with protestors, giving crash-course instruction on personal conduct. If arrested, do not resist. If met with physical violence in a situation of imminent bodily danger, fall to the ground and curl in a ball; use hands, arms and legs to protect head and vital organs. Instruction on dealing with hecklers is given, anti-demonstration groups said to be in place along the parade route. ACLU local hotline numbers are provided, protestors given a special ACLU code, prearranged with HPD, identifying an individual under ACLU protection. Marchers are warned not to leave the street once the march begins, not to go onto the sidewalk, not to engage bystanders in discourse of any sort under any circumstance. Bottled water will be provided during the march. Mounted officers will escort for safety. Neutral observers and ACLU members—both, clearly and visibly identified—will circulate through the ranks during the march. Camcorders will videotape the entire march. The march will be non-violent; trouble will not come from marchers. Stay with the march; stay in the street; avoid discussion with anyone, especially police; in the event of a problem, get the nearest ACLU volunteer. Don't hesitate—act quickly!

Mood in the park changed to one of readiness, a heightened sense of awareness—an event in the making about to unfold.

Word came. A cadence of drums cracked the air. Mounted officers stiffened to alert. Four horsemen moved to the lead. Protestors streamed onto the street. Row upon row file abreast the width of Fannin—more coming. Horsemen flank the marchers. Banners are unfurled, death flags raised. A chant rises under the bright Texas sky—the march begins.

Fight Back, Fight AIDS, Act Up! Fight Back, Fight AIDS, Act Up!

JC and I march near the front of the parade. I wore a pair of new shoes bought earlier in the day—unwisely opting for a smaller size. My feet are in pain. I will be nearly crippled before the march reaches its goal. I look back several times toward the park. There are too many rows of marchers for me to see clearly. I glimpse protestors still moving onto the street. What earlier may have seemed a ragtag band forms a well-ordered army, an army without shining uniform—one of misfit and degenerate; one of gaunt limb and sunken cheek; one of suffering, one of pain; an army that marches not on its belly, an army that marches with death; yet, an army that marches with a single voice, strong and clear under a late-day Texas sun.

Fight Back, Fight AIDS, Act Up! Fight Back, Fight AIDS, Act Up!

Fannin lined with onlookers. People gave little reaction, their faces showing confusion. They may have been sympathetic; simply, it could be they were stunned—Houston had never witnessed such an event. Nearing the Medical Center, crowds became larger, still showing no reaction. I look again across our ranks, the march stretching up the street far behind. I get a sense we are on our own, cut off from the park, cut off at the umbilical; we, no longer connected to the earth, moving onto a street become now a river; moving onto a page of history, moving beyond, moving to a larger realm; we, the ones someday spoken of through praise and in song.

At prearranged locations, bottled water quickly handed to marchers is passed among us. ACLU volunteers and neutral observers move through the ranks, identification badges prominent. The summer sun is hot and the march moves steadily, a cadence of drums sharp in the air. A horseman flanking on my right holds his steed to our pace. I glance at him from time to time, his demeanor calm and relaxed. I can't see his face clearly. He seems to smile, possibly relieved it is him riding and me walking. I get a feeling with this horseman nearby, one more of assurance than mistrust, glad he is on duty and glad Houston cares enough to send their best. I may have tired from physical exertion—I lowered my guard.

Fight Back, Fight AIDS, Act Up! Fight Back, Fight AIDS, Act Up!

In the deep gorge cutting through the Medical Center, crowds lining the street become large. Caught between towering walls, the words of our voice bounce and boom, echo to heaven,

Fight Back, Fight AIDS, Act Up! Fight Back, Fight AIDS, Act Up!

Suddenly, cheers from the sidewalks, from open windows and low rooftops greet us. Medical professionals, hands held high, applaud. Waving and whistling, smiling, they cheer us on.

Fight Back, Fight AIDS, Act Up! Fight Back, Fight AIDS, Act Up!

My heart leaped! Men and women who face with a clinical face that which we face with a nameless face, know our fear and frustration, know our pain and grief. They who know our reason, who know our need, cheer us on.

Fight Back, Fight AIDS, Act Up! Fight Back, Fight AIDS, Act Up!

Through the Medical Center we march and through the Medical

————— Σ —————

Center we are cheered and through the Medical Center applause continues, echoing behind us in a cadence of drums. I think of Jim, lost in the early days of the war; Jim, who I let go alone, for whom I never wept. Tears finally begin, roll down stinging cheeks; tears, not stop this day, not stop this night.

Fight Back, Fight AIDS, Act Up! Fight Back, Fight AIDS, Act Up!

Beyond the Medical Center, not yet in sight of the Dome, we march through a derelict area shabby and deserted, one harboring unkempt quick-stop shops and darkened buildings, boarded up and empty. Day is fading. Few bystanders wait in this wasteland. We encounter hecklers, cowering in twilight, amid rubble near the outskirts of town. Bible in hand, they preach God's love is hatred—AIDS, his punishment. We chastise. *Shame on you! Shame! Shame! Shame!*

On we march in failing light, urged by an ever-present cadence of drums, spirits high. Weary and tired, men barely able to continue lean on a friend and brother. My feet are nearly crippled. I still cannot see the Dome. Our voice commands the air.

Fight Back, Fight AIDS, Act Up! Fight Back, Fight AIDS, Act Up!

The four horsemen lead us from Fannin onto a lesser street curving to the right. We pass near the Blood Center. I wonder why the march left Fannin, a street leading to the Dome. On we march, curving with the street, led onto a still lesser street. I wonder why I cannot see the Dome. On we are led down a narrow street, led now in darkness. I wonder why I cannot see light. On we are led, past a grassy lawn; turned into a narrow alley; funneled alongside a concrete wall; squeezed against a chainlink fence; brought to a halt at wooden barricades hidden from light. Darkness fell.

JC and I stand against the barricade, marchers behind pushing forward. This darkened place is no public place, no Free Speech area. Beyond the barricade, large steel doors provide service access to the Dome. Dark vans and enclosed trucks, some with identifying marks, are partly hidden. Mounted officers who guided and protected maneuver their steeds past us to the barricade. Waiting officers swing the wooden beams enough to allow the horsemen entry, then return them to place. This happened carefully and deliberately, in silence.

A hush fell over us, confusion. In the quiet of confusion, a rustling sound came from inside the barricade, and another sound, one more a clickety-clickety-clatter. Mounted horsemen, rigid and disciplined, emerge

——————— Σ ———————

from shadows in darkness. Well-formed, they are commanded by one who gives the appearance of a general. He leads them forward, halts them against the barricade, facing us across wooden beams. Behind the horsemen, troops on foot march forward. They are dressed all in black, wear heavy boots and thick gloves. Their faces are hidden behind thick shields that extend to cover breast. They do not look human. They are many—they are legion.

The black army behind the barricade in position before us, the general high atop his horse at the head—we were tricked by a wooden horse. Men push forward crushing against the barricade in an effort to hold a rally. Placards, including posters of George Bush, are piled before the barricade and set afire. Chants sound. Demands are shouted. The Death Flag, a facsimile of the US flag having skulls and crossbones for stars with blood dripping across black stripes, is held above the fire. Ignited, it burns. Flames rise high. Protestors press forward, eager to fuel the fire with our symbols of oppression. Anger is erupting. Something on the brink is happening.

George Bush does not want his hands dirtied! We are dying!

An empty water bottle tossed toward the fire sails through the night darkness, flung from the crush of men behind JC and me. It skips across the fire. The general's arm begins a slow arc from his side, riot stick in hand. His stiff arm in a rearward motion begins to rise, a motion I perceive will terminate above his head, the stick leading forward. I grip JC's arm, "We'd better step back from here." Caught in the excitement, he makes no move to retreat, having no belief that what may happen can happen. I dig fingers into flesh and spin him round, "Move, JC! Now!" The riot stick reaches an apex above the general's head. A terrible, terrible sound barks through darkness. *Charge!*

I drag JC along the chainlink fence to a corner opening onto the grassy lawn. We hardly turn the corner before horses jump the barricade onto protestors and plough through them. Well-trained riot sticks seek their mark and find it, foot troops close at their heels. Horsemen plunge forward at great speed, knocking protestors to the ground. Horses race across the grassy lawn in pursuit of those seeking escape. The general shouts, "Go for the cameras! Get the film! Knock out those damned cameras!"

JC breaks into a dead run across the grassy lawn. From above, I see my body running wildly in front of me. I, in time that moves slower than that of events proceeding around me, look down on a scene unfolding.

———— Σ ————

Horses bound forward on either side of my body, felling marchers. Riot sticks split the air, a loud crack against skull, a dull thud against flesh. Screams thicken the night. Cries and yelps follow; then, moans; now, groans. Bodies litter the grassy lawn. ACLU members holding forth identification are struck; neutral observers demanding neutrality, beaten; a woman holding a camcorder is whacked atop the head, her camera demolished.

The legion comes quickly, a dark force, manner grim. They set about their work methodically. They bludgeon the boys on the ground. I see this clearly, from above, from behind my body running wildly across the grassy lawn. Boys felled to the ground, begging for mercy, bludgeoned; boys pleading, arms upstretched, bludgeoned; boys crying out where they lay helpless, bludgeoned; a slaughter of seal pups—bludgeoned.

Man in his darkest of thought, thought too dark to name, revealed; in his heart, darkness; his final solution, extermination. How can the mind react, the heart respond? What word to describe such evil, what deed to cleanse? Bludgeoned. What path this way led? *Bludgeoned!*

——————— Σ ———————

Σ

You're not wanted

Alone, unable to connect, I felt like a jerk, haunting local drive-in hangouts. Two holiday weeks passed suddenly, the promise of high hopes now vapor. I was lost, no longer part of a familiar crowd—a college guy is supposed to have fun. What is there to do in Bay Prairie? Drive. Drive on. Drive away.

Excuses are cliché; the truth, awful. A chance lottery, birth, thrust us together. The thought is hideous—they were never friends. I'm not a good liar, no good masking feelings. The roller-coaster fall in my voice betrays.

I made myself a prisoner on the road, traveling to the coast two of every three weekends. I'd be fretful for days—disappointment angered. I felt stretched on a high wire, my life a catch trap, no net below. I was all too aware—my balance was not improving.

Branded an outcast, made to feel the pariah, I was not chosen or chosen last—chosen last bruised more deeply. Slowly and finally standing alone became harsh judgment, a glaring announcement, *You're not wanted!*

Drive. Drive on. I kept driving until there was no further place to go. Along a desolate ribbon of sand stretching forever, reaching nowhere, gulf waters churned. In darkness, I gave in to anger, flushed with a feeling of anguish I couldn't comprehend. Cased in heavy damp my body trembled. Across the sea's cold vastness I felt my emptiness naked. I spiraled into a bleak orbit, majestic mystery.

Somewhere, deep in the far spinning of time, a star exploded, another world arbitrarily ended. There would be fewer weekend trips. What awaited at the distant end of this highway, distasteful though it might be, was preferable to misery in Bay Prairie. This chapter done, the final episode inked, the book closed. Bitter tears mingled with salt from the sea.

I remember things done to me by classmates, a dead snake coiled under the clutch pedal of my '50 Chevy. Leaving the school parking area I suddenly saw the damned thing. I panicked, leaping from the car onto the

———— Σ ————

pavement. My old jalopy continued without me. It crossed the highway and stalled nose-down in a ditch.

Sophomore year the boys nicknamed me Jack-off Mouth-whore Queer. Aloud in class, in front of everyone, they called me J-O-M-W-Q. After three days of guffawing, the chemistry teacher demanded meaning of the acronym. I sat red-faced, all eyes on me, refusing to answer—the boys snickered and snorted, making loud sucking noises from their mouths.

The most biting memory is rejection I felt being excluded by the other boys. Always left out, at any opportunity I was reminded, sometimes forcibly, I was not one of them, not one of the guys. On a weekend field trip, kicked to the floor of the vehicle, I was stomped into submission. Pinned facedown beneath boots, I was forced to ride for hours cramped against the floor breathing exhaust fumes—I had asked to sit by the window.

On a Future Farmers summer camping trip to a national forest, I conceived a glorious bonfire—envisioned to supremely crown our last night. Park Rangers agreed, with the proviso that no living tree be cut. "Scour the woods," one of the rangers told me, "there's plenty of deadwood laying about. You'll need a mighty sharp axe if you expect to cut it."

I chopped and hacked logs deep in the forest and hauled wood by hand for days. Early the following morning I made sure the stack was neat in ready, then hiked to the Ranger Station. Shortly before noon I returned to camp, stunned to find the pile ablaze. My campmates stood smugly around leaping flames, highly satisfied. They laughed at me while it burned. It was mean, a senseless act. Once again, they cast me aside. I searched faces behind leers and grins. I was saddened, they were unwilling to let me share. I retreated to the silent forest, buoyed by stillness in which I hid. I couldn't escape a feeling—I was being cheated.

Taste for suffering and desire for punishment didn't keep me at their heels, trying and trying again. I wanted to be accepted, to belong. I was easy prey, my skinny body outmatched. I didn't possess the physical strength and coordination their competitive edge demanded. I didn't like being pushed to that edge. My needs dictate a gentle response, skill the other boys lacked—they were not equipped to function on my terrain.

I felt more than loneliness. I felt desolation cut off from others—a feeling of desperation, never belonging. Underneath lurked fear, somehow I was different. I grew from childhood in the shadow of that doubt. In

———— Σ ————

childhood I met the beast. In childhood, impoverished and ashamed, I died.

The cry rose with a shout on the playground , my crime proclaimed in a din. "Those are *girl's* shoes! *Sis-sy...sis-sy...!*"

Suddenly, I was singled out. The boys formed a ring around me, prancing in mock attack, skip-dancing the awful chant, *Sis-sy!...sis-sy...!* The words stung. Judged and found lacking, the unfit are excised. Crisscrossing forefingers slashed at me, *Shame! Shame!*

My cheeks flamed. Fear collided with panic. Tightness seized my gut, wrenched at my throat, squeezing for the cry I choked back. I wanted to run, desperate to flee the accusatory noise. The ring widened two, then three circles deep. It closed around me, suffocating escape. Within, there was no place to hide. The ring narrowed, the game not a game—I was the sacrifice.

Was I different? The prospect didn't occur to me until this autumn morning. Six years old in second grade, I thought I'd gotten anxiety under control. I was timid and shy, a nervous bent, described as sensitive—some boys are turned that way. It wasn't school that tested me. My confidence faltered face-to-face with other kids. They terrified me—especially boys.

From early age I sensed inability to measure up, whatever that means. Irrational, an inborn fear; primordial, a primary dictate; it imparted no recognition. My timidity with its concomitant fear should not be surprising, should with high probability be anticipated. The place where my childhood idled, rural in nature, was isolated in essence.

I do not come from advantage. I was a war baby, born between the invasion at Normandy Beach and the bombing of Japan. Hiroshima, Nagasaki and *The Enola Gay* were history before I was a year old. War brought hard times atop lingering reminders of economic depression— deprivation was as much legacy as lesson. Work tempered with thrift was my spoon. Honest though it was, it left little time to challenge or to chance.

War was a provider, bringing urgent need for Texas crude. Japan's surrender did more than end the fighting—it set off a petrochemical boom. Construction jobs with badly needed paychecks spawned a blue-collar army and my dad joined the ranks. He was gone before sunrise, not home until well after dark. He regarded the job a necessary evil. It continued to remain secondary, the farm always first.

I had no community. Any semblance centered on a general store, the Baptist Church, and U.S. Post Office, scattered the length of a country

———— Σ ————

mile. The post office typified my ambivalence, its refuge a crusty building that sometime ago ceased selling gasoline and oil. Prominent on a rusting shield overhead, a flying red horse looked as though it had been snared.

The near part of the world surrounding me had no wings—it was altogether practical. The shoes that caused my scorn—barely scuffed and bound to fit—a cousin outgrew. They came to me an early summer's day, hand-me-downs amid the shelling of black-eyed peas.

Leather sandals, flat sole and open toe, a strap buckled around the ankle, a wide band perforated with pinwheels arching the foot—I was skeptical. "Aren't those girl's shoes?" I fretted.

"With socks," I was told, "no one will notice!" That settled it—they were indistinguishable from boy's sandals *except* for being *white!*

They *were* smart shoes—I was proud of them. What I didn't realize dressing for school that September morning was my bad choice selecting socks—brown argyle was not camouflage.

Inside the narrowing ring I felt helpless being set upon. Images grazed my mind, a savage taste purged my mouth. I was urged by a blind mechanism, rage. Knowledge of death struggle is imprinted—permanent, within genetic makeup.

Reeling in confusion amid dust and noise, I slammed my body into the circling ranks, hitting full force, arms flailing. My spinning momentum broke free. The ordeal at last over, its aftermath blurred. What has remained with me does not blur.

Sissy! Girl-boy! Limp-wrist! I was never allowed to overcome lack of skill and prowess on the playing field. That was a large part of it, physical attitude. Inside me was another attitude, equally large—I did not care to compete within that arena.

Spring of my final year in junior high, a voice cracked loudly across the baseball diamond. I was sure the entire world heard. "He can't *pitch,* he *throws* the ball—*like a girl!*"

I was angry, my face flushed. I couldn't win alongside the other boys and I couldn't win competing against them—they wouldn't even let me lose fairly. I tossed a wild ball broken-wrist over my head. The ball crazily lobbed somewhere near home plate, sending startled players scrambling. I walked off the field amid touts of *Quitter!* I didn't look back. Doing so would have been defeat. I admitted to myself I could never be like other boys. Through

———————— Σ ————————

that act I leaped a first great hurdle—fear of being different. Loss of fear is not defeat—it is the window through which I reach for identity.

No single incident can deserve credit or take blame. Whether one is or might be different remains, like those shoes, a matter of context. The most lasting of damage was done to my classmates. Through the years that followed, as I struggled to gain acceptance, I struggled for something more. I struggled for return to them something they had lost—my trust.

* * * * *

Vandal Lake, once a railhead shipping longhorns, was little more than the public school I attended, it's biggest attraction, cheaper rent. I envied boys living in Vandal Lake, their lives appearing more normal than mine. They rode bikes in neighborhoods and palled with other guys.

Vandal Lake's single campus, like one-room schools it consolidated, remained small. My graduating class stood twenty-five from a school of ninety-four. Such numbers don't justify curriculum outside the basic—a compelling disadvantage. I found nothing beyond the school band to stir creative imagination.

I was no athlete. Chance to pursue other interest better suiting was limited. Little opportunity for contact with others whose temperament, like my own, was slightly bent precluded blending within a larger fabric.

Seven miles beyond Vandal Lake was a larger fabric—Bay Prairie, a thriving town, everything Vandal Lake was not. Transfer between schools was not an option—Bay Prairie wanted nothing to do with Vandal Lake. Hostility was more than school rivalry. From Bay Prairie, we were looked down on in Vandal Lake.

I passed through Vandal Lake an outsider, developing ability to move among cliques and groups. I drifted into one and faded from another as agile as a weaver. I perceived my life nothing more than a thread shuttling back and forth on a loom. I was tolerated on those terms without ever belonging. In masterful irony, senior year my classmates elected me class president and their favorite boy. I've never been sure whether it was final mockery or sublime apology.

I was not awash with popularity, especially with girls. I didn't have a particular disliking for them. We tended, rather easily, to become buddies, great pals. Girls didn't turn me on sexually. I didn't get from being near them a thrill I found exciting in boys. Dating girls was not my idea of fun. I

———————— Σ ————————

was ill at ease and felt awkward those times I was pushed into a date.

My boldest adventure in the dating game courted disaster. I asked a girl from Bay Prairie one Saturday evening to a movie. I picked her up and fumbled with the car door, all but closing it on her ruffled skirt. Barely away from her parents' curb, my grip on the steering wheel tightened with clammy palms—she slid across the seat toward me. Though Bay Prairie had all of two movie houses, it became a big deal when she asked me what was showing—I hadn't the least idea.

"Gee, I don't know," I said nervously, afraid to take my eyes from the street. "I'll drive around the block, we c'n see what they offer."

I wasn't a cool guy. Intently reading the marquee at the first theater, I veered my car into the opposite lane of traffic. She yelled loudly and startled me. We were aligned for a head-on crash and I froze at the wheel. She pounced on me to take control, whipping us from the path of danger. Tires squealed and horns blared—there was no saving face. I wanted to die. Really, I wanted to shove her out the door and speed away into the night!

The near-catastrophe fairly ended my career at dating without my ever having fallen in love—at best, never having become emotionally stricken. With present vision, it is a certainty my failure as a teenage lover did not blossom overnight.

In third grade I *did* develop a blushing crush on Eileen—all the third-grade boys had a crush on her. Eileen was easily the prettiest girl in class. I must be careful. My pre-adolescent feelings, though sincere, totally objectify her. She was the prize, a doll to be won and worshiped.

Isn't that the plan? Meet a beautiful girl and fall in love? Get married—thence go thither down yon blissful path of life?

For some gentle reason my heart was not in it. Until I did fall in love, at a much later time, I was unaware the blueprint could be changed. Eileen opted for another boy. I had my first tender hurt. It was really more a bruise—in fourth grade I met Johnny.

Johnny came in after the term began. He was a year older than me and had difficulty staying in school—his dad followed the oil patch. Johnny was shy, a quiet boy, soft spoken. He appeared nervous, may have lacked confidence. Being a stranger in class, he also was excluded.

Johnny and I began with much in common, shared rejection being what drew me to him—I did stride boldly up to him. I must have acquired

——————— Σ ———————

some self-assurance—it was an odd thing for me to do. "Hi," I said. Johnny immediately smiled and I damn near burst with surprise. I was unaware my presence could truly inspire another!

Johnny was stocky. Sandy hair tossed wispy in a breeze, strands of it falling about his eyes. They were an unusual shade of brown, tending toward green. His eyes held a mellow quality I equated with sadness. I remember Johnny's face somewhat cherubic, fleshy cheeks and a slight thickness to his nose. When he smiled, his whole face beamed. Johnny didn't give away his smiles. They were private, reserved to a special place kept within. My reason for thinking so—if ever I had reason—is long gone. Johnny's smiles are not—the ones he gave me I've strung like pearls.

Johnny and I soon became fast friends, at school inseparable. By a stroke of luck—call it fate—our desks were side-by-side, spaced only by a narrow aisle between us. We queued together, ate together, played together —though in truth, we didn't play at all. Recess was our time. We talked, sometimes leaning against the schoolhouse wall; at others, sitting in the grass or lying on our backs, drifting through the sky; oftentimes walking, simply because there was need.

Whatever stance, we always held apart from the other boys—distant is the word that comes to mind. It was never possible for any of the others to invade our universe. They posed no threat—the space we occupied, not territorial. None among the others traveled a distance we'd already been.

We talked, though I can't recall any of the words. The usual things ordinarily expected were unimportant. Johnny was not a sad boy. He was a hurt boy, a hurt boy and a hurting boy on his way to sadness. "My dad'll hit me, he'll hit me again. He beats me." These are the words I remember, along with a choking sound as Johnny's voice tightened. "I don't cry anymore. Not 'til he's gone. 'Cause when I cry, he beats me more."

A grieving pain clawed my gut. I had no understanding more than what I felt for my special friend. That he told me, said much for his need. It said much for our relationship, one together we crafted from separate alienation. I would be foolish to dwell on what our friendship may have become, our feeling of an intensity that can soar to trembling heights. Words needed were too far away for me to grasp—I fell in love with Johnny.

Johnny was taken from me in a way that had its own cruelty. Trouble with school wasn't a question of his being bright or slow. At home,

——————— Σ ———————

kept from his lessons, he was severely punished when homework wasn't done. At mid-year tests, Johnny confided in me. "I'm scared," he told me. "If I flunk fourth grade I'll really get beat. We'll have to move again. I'm so afraid." The thought of separation from Johnny alarmed me, but I was greatly troubled by demons he faced. His was a situation in desperate need. I was overwhelmed, not equipped to recognize the awful burden cast on him. Johnny was not the failure, not yet—he only took the bruises.

Next day the honor system was explained and papers distributed for grading. How could it be possible I was handed Johnny's? Answer after answer was wrong. I was forced to pencil "F" across the top. At recess Johnny slipped out the side door, alone. "Why me," I wondered, *"why!"*

I followed and caught up to him. "Johnny!" I wanted to apologize. Johnny didn't say anything. He turned to me and folded his arms about my waist. He lay his head on my shoulder and squeezed the cheek of his face against mine. He held me tightly and he cried. "I'm so scared," he whispered. "I don't want to go," he sobbed. "I don't want to leave you." I didn't know what to say, what more to do. All we had left to us was my holding him.

I did hold him, arms clutching him about the shoulder. I touched softness in his hair, brushed damp warmth at his cheek. I smelled at his skin a sweet-sour scent. I felt nearness of his body close to mine, nearness of his body pressing to mine.

I have a sense of us clinging to one another entwined in embrace a very long time. I can't recall anyone noticed. For all the world, I would not have cared. It was a good feeling, holding Johnny, being held by him.

After awhile Johnny cocked his head to one side and locked eyes with mine. "I'm glad you're here," he said, and he smiled. It was the last smile Johnny gave me, the last time I saw him. He didn't return to school. I stared at his vacant desk, the shelf beneath empty of books. Timidly I went to the teacher. "Where's Johnny?" I quietly asked. She leaned toward me and spoke softly. "He's gone. They moved away. Johnny isn't coming back." Then she touched my hand and said, "I'm sorry. I am so sorry." A sense of pathos escaped her voice—it betrayed understanding she herself would not admit. I stole back to my seat beside the vacant desk and fell alone into emptiness. The place Johnny occupied grew misty.

Different? The question does not beg for answer, though I didn't know how or in what way different. I stepped, in Whitman's phrase, to the

———————— Σ ————————

beat of a different drum, a beat no amount of struggle can change—the drummer offers no choice. I wanted more than anything to be like other boys, not to be different from them. Different can lead to indifference. I was not indifferent, a clue in the puzzle of what kept me going.

Emptiness remained, hollow space felt deeply within; dark and unfathomable; a void crying to be filled. It was emptiness of unknowing and uncertainty, bleak emptiness, having no steering currents, no stars by which to guide, nor any fables in which to hide.

Once, when the world was new, summer young; when innocence walked barefoot in green grass warm; once, when bright eyes and bliss were one; when the air smelled sweet in a clear sky deep; once, in a time untroubled a time in sleep; once, a brilliant ball clear as liquid light hurtled from the east, touched earth at the feet of a child at play, bounced teasingly once round the child, sparkled and spoke, *I am Iphigenia from Tauris–I come from Aulis–I'll be your companion;* bounced once more at the child's feet, then beamed upward around him into him throughout him—once.

* * * * *

To ascertain from this map of memory the point at which my looking at boys and my noticing them interchanged is hard. Situations with flesh exposed made me self-conscious, in part due to a depressed sense of self, owing equally to desires I was unable to understand. In the locker room and showers I dillydallied in futile attempt to avoid boys in undress for fear it might seem to them I looked too long. Circumstance made it impossible *not* to look—in that steamy jungle I pretended *not* to see.

One hot July afternoon self-consciousness momentarily melted. Swimming in an abandoned sandpit, a boy on summer's visit stripped to a jock strap. He liked showing his body, didn't mind having it seen. He asked would it bother me, would I mind watching him pose. My watching wouldn't bother him—he said he'd rather I look.

At a scout jamboree, age eight or nine, I glimpse the image of young warrior braves, two boys standing tall and sleek, slender bodies naked to a scrap of cloth at the loin. New feelings are excited within me, feelings I find pleasurable—desirable. I hold back in the crowd, wanting to satisfy my gaze.

I *did* look at boys. I *know* I looked. I *looked* at them differently from the way they looked at each another. I looked at them through the silhouette of Levis, the taper of waist and trim of thighs. I *noticed* boys, their faces,

——————— Σ ———————

their lips, their eyes. I *saw* them differently from the way they saw themselves. I saw in them what their own eyes overlooked—their beauty.

Attraction to male beauty set me apart from the other boys. Like them, I was developing focus outside myself. The focus of my attention differed from the focus of theirs. While my male classmates fantasized about girls, I daydreamed about one or another of them—desire that felt *natural,* the feelings, comfortable. The boys, accustomed to pushing me aside, never noticed a subtle shift. I was for them an object of scorn and abuse, their aggression fueled by intolerance, attitudes that do not mirror. They lacked emotional capacity to relate on deeper levels within their same gender. Names they called me were hollow, words empty of meaning. I was not what they feared, not what they made of me. What I would be, I would become. What I am, they are unable to understand.

Senior year I developed a burning crush on a boy named George. He wasn't popular among the "in" crowd, not an athlete. George was bright and witty. He didn't regard me with disdain. I found him likable—his gentle nature appealed. I became more and more fond of him—tediously so. I longed for his attention, imagined in him passion and tenderness. Our relationship was in no danger of tumbling into bed. Within the confines of my discernment, sex was as vague as stardust—and just as far away.

Sex to me was a fist—my own. At age thirteen I figured out—with the help of an older boy at school—how to masturbate. He gave me facsimile instruction, making an open fist on one hand, demonstrating with forefinger from the other. Alone in bed later that night I gave myself incredible sensation. Muscles suddenly tensed and my penis jerked in spasms. Globs of slimy liquid shot through my hand, splattering my belly, streaming onto the sheet. The explosive event was shocking—the temptation for repetition, greater than the shock.

Jack off, jerk off, beat off—my five-finger obsession was a private pleasure practiced to perfection, exploding the word ecstasy with superb meaning. Satisfaction derived from whacking off did not fill the emptiness I kept inside. My starry-eyed crush on George came most near, giving it definition, my need for affection—affection I felt most absent from my life.

I struggled to balance self-gratification and deep need, sensual and emotional. The one attends physical needs of the self; the other, spiritual; both, believed entwined in a portion of the brain dominated by instinctual

————— Σ —————

needs and drives. That the two are entwined, allows them to function in a social context—it's a Pandora's box.

A child, I got a mix of self-hate and guilt in the Baptist Church. Robed in a guise of love, revilement thundered from the pulpit, a revelation of Old Testament sin and damnation. Fevered revivalists overwrought with smoke and burning brimstone fired up week-long tirades. I labored in vain to reconcile worldly ways—of which I knew nothing—with undisturbed innocence. I, too, grew fevered and overwrought—with terror!

What is there for me, one shunned as different? I am lost—totally, forever lost. Where can I find hope? How can I be loved?

A pubescent teen with racing hormones and randy hands, the vileness of flesh had a nasty habit during worship, catching between my legs and sticking straight up. My ears burned from embarrassment—throbbing erections can't be controlled. I ducked my head, afraid to look up for fear the whole congregation was staring—my red face betrayed me. Why an erection should have been my fault was hardly the concern. Love is promulgated on penis denial and castration—the Galilean, emasculated. There sat I, with an out-of-control boner—I crucified myself with blame!

One Sunday, guilt particularly revulsive, I had a sudden terrible compulsion to jump up and rip down my pants, to charge in full tumescence down the aisle and face the faithful head-on. *See! It's there. Admit it!*

The thought was dirty, wicked. I became convinced I couldn't survive a hypocrite's path to salvation. I turned from demoralizing religion incapable of tolerating love. With no assurance beyond blind belief, I fashioned faith of my own feeling. God loves me *in the way* I love Him, *because* I love Him. I did not reject God—I rejected hatred.

Senior year my demons knotted in a roundhouse of turmoil. I looked to college as escape from Vandal Lake and Bay Prairie, eager to go as far away as possible. Out-of-state was out-of-mind—as far away as possible became The University of Texas. One cool spring day, armed with the approved rooming list and a strict budget, I set out for Austin.

I expected a private room. Having waited too late, I was forced to pick from leftovers. Ferrell Cottages, a block from campus, had one vacancy remaining—two boys occupied a room. Upstairs rear in the rear cottage, the room was drab. One student, the elderly lady explained, "a nice young man," sent his deposit. "All my boys call me *Mother* Ferrell," she insisted.

———————— Σ ————————

Graduation with its round of festivity dimmed. Summer was passing abruptly. I became increasingly curious about my soon-to-be roommate. I conjured an image blond and beautiful—Adonis, had I *known* the word.

Blond and beautiful—the first night, lights out, he stretches his hand across the shallow gulf separating our beds. He reaches out in darkness, his hand finding mine. He clasps my hand firmly, draws me gently across to his bed. Then—I drift to sleep holding his image!

Reality is a dream, a myth—whatever one wishes. The hard fact—I arrived at Ferrell Cottages an early autumn afternoon to discover a lanky Ichabod jester-like on the porch railing, Jim somebody, from north Texas somewhere. Whatever else he said I didn't hear, bewildered by his appearance. Escape from Bay Prairie landed me in the arms of defeat. I wanted to turn away and run—dark hair and sallow complexion was *not* Adonis.

Jim, already settled in the room, offered to help get my bags. He chattered about my taking the bed nearest the door, whether or not it suited, about the closet, the desk, and more. I clumsily began putting things away, dreading by long minutes the hour lights would be extinguished.

Dreaded night, time of darkness and shadow, time of refuge and hiding. Dreaded night, time I most despised—until Adonis shared my quiet. A brief time, I eagerly awaited night, welcomed sanctity in his embrace.

Finally, in stillness, the dreaded time came. "Hey, Roomie," Jim announced, "I'm ready for bed. How about you?" The hour could no longer be forestalled—my heart froze. I lay tense in bed, fearing to breathe. I tried to conjure my blond. He had evaporated—in his place, emptiness.

Escape again met disappointment—fate is cruel. I tried to speak to God, my belief hazy and rarefied. The power of prayer not my strong point, I was unsure *how* to pray. I *talked* to God—not aloud. My lips moved, whispering word-shapes ever so mute.

Jim was restless. He tossed and turned, beat his pillow. At last he leaped up and charged to the window. "I've got to turn this thing on." The evaporative cooler on high, then superhigh, whirred and gurgled. Returning to bed, Jim snapped the waistband of his briefs against flesh. I caught a glimpse of white, iridescent in filtered streetlight—neon to olive skin.

Masked by noise from the cooler, my incantation grew bolder. Talking to God was wearisome and one-sided. Never did I get a hint of revelation, not a slight tinge of solace. I talked and cried myself to sleep.

——————— Σ ———————

Moisture blew from the window cooler all night. By morning, brittle wallpaper bulged from walls and ceiling. "Mother Ferrell will *shit!*" Jim shouted. There was no polish to him. I was sullen, depression lasting for weeks. I avoided Jim as much as possible, hardly spoke to him beyond necessary civilities. Jim tried. He fought hard to get through to me. I was isolated, far from home, feeling lost and rejected among strangers. I ached for hot July sand and gulf beaches.

Phil, a raw-boned boy from the Panhandle, shared the suite next door. His roommate, Al, a senior, spent most of his time away from the Cottages, on campus or with his girl, LaDonna, or both. Phil was tall, with blond hair and blue eyes. His body, a trim sort, looked good in anything and better in nothing. I know—Phil was immodest, parading about the room as comfortably naked as not. I wondered if it was done to test or to tease—Phil, oblivious of others, was too wrapped in himself to give me such attention.

Phil and I had nothing in common. He was a physics major, slide rule always in hand. He was hyper, outgoing and loud. He was rude, he was vulgar and he was crude. Blond and beautiful was his attraction. I gyrated toward him on the precarious strength of his beauty. He was a ready-made escape from my disappointment with Jim.

I did not fall in love with Phil. He was crude, that is so. He also was without shame. I've said that. The first time he stepped through the room naked I was enthralled by his body—detailed, endowed and sharply focused. I wanted to reach out and touch him, as in fantasy I touched Adonis.

I hadn't actually *touched* Adonis, the fantasy satisfied holding and caressing—an image of lover and beloved. Once, I dared to kiss Adonis. He responded, touching my cheek. I *supposed* love would happen next, of its own accord. Sex as arbitrary entity, the connection between kiss and cock—a penis held and caressed, fondled and manipulated in a scenario seriously sexual—was a concept I didn't know. I hadn't yet gotten to sex. I didn't know sex could be had with a beauty such as Phil. There, now I've said it.

Ignorance served me well in not lusting for Phil's body—he was ungainly gross. Door open, facing full forward, he would sit stark naked on the john having a bowel movement. Certain things, despite army etiquette, belong behind closed doors—Phil's lack of decency repelled me. Alas, that idols be made with feet of clay!

The barrier between Jim and me finally broke, involving Mother

——————— Σ ———————

25

Ferrell. Jim was busy acquainting himself with some of the other boys. One evening, a bull session developed in our room, the main topic Mother Ferrell and what Jim termed the Mother Ferrell Conspiracy.

Mother Ferrell patrolled cottage sidewalks well into night, stiff-leg arthritic poodle at her side and nerve-deaf husband John in tow. She was compelled to keep an eye on things. We learned to avoid being waylaid by her—as Jim put it, "she talks the dead to sleep."

Convinced some of the boys were doing "bad" things, Mother Ferrell hid in shrubbery at night eavesdropping. She determined to find out which boys were involved. "It's a plot, mark my word," she said. So great was her sense of imagined threat, she ordered John not to sleep on his good ear, "lest he be caught napping."

One night in sleep the poodle died and she forbade John to sleep at all. "Murder," she said, "as I suspected. A conspiracy. Mother Ferrell will be next." From that point, shrubbery vigils lasted through the night to dawn. What set her off was never clear, the greater disturbance in her mind.

"If that old lady ever sees anything, peeping all hours through windows," Jim said bluntly, "she'll shit!"

Her antics provided fuel enough to ignite raucous evenings, usually in our room, it being the more isolated. We didn't always have the same cast of conspirators, one boy, Joe, a regular. He was on the UT swim team and occupied a small, third-floor room in the big house. Joe was a copper-tanned beauty, smooth skinned in a pair of pajama bottoms worn thin. Cotton fabric hugged like cheesecloth with a fit to match. The legs were short, striking well above the ankle—boy mystique added to his appeal. Nightly, nocturnally, he sprawled on *my* bed, occupying a position *close* to me—regardless of others present.

The Mother Ferrell intrigue finally wore as thin as Joe's jammies. Besides exhausting the humor, *Paradise Lost* had to be read, papers written, pages on pages on pages. Eventually the rear cottage sessions ended. Joe continued to visit in the evenings. Later, he began dropping by those after-noons he knew I was in and Jim out.

Autumn in Austin came as a shock. Subtle on the coast, at times taking summer skipping into winter, autumn became authentic. Suddenly the air bristled and summer swirled about my feet. With a changing season, Jim and I at last made a better beginning. My loneliness continued.

————— Σ —————

Late one afternoon I was sitting on the stairway to our cottage, feeling for all the world forlorn. Jim was napping—he cut class. Joe strolled down the sidewalk, climbed to the step below my feet and propped against the railing. He was casual, his voice soft and mellow. "Why so sad? Lose your best friend?"

"Maybe," I said, my word empty of feeling.

Joe was calm. "Ever think of turning queer?"

I looked into his eyes piercing mine. "Would that help?" I asked, in a tone of brilliance I found surprising.

Joe leaned slightly toward me. He didn't hesitate, his answer confident, his voice reassuring. "Maybe. You never can tell."

I dove into his eyes. Words formed, pressing against my lips.

Suddenly, from above, the door burst open and Jim bounded onto the porch. "Whatcha guys doing?" he chirped.

Jim's timing by gross coincidence could not be more precise. I was enraged, a moment of discovery almost in reach smashed indelicately. I failed to notice Joe's reaction. He managed to recover quickly, as though our brief words were never spoken.

"I've got a swim meet tomorrow," he replied, "I don't want to sleep—*over* sleep," he corrected. "Do you mind waking me?" Joe directed his question straight at me.

I took awhile to surface from Joe's eyes. "Yeah, sure," I slowly answered, drowning in disappointment, stupefied—wondering, *wondering!*

"About 2:30," Joe's eyes were intently on me. "I'll leave the door open." He turned and, as casually as he arrived, strolled up the sidewalk.

My distaste for Jim boiled again. I'm sure he felt it—he was fidgety. "I think, I must've—," he began haltingly.

"You must've!" I said curtly, cutting him off so flatly it ended what might have become a conversation.

Exactly 2:30 the following afternoon I slipped into the big house and climbed the stairs. I felt my heart pounding. The door to Joe's room was ajar. My hand trembled as I pushed against it, not knowing what to expect. Yes, eager—I wanted to give myself to Joe. I whispered, *"Yes, Joe. Yes!"*

The room was dark. Joe lay on his back, his body naked to white Jockeys. I crept to the foot of his bed and slowly reached one hand to his feet. My fingers closed on toes. The feel of them, warm and firm to my touch,

————— Σ —————

excited my all-but-racing heart. I shook his foot in a careful rocking motion. "Joe? Joe?" was all I could utter from a voice barely audible, one seeming not to belong to me. "It's 2:30, are you awake?"

Those are not the words I wanted to say, ones I should have said. *Joe, I'm here. I came as I promised, to be with you.*

Joe opened his eyes and yawned. He raised his arms and arched his back. He stretched his body and thrust his pelvis. "Yeah, yeah, I'm awake."

I was crystallized at the foot of Joe's bed. Holding his firm, warm toes, I gazed the length of his body, entranced. Joe said, "Thanks. You can let go now." Nothing more was said, nothing happened. What did I expect?

I released his toes and shuffled from the room. From the hallway, I ran downstairs and raced to my room, burying my face in the pillow where I hid in shame. Terrible loneliness gripped me. *You're not wanted!*

* * * * *

Winter months are capable of etching despondency, closed space intolerably confining. Holidays in Bay Prairie pushed disappointment to disaster. I was irritable, demanding everything be so-so. To calm my stomach I chewed chalky tablets by the pocketful—an ulcer, I was told at the Student Health Center. In the evenings I took solitary walks down North Congress as far as the Capitol, those few blocks deserted at night.

By spring my walks were constitutional. One Sunday evening I walked through the Capitol, underneath its massive dome and out the front doors, down to curbside at South Congress. I decided to return by way of the surrounding grounds. On narrow streets laid out originally for carriage travel, lighting was subdued. A pale green sedan crept from the curb. It cautiously eased alongside, its driver opposite me. He leaned across to the open window to ask directions. He seemed harmless, though the destination obvious. He offered me a ride. "No, thanks, it's only a couple o' blocks."

"College kid, huh? Me, too—once that is, not now. Hop in anyway!" He thrust open the door, a squat little man well into middle-age, balding, paunchy and round-faced. He was pleasant—he *seemed* decent.

Against better judgement, I got into the car. A salesman in town on business, he said he should be headed home, "the Mrs. is expecting me."

Were comments about the Mrs. tossed in to gain my confidence? "Hey, I'm just a regular blow with my own grease bucket at home." Was she popped about to bolster his self-image, "Hey, whaddya think, *I'm* that way?

—————— Σ ——————

Look again, Bozo!" Was it as he purported, only small talk, after exhausting comments about the weather?

The Mrs. at home expecting him and a big client he waited to see, he was insistent, "Ride with me out to his house. Maybe I c'n git 'im there—Aw, c'mon, it'll only take fifteen minutes!"

Already in the car, I rode with him. Small talk became bolder, interspersed with corn-ball jokes. "Oh! Here's a good one. Know the difference between a hotel and a motel? Know, huh? A motel has no *ball* room!"

He suddenly grabbed my crotch. His hand cupped *everything* and he began a squeezing, massaging action. My knees slammed reflexively and my body tensed in a spasmodic jerk. I pried at chubby fingers. His grip tightened, groping in earnest. "A motel has no *ball* room. Huh? Git it? You got any *ball* room there?"

He stopped the car on a quiet, dark street in a residential neighborhood. Lights from family homes twinkled without distraction. He begged, "Le'me suck it. How about that, huh? Ever had it sucked?"

I shook my head *No!* still prying at pudgy fingers.

"Le'me take it out, le'me git a look. How about it, huh?" He gave another squeeze, "No *ball* room, huh!"

I felt his grip begin to relax. "No...no...no...," I said in a hoarse whisper that barely made it to my ears. My mouth cotton-dry, I couldn't spit for salvation. "...nothing...," the tiny voice drifted away.

Finally relenting, he put the car into gear. Driving like gangbusters downtown to the Capitol, I thought of Joe. My feeling with Joe was wonderful. I didn't feel dirty. *With Joe, oh, Joe, yes! But not you—not with a queer!*

I lied about the Cottages, frightened he would follow to my room. He stopped on the street in front of a rooming house a block away. I slipped hurriedly into the dark. I felt violated. Disregard for sensitive feelings I regard in a special way cheapened. I wanted to wash my hands. The dirtiness I felt inside soap was unable to scrub. I couldn't go to my room. I couldn't face Jim. I needed—closeness.

Phil was sitting at his desk, slide rule in hand. I tapped at the door and let myself in. "Take a chair," he said, not glancing from his book. My lips trembled, tears filled my eyes. Suddenly too much—my loneliness, Adonis and Jim, Phil's body and Joe's tenderness; emptiness, desire, love. *Is queer what I want, who I am? I don't know where to find the answer!* The swirl

———————— Σ ————————

tangled, hopelessly snarled. The room whirled and flipped, lights went out.

Phil and Jim stood over me—Phil helpless, Jim perplexed. "I dunno," Phil said, "he walked in and went out cold. Scared the crap outta me. I jumped up and called you." Jim put a cold cloth on my forehead. The two of them carried me to Phil's bed.

Jim stayed with me. After awhile I told him I wanted to sleep. He helped me to our room and I slumped into bed. Jim was patient in his concern. "Are you sure?" he asked. "Are you okay?"

Jim turned out the light and sat in bed a long time, sat with feet pulled into him closely, knees tucked under chin. Smoke from his cigarette flooded the room, curling into mysterious vapor. Each time he inhaled, a reddish glow momentarily flared, having about it reassuring warmth. In a strange way, the small fire gave me comfort. I should have realized it wasn't from the fire of Jim's cigarette on which I drew. I wish we had talked.

* * * * *

Tender budding in the unmistakable urgency of spring, my life was finally falling into place. Jim and I found steady ground the night I fainted. Our relationship changed; the difference, a sharing I previously denied. We began doing things together, movies, midnight caffeine runs—tame things for college freshmen. We laughed and joked, we poked fun at one another. More importantly, we talked.

Fears and frustrations, hopes for the future, dreams—*dreams,* not goals. Communication sprouted between us. One area remained taboo—sex, a frivolous subject, lower case *s-e-x.* The nearest we got to *s-e-x* were Jim's sporadic outbursts, "Roomie, I must be horny—my hormones itch!"

Jim was a sort of person I call self-reliant—he scratched where it itched. If he scratched this itch, I don't know where he did the scratching. One occasion he declared, "Roomie, I'm going to Dallas, I'm going to get laid." I asked on his return, "So, Jim, how did it go?" Jim shot me the finger. "See this? Sit on it, rotate and FUCK OFF!" He easily answered my question.

S-e-x, insofar as I knew, was exclusively girl-boy. The other, specifically boy-boy *s-e-x,* didn't exist—one had to know where it lurked. I didn't have a clue; Jim may have. Unless one lurked where it lurked, boy-boy *s-e-x* was the first Black Hole—cosmically all around, completely invisible.

The unspoken rite of passage from boyhood, as Jim phrased it, is getting laid. The path may wander across fields of wild oat before landing in

——————— Σ ———————

the marriage bed. Sex outside love, in that context compartmentalized, is socially tolerated—with a wink and a nod.

Homosexual love as a concept was nonexistent. Like-gender partners having full range of emotional capability the equivalent of heterosexual partners, was unheard. The love that dare not speak its name, presumed lacking sufficient courage to do so under threat of disastrous confrontation, truly was silent. Prominent was an exaggerated notion of overindulgence in sex, compartmentalization in the extreme—this, with no wink or nod.

Queer sex and forbidden love were perverse and unnatural; ungodly and unholy; hated, feared, despised; distasteful, repugnant—nothing positive about it. Under pall of such absolute denigration, pursuit of queer sex as integrated expression of emotional fulfillment was hardly a choice. My hormones weren't so itchy—I may not have lurked in the right place.

*   *   *   *   *

Innocence corrupted English 601.b and Koestler's stirring account of Communism—innocence very real and very urgent. A girl named Jackie seated behind me provoked anarchy while we experienced the thrill of Politics Red. Jackie is what most red-blooded, non-Communistic males call *nice!* By way of description, don't expect more. My red blood, unlike that of other non-Communistic males, isn't pre-conditioned "hot" for girls. Cold Cock and Cold War are tenants—they sleep together. It's un-American to be hot for boys.

I *can* depict Jackie the person—unexpected sophistication, no odor of snobbery; social and intellectual refinement her attempts to subvert can't hide; clinical in humor, optimistic otherwise; essentially open with those whom *she* has chosen. Jackie was not bound by Chance—it served her.

Jackie, finding one of Dr. Jones' lectures boring, lazily played the eraser of her pencil through my hair, haphazardly allowing it to creep bristly down my neck. Her activity, lightly done, continued at an altogether casual pace, more absent-minded than determined. She did it to toy, not to tease.

I tried to ignore her pencil, the antic not bothersome, more akin to stroking a cat. Unexplained itch or generous erection, the playful pencil grew unbearably tingly, amusement headed to arousal. Jackie's stroking sent sexually thrilling shivers shooting throughout—I got a hard-on.

Precisely that was Jackie, bold and daring, secret but not private. Frankly her flagrantly suggestive antic incongruous with Communism or

———————— Σ ————————

Koestler pleased me. It amused me. Finally it got to me. Shoulders hunched in contrite convulsion, I grinned, spitting a loud giggle. Jackie lost composure. She smirked with a throaty grunt and dropped the pencil. It clinked on the wooden desktop, practically purred on its journey downward. At the lower edge, it paused precarious, then dove with a splat onto the floor. *Whee-ee* it rolled across the aisle and stopped *thonk* against the leg of a co-ed's desk. The girl stared pitifully at the pencil trapped near her foot, as though fresh dog shit had been rolled her way.

Jackie collapsed, burying her head. It was useless to attempt hiding laughter—she was hysterical. When she smirked and the pencil launched, I turned around—everyone not sitting rearward of us turned around. No one stared at Jackie or me, all eyes intently, *suspiciously,* focused on the innocent co-ed and her dog-shit pencil. I exploded in laughter.

At the same moment, the hallway bell set off its growling jangle. Dr. Jones paused picking up his notes to glance toward us. An unmistakably non-tutorial smile escaped his lips. His class scrambled for the door, keeping safe distance from the anarchists.

Inaction the safest choice, I remained behind, Jackie's collapsed form buried to the elbow. Suddenly she bolted upright, hands firmly planted palm-down. "Would you like a cup of coffee? That's all I wanted to know!"

What began our relationship sustained it—a standing coffee-date after Dr. Jones' class. The Commons was conducive to coffee and chatter— we indulged liberally. Seldom a night passed without one of us phoning. We never had a *real* date. Jackie didn't bring it up, neither did I. Pals from word go, nothing sexual unbalanced our affair, both thoroughly comfortable in the arrangement. Inward contentment comes with familiarity—an old hat hangs better, fits better, feels better. With few others have I felt such ease.

Jackie gave me more than a three-letter romp. She gave me a world of books, names I never heard, *Your Turn to Curtsy, My Turn to Bow; Lord of the Flies; A Separate Peace.* She recommended, I read, we talked. Ideas painted with words, thoughts enlarged and defined, with power to limit or expand—Jackie opened for me a door that since has never closed.

Dr. Jones regularly assigned papers. Jackie composed one theme around a white lily, weaving symbolism into any conceivable scrap of imagery no matter how obvious or sublime. She concluded her paper, "I crushed the lily underfoot. I stomped it." Before Dr. Jones' next class, she tacked a

———————— Σ ————————

fresh white lily to his office door with a note: "Dr. Jones, It could be you."

The week before finals, Jackie leaned forward and whispered at the back of my head, "Let's pick up our books and walk out." Rude and stupid, we picked up, stacked up and packed up our clutter. We marched defiantly toward the rear door. Dr. Jones didn't drop a syllable, his tone unchanged from lecture. "Miss Golden, Mr. Hamilton, you needn't bother coming back to class again." His delivery was smooth—the full extent of meaning almost shot past me. With sudden grip, the words pierced like icy steel—*Eeow, shit!* Civility begged for response. Over my shoulder, as smoothly as Dr. Jones, I replied, "No bother at all, Dr. Jones." A look of bewilderment from the rest of class, Dr. Jones continued his lecture. I closed the door behind us.

Jackie was unnerved. I said, "What the heck, it's done." She was unwilling to concede. "Let's talk to him, at least apologize." We were sitting on the stairway landing outside his office when Dr. Jones returned. He called cheerfully, "Miss Golden! Mr. Hamilton! Come in, come in!" Jackie at once began apology. "No, no, no," Dr. Jones dismissed. "No need for apology—what a good show! You two have guts, the other sheep afraid to follow. I like it! You two have had fun all semester—now, I've had mine."

Jackie caught my eye, neither of us sure what to make of Dr. Jones. He continued, more seriously. "I mean what I said. Don't bother coming back to class—or to my final exam." Queasiness rimmed my stomach. I felt I'd puke or pass out, maybe both. Jackie's face pale, she was near collapse. Dr. Jones paused reflectively, then pulled his punch. "You both have A's!"

Jackie and I were determined to take the final, Dr. Jones equally adamant. "No, no. Let the others remain in darkness. Perhaps your antics will inspire just one of them." We remained with Dr. Jones until his next class—the only coffee date Jackie and I missed. He gave us a fix stronger than caffeine. What began idly we moved into metaphor and manipulated to method, sheer philosophy—or utter nonsense, according to Dr. Jones. I stepped from his office standing a foot taller.

"I have a friend," Jackie mentioned one day. "A great guy, he's a lot like you. I want you to meet him."

A great guy, a lot like me, unmade, unformed, rustic and blasé—I didn't know *what* she considered *a lot like me.* "Yeah? Sure, Jackie," I said.

Mention of her friend began casually. More and more Jackie got back to him. "I'm sure you two will hit it off great!"

——————— Σ ———————

At first, I thought little more about it. "Yeah, sure," I told her. Her great-guy friend became a regular part of conversation.

"I *must* get the two of you together," she determined.

My lack of interest and enthusiasm no deterrent, Jackie developed new strategy. "I told him all about you—*he* wants to meet *you.*"

All about me—how *much* is there to tell? "Sure, Jackie, why not."

Efforts getting nowhere, phase three was deployed. "He's part of a group—not really a group—a bunch of guys—really great guys! Guys who hang out together—sort of, you know, friends."

I merely nodded. She continued. "Does that sound terrific?" Jackie eyed me scrupulously, intent on response.

"Yeah, sure, Jackie, terrific," I told her. What *could* I say in response to something that doesn't exist? *Wow! Look! A Black Hole—great!*

"Um-hm," Jim announced proudly, certain he solved the riddle of Jackie's group. "Commies. The whole bunch. That Koestler crud is creeping up on you." Here is a lesson in how the mind works. Given a simple unknown, it invents worse—in this case Communism. I was relieved to discover my greatest threat nothing more sinister than Nikita Khrushchev.

"The guys are terrific," Jackie coaxed. "You'll like them—I'm *sure* they'll like you. You'll fit in perfectly. *So* perfectly!"

Again, with only a slight shrug, I responded, "Yeah, sure, Jackie."

I had no reason to dislike the friends Jackie eagerly wanted me to meet. We could have met had she simply set up a meeting—*arranged* it. I had no suspicions about her friends, certainly none that were Red. Had the notion arisen of our ready-made compatibility being sexually inspired, I like to believe I would've moved at the speed of light.

I felt inferior and inadequate, imagining the group one of intellectuals. One on one with Jackie, I didn't feel threatened. She had *chosen* me, our relationship developing of its own momentum. That felt natural. Fear of rejection was more than I could face. I couldn't claim much, what little I had gained. I was unwilling to roll dice.

Meeting Jackie's friend almost happened. During dead week, Jim and I at the Student Union Cinema waited for the doors to open. The ten-cent price of admission guaranteed mob-rule, a wild clamor for seats. Push and shove at the entrance, Jim bullied us deep into the throng, assuring our survival in a deadly rush soon to begin. He knew to hold my arm firmly and

———————— Σ ————————

drag me beside him—crowds confuse me. "Plainly scare you shitless," was Jim's pronouncement.

Above a rising din in the crush of final seconds I heard my name shouted far back in the crowd; Jackie, her bobbing head a cork, leaping above the mob to capture my attention. "My friend is here!—My friend is here!—I want you—to meet him!" A sudden rush of bodies swept us inside, Jim dragging me by the arm. I tried looking back for Jackie, torn between breaking Jim's grip and my own fear. Cold feet won. We scrambled for seats.

I could do nothing to disentangle myself from the mob, the melee over in less time than required to tell. Before swept inside, I saw Jackie's bobbing face a last time, her expression one of disappointment and hurt. My chance to meet a friend-to-be vanished within seconds.

Jackie did not return to UT the following fall. I looked for her. A computer card check on her name with the registrar's office came up blank.

*   *   *   *   *

Spring nudged life at Ferrell Cottages. Jim, outgoing, kept me part of the crowd. Without him, I would've been left behind, hanging off the wall in our room like faded wallpaper Jim continually fought. That bull sessions never die, being truth unto themselves, is fact. They returned full-blown in the spring, one such event giving rise to the hard-on salute.

Several boys gathered in Steve's room, Steve being Phil; rather, Phil having *become* Steve—the handiwork of Mother Ferrell. By whatever unreasoned logic her mind worked is forever mystery. She determined Phil to be Steve and so he was. Mention Phil and she'd scowl, *"Who,* honey?" Mother Ferrell used *honey* when being personal. "You mean *Steve." Steve* was never *honey.* She disliked him from the start. It was no secret—he hated her.

Gathered in Steve's room, a difference of opinion developed between Smith and Hooper, both Chicagoans. Hooper, a new guy among us, transferred in spring semester, he and Smith previously acquainted. Both were drama majors—that in itself enough to quicken the blood. On campus, a microcosm of squeaky-clean dominated by frat rat and sorority deb, a drama major was held highly suspect, not necessarily of being queer—that, too; generally, of being "just *weird,* man."

I knew differently. Phil's roommate, Al, and Al's girl, LaDonna, were drama majors. They were less *weird* than most all the rest of us.

Smith and Hooper, each convinced his stance invincible, engaged

———————— Σ ————————

in mouth-to-mouth combat, their passion escalating from heated to loud. *Bullshit,* a favorite projectile in their arsenal, was flung prolifically, delivery remarkably the same—resonantly *schwooshed* from puffed cheek through fully rounded mouth, bwull-*schit,* emphasis on *schit.* Jim later remarked, "Chicagoans sprinkle *bullshit* loosely on everything—including cornflakes!"

It may be so with Smith and Hooper, who had remarkable ability to make of bullshit an entire conversation. Hooper finally said to Smith, *"You're* bwull-schit, Smith." Smith replied, "So I'm bwull-schit, Hooper—Hard-on." Hooper, unprepared for a sneak attack, blurted, "What?—What? *Hard-on!* Smith, what's that?" Smith, right arm stiffened high above crotch in heil-like salute, intoned, "Hard-on, Hooper—Big-Fucking-Deal."

From that time a stiff salute above the crotch communicated succinctly—we used it when the *schit* was on the rise.

The question *who is* and *who isn't* crept from the woodwork with astounding frequency during bull sessions, speculation never about individuals known to us. Two guys roomed in the front cottage, lower floor street side, theirs the only room with private entrance from the sidewalk. Why is that? Does anyone know them, their names? Why won't they join in—has anyone *seen* them? They leave early, stay gone all day—window blinds *always* closed and lights out *early.* Yes, assuredly they are—*odd!*

Directly above them, Cozby and Blair. Something's the matter with Blair, not so much as *fuck off* when we meet, just pass and stare—Jim's contribution. Yes, strange. Cozby—he *looks* peculiar!

Gale, front cottage, upper floor rear. Does he have a roommate? Yeah, sure, who? With a name like Gale—he's an *architect* major? That explains it—he *must* be funny!

Thornton in the garage apartment paid double room charge for privacy, no roommate. He comes and goes by the driveway, never down the sidewalk *we* use. Has anyone *ever* seen him? Lights on all hours of the night. Pretty *weird,* wouldn't you say?

Mother Ferrell was the thread tying this knot. Spring renewed her conspiracy espionage. The guys, weary of her nonsense, dismissed her a genuine basket case. Jim and I relished the insanity. Were he alive, we could restage the events, he with Seven-and-Seven, me with Johnny Walker, the two of us going through the night—at some point Jim suddenly jumping up to declare, "My God, the sun's coming up! We've been at this all night!"

——————— Σ ———————

Some thoughts are dedicated to an individual—these belong to Jim. Had it not been for his declaration so very many nights, the two of us might easily have gone on forever. I often wonder if at his last moment, Jim may suddenly have looked out from sunken eyes over hollow cheeks for a final time. *My God, the sun's coming up! I've been at this all night!*

Jim and I returned from dinner on a Sunday afternoon, the last day of Easter break. On North Congress Avenue, Mother Ferrell blocked our path and laid a fast grip on my arm. She commenced, "Fuck. Four times. *Fuck-Fuck-Fuck-Fuck!* Mother Ferrell doesn't use such words. *You old son-of-a-hmn, hmn, hmn!* Mother Ferrell doesn't say those words. *Fuck-Fuck-Fuck-Fuck!* Would Mother Ferrell go out there alone, a defenseless woman with a hot young buck? Not on your life! Mother Ferrell went straight to Dean Arno's office at The University. *Fuck four times, Dean Arno. Fuck-Fuck-Fuck-Fuck!* Mother Ferrell was eager to tell."

Jim tried to pry me away, her grip set. "Mother Ferrell's been hiding in the bushes and she's heard plenty. Oh, yes, it was Steve. When he said *fuck*, Mother Ferrell knew, he's the gang leader. They have night-vision equipment to see in the dark. Last term I heard one of them say, 'Where's the old bat?' The other one said, 'She's on the floor, with the dog!'"

Jim choked, Mother Ferrell having misunderstood the implication. She looked at Jim quizzically, staring him dead in the eye. "Why, honey, how else could they know I was sitting on the floor with a sick dog? That was when they murdered him."

Jim tried again to break her off, "I thought the dog went to sleep." Mother Ferrell glared at him harder, "Honey, he did. They fed him poison."

Something had changed. "It's sad, that old woman," Jim later said. "She finally has lost her mind." He said no more. A sadness, yes; a rue for the perceived closing of a circle—we both felt it. We both were genuinely fond of her. Afterward, Mother Ferrell was taken somewhere and put away.

The rational part of my brain dictates a sequence of events, beginning with Fuck Four Times, is related. Rather like a china teapot accidentally smashed on the sideboard—all the pieces, carefully gathered into a box, are a puzzle, yet remain a riddle.

Brief renewal of enthusiasm for the Conspiracy Saga brought back the old sessions. Retold and sifted again for the last scrap of humor, the question *who is* and *who isn't* came round. The gang was in Phil, Steve's,

——————— Σ ———————

room. It so happened Thornton was spotlighted. It further happened, which none of us knew, Phil had become friendly with Thornton. "The guy's a physics major," Phil offered in defense, "sharp as a tack, one helluva nice guy. I met him and we talked, simple as that. He offered to help with some of my problems. *Physics* problems," Phil added pointedly. One thing led to another, Phil got mad. Loudly and abusively, he threw everyone out. Jim, as usual, capped it with perspective, "Steve's got a hair twisted up his butt."

A few days later Phil, Steve, moved into the garage apartment with Thornton and we never saw him after that. Jim observed, "The light over there sure as hell goes out early now!" He merely nodded, making a clicking sound from one corner of his mouth—the rest, he left alone.

Sandwiched between these two events, Phil said to me one afternoon, "We're thrown together in nonsensical nonsequential randomness, no reason to be friends." He returned to his slide rule. Nothing else had been said, nothing more said. I stood perfectly still, stunned in disbelief, uncertain of Phil's meaning. He kept his back to me. I felt a door rudely slam shut as I quietly closed his behind me.

Nonsensical nonsequential randomness, perhaps—any set of circumstances, events or occurrences, no matter how random, will, when given enough space in terms of time, plot a normal curve.

Into this puzzle Jim brought Cozby and, through him, Gale. By semester's end it had come down to the four of us. Exactly what gelled among us may never be deciphered. Jim, from seated fetal position, knees tucked snugly under chin, once said to me, "Roomie, you really are a gentle soul." *Gentle* may have been part of what we shared. I prefer to think of us as being the normal curve plotted from random circumstance.

"We've come full circle," Jim said at such times a describable ending, a summing of parts, was achieved. It had an air of authority and finality. Every raw edge rounded and loose end neatly tucked, events could proceed unhindered. Life, freed, can go on smoothly. The fallacy of my perception, what I failed to recognize, was critical. One circle looped with another much the way metal hoops tangle in a familiar stage trick. A chain ever so subtly forged, any given result cannot exist without all the links coming before.

Change—plodding, tenacious; sometimes tedious, always stubborn; adaptable, elusive and certain—captured Jim and me. We eased into it with unnoticed direction. Once there, anything else felt clawed. Jim put up with

———————— Σ ————————

much from me—my scorn and abuse, the rebuke I wallowed from self-pity. He waded at high tide my sewer of self-esteem trapped in a toilet of anxiety. I was a pathetic mess. Why Jim didn't long before throw up his hands in despair and concoct some shameless scheme to effectively excise me from his life is a wonder. More can be endured from family than tolerated from outsiders, even friends. Of this I am certain—Jim and I were brothers.

What was our chemistry? We should have been a perfect couple. The night I cringed while he pondered, suppose we had talked? Suppose there had been a subject to discuss instead of a Black Hole?

Now common, Black Holes contain energy in ratios nonequivalent to mass or volume. Consider this ratio, "Mom! Jim's takin' me to a movie!" Or its equivalent, "Mom! Jim's asked me for a date—*Who's* Jim? *Mom! Just* the *dreamiest!*" Or further consider, as co-product mass into volume, "Mom! Guess who just asked me to the prom—*Jim!*" Or, simply, energy, "Mom! Dad! Jim proposed, he asked me to marry him—*I Said Yes!*"

We were unable to lead complete lives, only parts. Even those parts were not our own. Except for the advantage of skill or luck, the chance of winning—or the risk of losing—*must* be the same for all participants. I didn't even know that I could love.

Jim mentioned our rooming together the following year. I said, "Sure, Jim, why not!" That settled, his enthusiasm sprang to action. Jim was resourceful, especially in getting something he wanted. I didn't have his knack, never able to put into it that extra bite—a little dishonesty. He was adept when he chose to apply himself. I was the dreamer—neither of my feet touched terra firma.

"Roomie, I've scoped it out. The best room in the whole place is front cottage upstairs, facing Congress." It was the room Cozby and Blair occupied. Jim boldly knocked at their door and said bluntly, "Can I see your room?" That was how he met Cozby. I think it probable Jim intended us rooming together all along. However managed, Jim was jubilant. "Cozby and Blair are taking an apartment for fall semester—we've got the room!"

Boundaries of definition were never placed on our relationship, not in all our volumes of words. To define a thing is to know it implicitly, to rob it of spontaneity and mystery—magic qualities that intrigue. Definition harshly signifies, "Yes, this is done." That Jim and I weren't done was the mystery—that we'd hardly begun, the magic.

————— Σ —————

"I'm afraid," Jim said to me. "I want my life to be something more. I don't want to wake up and find myself in north Texas, like mom and dad, trapped in those dirty mills." It was a brave admission, what is given must ultimately be taken. We are doomed to repetition, mistakes embedded in the past. Sadness gripped me. I suddenly wanted an end to hurtful things. Jim, only human, touched me with ethereal breath.

The week of finals Jim got a car, the family Chrysler his folks promised. I had a geology final 7:30 Friday morning. The four of us, Jim, Cozby, Gale and myself, Thursday evening piled into Jim's car, headed for a drive-in movie—any movie. Someone shouted *"Beer!"* and we chipped in.

The old Chrysler rocked dangerously, lost in a billowy cloud of cigarette smoke. We whooped and hollered with all doors open. We laughed, we shouted, beer kept flowing. We were in, out, around; sprawling, hanging, dangling. My stomach was feeling funny when Jim called out, "Hey, Roomie needs another beer!" From the rear seat Gale thrust one at me and I took generous gulps. My head determined to launch itself and funny within my stomach grew violent. "I on't thing...I me'n, me...no too goo...." I sloshed and Gale giggled out of control. "Me-me no-too goo-goo!" he mimicked. Jim was frantic, "Ooh, ooh, is 'e gonna be sig? Cozby, do something, get 'im outta here!" Gale went from giggle to hysterical. "Ooh-ooh, too-goo!"

Crouched at the door, Cozby cradled my wobbly head between outstretched palms. He brought his face near to mine, so near lips barely, barely touched. "Yup," he said. Outside the car he held me, arms securely about my waist. I bent double, puking splashing globs. I pulled my first drunk. I don't remember much about it—I passed out.

Next morning I made it to the 7:30 geology final and whipped through the exam, grabbing an easy A. I packed my car, in ready for return to Bay Prairie. Jim and I didn't make much of this temporary parting. I noticed the small room we shared looked forlorn.

"Hey, Roomie, don't forget to write!" Jim called brightly.

I blew a hefty sigh. "Whew! I made it—I *really* made it!" Part of me did not want to leave, another part urged me on—both parts ecstatic.

——————— Σ ———————

The vision made flesh

Life in Bay Prairie pressed onward, dull and plodding. What had I expected? My old room was neat and tidy, the bed ready with fresh linen. Things, much as I left them, weren't charged with the same familiarity. Friction with my dad stemmed from my lack of a summer job. In small-town rural environs, a summer job is coveted. I would have to help with ranch work, a distasteful compromise. For the moment, it eased tension, perhaps would leave time for the beach—a big plus.

I managed more time for the beach than a regular job would allow. On the East Bay of Matagorda Island was the pristine beach. I preferred a rugged, wild beach that lay beyond a sharp bend in the road, a bend called Sargent. Sargent had, Sargent *was*, a general store—gas, groceries, gadgets. A few miles beyond the bend, an old swing-draw bridge, wooden and creaky, crossed the Gulf Waterway onto an island. Gulf waters on Sargent Beach churn dirty brown foam. This piece of coast, always known as Sargent Beach, was fisherman's paradise long before developers came, sharks to blood. Planted on the gulf side of the island, a large billboard *Welcome To Holiday Isle* weathered—accelerated erosion swept it to the deep.

Before the billboard vanished, row after row of beach houses became waterfront property—complacent old-timers patiently watched "that ol' guff" gobble them all. Until the scheme was halted, Sargent Beach teemed with families of suckers who swallowed hook, line and sinker—like the "guff." It was a short summer for *Holiday Isle,* the island once more called Sargent Beach—the name it had always been called.

Surfers, searchers for the perfect wave, discovered the turbulence of Sargent surf. Dilapidated panel wagons accompanied by badly rusted Chevies and Fords drifted in on Fridays, packing whatever they needed—usually not much. They dug a two-day scene, then split with the weekend. Locals called them a bunch of mongrels, pleasure-seeking idlers not wanted. I saw little difference between hanging out on a board and hanging around

——————— Σ ———————

on a line—surfers are a far lovelier sight than tough-hide fishermen.

Surfing on the island never became legend, no Malibu. For me, it was the stuff of dreams. Isolated on a remote piece of land's end considered worthless, elegant bodies, superbly acrobatic, dazzled—daring dancers, solo in the sun. Summer on Sargent Beach doesn't end.

Long days with no companion passed slowly; humid nights alone, slower. Lost in a sea of turbulence, I didn't seem likely to find a friend. Days, I languished on Sargent Beach. Nights were unbearable—I was lonely.

I trekked along sandy, flotsam-strewn shore, poking in litter and debris. The beach was all my own, seldom a person to invade secret places I discovered, places known only to me, places that thrilled my senses. Thought in a primitive setting, eternity of sky and forever of ocean, is not tamable—its dreams, magnificent manna.

One day at noon, the sun hot, the sky above the beach a clear boundless blue, the surf lay still, perfectly level. Without a breeze, the water crystal green was without ripple. On bottom, waist deep and beyond, sand sparkled. Glistening grains could be counted. This haunting sea held me a long while in silence. It seemed to have calmed for me—a sea not before, never again after, have I seen at Sargent Beach.

I found a lagoon that day, trapped inland behind a barrier of low dunes, silent waters dark emerald and deep. I doted on its ephemeral spell and escaped—transcended the lackluster of my uneventful life. My body felt restrained. I thirsted for freedom. I stepped naked into fullness of mind and spirit. I was a breath, a whisper. I was the wind, the sun. I was lifted into the blue where mysterious forces abide—yes, *abide*. Another season this lagoon would be gone, leaving no trace; from this sand, my childhood steps erased, swept under surf and spreading foam. To future seasons we each belong.

I returned to the lagoon often, seeking refuge from my troubling and anxious world, one I felt catapulting beyond control. My initial experience was never repeated. Instead, I found a feeling of peace, one of quiet calm infused with awe. I sensed an understanding—the lagoon was my place, caught in time for me. Through the years since, no such perfect moment has touched me as did the lagoon.

I discovered a second island on Sargent Beach, perched on the gulf side of the Waterway. The Driftwood Inn, a wooden shoe box weathered dull gray like its surroundings, seemed unimposing. Under a flat roof, rows of

————— Σ —————

screened windows commanded a view of water east and west. Inside, simple chairs had scattered among square, straight-leg tables, each covered in red-checker oilcloth, each with its own candle jar—red or amber. In a corner at one end a kitchen was partitioned and a jumble of tall stools lined a high counter serving as bar. Centered on the wall at opposite end was an old Wurlitzer, its cathedral-shape facade swirling in whorls of soft rosy color. Table and chair never migrated to this part of the Inn, wood-plank flooring as smoothly worn as glazed tile.

Kay and Fred owned the place. Not without age, they were ageless, seeming neither older nor more weatherbeaten than their surroundings. He, a swarthy man with ruddy face, always sat at "his" table near passageway to the kitchen. His table, a clutter of long neck empties often in company with a bottle of whisky, stood apart from other tables. Fred rarely spoke, seldom to Kay. Periodically rising from his chair, he collected whatever empties he could manage, knocking his table about in the process. With moderate control, he shuffled behind the bar to deposit empties in returnable cartons, fetching himself a cold one and returning to his table. The same no matter the time of day, Fred wasn't rushed in drinking—he kept steady at it.

I got an odd feeling from him. This piece of humanity, for whatever reason, disappointment too large or event too sad to handle, one day shut himself off in a world moving now only to the pace of his shuffle.

Kay was the cheerful one. A small, fragile woman with shining eyes darting bird-like with a disposition to match, she was a talker. It didn't take much to figure out checker oilcloths with candles were hers, probably the jukebox as well—things *she* needed, not Fred. Whether Kay drank, or what she drank, I was never sure. She seemed always tipsy in a manner perhaps clumsy. Her wispy, slurred speech and outward appearance did not much show effect of alcohol. Kay was a romantic, a person swept through life on a vision of remote imagery. Where it had swept her was the Driftwood Inn.

Kay ran the place—she did the *work*. Whatever that amounted to, I was never certain, the Driftwood deserted each time I was there. For me, it became a regular stop—I formed addiction to Kay's vanilla malted. Talk between us was easy—*she* talked. Kay needed no prompting for conversation. Her yarns no doubt were truthful; once, at least; or partly so—trapped in characters of other circumstance. I laughed with her, not so much over the stories as at her quick, animated way of telling them. I think Kay adored

————— Σ —————

having me there, someone to let her talk—someone to listen.

The old jukebox featured honky-tonk, drinking songs slow and sad; loving songs lonesome and blue; songs that fit my every mood, sending echo into emptiness I couldn't reach. I never had enough quarters and Kay would slip behind the bar to hand me a fistful. "Here, play some more. Then le's dance." We did dance, me more clumsy than her. When I made an excuse to sit one out, she continued alone, gliding beautifully, lost in reverie on the polished planks. I could almost see her striking partner.

Nighttime spoke with many voices, more so on the beach. I preferred a silver moon with attendant symphony of stars to dull lights and crackling neon—such aloneness on the beach, better than abject loneliness in Bay Prairie. Sounds of the sea, be they gentle or rough, compel. Cool, salty breezes tease. Under a full moon the rain of phosphorescent creatures wildly tossed and re-tossed across a glimmer-streaked mirror is poetry. This milieu I played, a vista that dwarfed sense of self—shot it to infinity.

My life will not be ordinary, shackled in sameness. I will be a prince, among men. A prince—not from towers, not from above; a prince—*among* men. I will smell their dust, taste their sweat, feel the sting of their tears. A *prince*—my blood spilt among them. Touch my garments, soil them—take them from me. I'll walk naked among you. By my nakedness you'll know we are not different. We're of the same dust—the dust of princes.

Words came loudly, someday a question put, "Who's been among them as I would be? On him I lay my mantle; in his hand, place my staff."

* * * * *

I had never *seen* a sailboat. That summer, I set out to build one, using an empty barn for shipyard and any scrap of lumber on which I could lay hand. I had no plan or diagram, no sketch and no experience. Basic handiness with simple carpentry tools was my only qualification. I had only a vague mental image, the reason itself for my project equally vague. In part to compensate my feeling of being lost, I think it also filled a need for *positive* industry. I have to admit, I fell under the spell of the ocean. What boy in adolescence doesn't dream of running away to sea?

By midsummer the boat was all but finished, lacking its rudder, a keel, some paint and sails. My fantasy to share the adventure with a mate, what good was the boat to me alone? Discouraged, ready to junk the whole project, Ronnie entered my life—*because* of the boat! He dropped by one

——————— Σ ———————

noon. "I heard about your boat, can I take a look?" There *had* been talk. I was aware of snickers—a *flat* bottom *sail* boat!

Ronnie lived nearby, on the road to Bay Prairie. Two years younger than me, fall would begin his senior year at Vandal Lake. I knew Ronnie, knew *of* him, through school—with ninety-four students, one *knows* everyone. Ronnie's hair was blond, cut flattop; his build, slight but firm. Between hazel-blue eyes and dimpled smile a touch of freckles bridged his nose. A bit shy, Ronnie preferred the ambiguity of being a face in the crowd.

"Wow!" he exclaimed, touching the ship a second time over, his face beaming. "You really *have* done it!" To be fair, the boat fit somewhere on a scale far-less-than-perfect to something-more-than-crude. Ronnie's excitement was contagious—through his eyes, I too was seeing for the first time. Straight-out, he took me by storm. "Can I help finish 'er?"

Suddenly, I was thrilled. "Wow, Ronnie, sure!" I shouted—plainly, simply, utterly *thrilled!*

Jim once said, "It doesn't take much to please you, does it. Simple things, they do it, don't they." Yes, dear Jim, simple things—the hardest to attain. How many times in reach, almost in grasp, how many? How many times touched, how many? How often the promise, how often, pain?

Ronnie proved his zeal with piracy. He slipped through a window in the vocational shop at Vandal Lake, chalked a keel freehand on a scrap of metal plate and quickly cut it out using a torch. He fashioned and welded brackets to fasten it onto the boat. He *borrowed* paint, a gallon of white and a quart of vivid orange. He began giving me directions to an Army Surplus Store. I said, "Hey, Ronnie, why don't *you* drive?" From that time, Ronnie drove us in my car wherever we went.

A parachute was salvaged as sail. Its tough, braided cord made stout line for rigging. Ronnie had a better sense than me how these things should be. He outlined on plywood a shape for the rudder. I worked at that while he painted. In barely a week we were done.

On the afternoon of that particular Thursday, I was on my knees at the stern tightening screws to secure the rudder. Ronnie was busy at the bow attaching final rigging hardware. I stood, looking at Ronnie across the length of *our* boat. I was seeing him through a different eye, one unfamiliar to me, one whose scope extended beyond mere vision. A single eye, centered slightly forward on my forehead, it was larger and brighter than ordinary eyes. A

——————— Σ ———————

powerful beam seeming more as energy than illumination arced through that eye. I perceived myself in its energy, completely me. I was not completely in molecular form, my head vaporized in a silvery gray haze. I felt I was *seeing* directly *through* self.

Suddenly, with a jolt, I saw Ronnie, busy at his task. I *saw* Ronnie, my whole being focused on him. For an instantaneous flash—or awhile that had no relation to time—I was altogether my *self* without being at all *in* my *self*. Brilliant, clear light surrounded me, encompassing Ronnie.

A certain *knowing* pervaded. More than thought, more than realization, *awareness* engulfed me—love for Ronnie.

I didn't move. I stood as if in granite, my body pitched at some high level of vibration I can't describe. This is the *funny* part—what just occurred struck me as commonplace, perfectly *normal*.

Soon, thought made a crash landing—my love for Ronnie, a boy, would brand me. I knew the word such love was called, a hateful and despised word. What I experienced in that extraordinary moment gave me comfort. A feeling of profound love exploded throughout emptiness I carried within. I knew then the power of love could heal darkness. To become whole and complete, to feel love, is not wrong. I would be branded, hated and despised. No matter the names called—*love* is not queer.

This is the *peculiar* part—none of what I realized bothered me. If one stubs his big toe or bangs an elbow, right away it gets his attention, *Ouch!* It didn't hurt so very much after all. He carries on with whatever he was about, a little sting carries right on with him—a *reminder*. That's how it is for me, my little sting, my *reminder*, part of my life—a large part.

This is dangerous ice on which I skate. In other circumstance, the sight or smell or proximity of his body turning me on—had I merely gotten a hard-on for him, or been *fooling* around with him—my sudden *queer* feeling for Ronnie would be easier to swallow. Lust, sex, depravity—the world is an eager marketplace. I said so already, I had no concept of sex, not a vague notion, nothing beyond a mysterious man-woman marriage bed following I-do's and rice. Ronnie and I hadn't been *fooling* around, *not* up to this point—to be blunt, I had never *fooled* around with anyone.

I was ignorant, stupid. Jim said so—maybe he didn't. "You are so naive. Or else totally *stupid!*" He knuckled the top of his head with both fists. Jim did that to show the limits of his frustration. "No one is *that* naive.

—————— Σ ——————

I don't believe anyone is that *stupid!"* Look again, Jim. One thing I forgot to mention—ignorance is *not* bliss.

Life has a way of sneaking from the rear rather than leaping suddenly in one's face. Is there pulsing undiscovered spiritual code hidden within undiscovered spiritual gene? Why things come as sometimes they do, is mystery. My vision of love came on Thursday, time and place firmly fixed. I could little guess how far it would take me.

* * * * *

At noon the following day we launched our boat in the Gulf Waterway. Trimmed in vivid orange and gleaming white, the sixteen-foot hull easily rode the water. Our twenty-foot mast carried a fourteen-by-sixteen-foot mainsail and its nine-by-twelve-foot flying jib. The single hatch we painted bright orange—it proved a perfect touch. We hadn't christened our craft. Ronnie's mom sent along an unlabeled bottle, homemade wine made from wild grapes—*that* we saved for later.

Somewhere Ronnie laid hands on a conch the size of a ripe melon. Spiral tip abraded, a mouth-size hole entered directly its deepest chamber. He said it would make a good horn. My contribution was a yacht ensign no bigger than a bandanna. It flew proudly from a staff Ronnie fixed at the stern. The sky clear, the sea calm, the air bright—our adventure began.

We launched our craft from a ramp on the mainland opposite the Driftwood Inn. A young couple, Raymond and Dee, had an old bait camp there. He was a sometime shrimper—Dee supported them from a small cafe enclosed within pilings supporting the house. It sat on water's edge, a slight harbor dredged from the bank of the Waterway. Framed by remnant of a one-time pier, the harbor faced the old bridge, fronting the road where it abruptly ended. Though it wasn't much, Raymond said we could tie up there—our own marina. The creaky pier was mostly skeleton. Ronnie and I, reckless and daring, danced across it.

A crowd of curious onlookers gathered while we were rigging. We pushed out to deep water and hoisted sail. Kay, outside the Driftwood Inn, was all smiles. She was birdlike, hopping, jumping up and down, slap-clapping her frail hands. She shouted, "Give in to 'er, mate! Lean to it, hard 'round! Heave-ho! Heave-ho!" From her apron she whisked a dishcloth, flung it round and round overhead, delirious.

It took a few tries before we got the hang of it—we were sailing!

——————— Σ ———————

47

Down coast from the bridge on the Waterway—we were sailing! Sailing on the bounding main, alone with my love—near him, at his side, all I needed. We were together. We could make it, could survive. We had each other, my beautiful blond, my beautiful boy, and me—the simple things!

Ronnie was not let in on our love affair, a fact of no matter. Love happens as it will, is sure to happen. Isn't *that* the way it is? I was rapt in ecstasy. Ronnie's presence, his nearness, was all I could imagine. More, I was unable to conceive—this love had yet to kindle desire. I may have wished for the touch of his hand in mine, may have longed for embrace of his body to mine, may have burned for the brush of his lips on mine—yes, this was enough, this satisfied. Ronnie *liked* me. It was telling; it showed.

The afternoon wore and so did we. We turned 'er 'bout 'n' steered for port. Rounding the last bend in full view of the bridge, Ronnie on impulse picked up the conch, cupping it with fingers well inside its wide lip. He intended to announce our homecoming. Feet wide, standing firm at the bow, he blew into the hole. *Tawoo, tawoo, tawoo* sounded in deep resonance from calcium chambers. Ronnie beamed at me one of his broad grins. Then, the big horn on the bridge answered, *Bawoo! Bawoo! Bawoo!* Access aprons groaned upward and the diesel engine revved. A sound from steel cable slapping tautly surface of the water preceded the old tub's crawling swing to shore. Ronnie looked ahead and I, behind. No other boat traffic could be seen, the old bridge swinging open for our dinghy craft!

We didn't know maritime code—we knew well enough not to blast for the bridge on a tease. Faces red from the sun, we sailed on through. Ronnie said, "I'm not blowin' that thing again—I'll find somethin' else to suck!" He gave me a big grin and scrunched his nose. A little farther up the Waterway we banked in a shallow cove to take down mast and rigging. We paddled back, slipping underneath one of the bridge aprons. The operator grinned at us, waving from the railing. I think he opened the bridge for the hell of it. In a carefree way, it was fitting climax to our maiden voyage.

The sun burned a red horizon, lazy shadows crawled. While Dee grilled us hamburgers, Ronnie and I discussed sleeping on the boat—she offered a tent. A bulky canvas wad of olive-drab army surplus, it became an octopus the more we tugged. At last set up, it commanded the point of a low bluff behind the boat ramp, overlooking the Waterway. Raymond dropped two bundles at our feet. "It ain't much, 'bout as good as we c'n do." Ronnie

——————— Σ ———————

and I unfolded the bundles, pleased to find camp cots. "Tell ya' what," Raymond went on, "later when it's good dark, one of ya' slip 'round to th' back door, over by th' bait box, 'n' give a knock." He winked.

The cots looked lost inside our roomy tent. We pulled on Levis, no shirts. Ronnie brought out the bottle of wine. "Ready?" he grinned. We drank some of it, not much. "Whee-ugh!" Ronnie spit. "It's sour as vinegar 'n' bitter'n hell. Downright *vile* stuff," he frowned, *"real* nasty."

After some discussion, we concluded it to be good dark. "Wonder what he wants, Pinchy?" Ronnie began calling me that—I don't know his reason. Each time saying it, he scrunched his nose and grinned at me—it gave me a cozy feeling. The sour wine had me warmed all the way to my ears. I merely shrugged, having no better notion than Ronnie what Raymond meant. Ronnie grinned at me and his eyes sparkled. "Wanna find out?" he challenged. "Sure," I said, and off we went.

Ronnie waited by the corner and I knocked at the door. It swung open and Raymond thrust a large, unwieldy paper bag in my arms. It was heavy, its contents chinked. "Here. Ya' little sons o' bitches deserve this—I don't know nothin', understand? Now git gone."

Whoever said there are no angels? The bag held a dozen bottles of cold beer. Ronnie was delighted. He danced around me. "Whoop-ee! No more sour grapes tonight! C'mon, Pinchy!" It was probably the best thing that could've happened. We had a fine day together, the whole night beckoned. It only lacked something to do, and we had it—cold beer. Ronnie was no stranger in that department. He drank long necks like a pro. This time, I was doing alright with beer, too. There was lots of joking, a good bit of touching, a fair amount of falling all over each other—my first time to get drunk with a guy, just me and him. This guy was more than just a guy. He was Ronnie, and it felt good—*all* of it.

Four bottles were left in the bag when we opted to go to the beach, a half mile across the bridge. There wasn't reason I can recall—it seemed the thing to do. I was pretty high. I guess Ronnie was, too. Barefoot in Levis we set out, Ronnie clutching the collapsed paper bag.

We skipped and trotted, ran foot races, faked games of tag—excuse to grab ass. Rough pavement became soft sand, warm in places, then cool, now damp. It tingled the bottoms of my feet. Warm shivers shot up my body. Cool breeze from the sea licked my bare chest. Ronnie's nipples were

—————— Σ ——————

tight, puckering buttons. We walked silently on the beach, me in my cosmic world, Ronnie in his, both worlds side by side. I got the sensation of a quick-start bump, like a boot from the rear. I realized Ronnie was smack inside my cosmic world, and I, in his. There weren't two worlds anymore—just one.

We sat on the rounded trunk of a large tree abandoned by waves and scoured as smooth as silk. Ronnie opened the last two beers and handed me one. Our fingers touched. The air was sweet. A full moon riding a cloudless sky reflected in gentle surf—streams of light.

We slipped to the sand, leaning against the tree, gazing at the sky, tracing with unsteady fingers patterns and outlines. We sailed the sky, roamed stars, spoke of dreams. Our course uncharted, we steered by night. When bare shoulders chanced a touch, I quivered in the calm.

We waded along shore, into the water waist-deep. We splashed in liquid night. An urging sea teased, tugging wet denim. Rivulets glistened on Ronnie's naked torso. He threw back his head. Salty spray streaked my face, taste of the sea heavy on my lips. *God! He is beautiful!* I wondered how my body looked through his eyes. I *thought* I saw the answer in his smile.

Ronnie flung an arm across my shoulders. He led us from the water, led us up the beach, back along the pavement. The night was ours. It belonged to us, held us still. Inside the tent, Ronnie shoved the cots side by side. Smell of old canvas copper coated was thick and musky. We didn't bother with damp denim. We dropped on the cots, side by side. I soon fell asleep, warmth from Ronnie's body near mine, a whisper of his breath on my cheek—it had been an almost perfect night.

It was a dream I dreamed, an image I conjured in darkness of wet-hot night. My blond, my beautiful blond at last lay sleeping beside me. He stretches out his hand through the night, reaches across darkness for me —reaches for *me*. He raises me to him. I feel his hands, feel him raising me. I feel him lifting me, holding me. I feel his hands, holding and caressing, fondling. My body is hard, quivering. Blood is hot, throbbing. "Oh, Ronnie, yeah. I'm coming. Coming! Ohhh, Ronnie! Yeah!"

It had been, after all, a perfect night. It had been the dream I dreamed. Fantasy that played in me a year before was here no fantasy, the vision made flesh. More than that, I leave for others to qualify. The experience is mine. I can live with that—after all, it *had* been a perfect night.

The tent remained on the point from the time we staked it. "Jus'

——————— Σ ———————

leave 'er up," Raymond said, giving us his sly wink. "You boys'll want 'er again." Sometimes another guy, maybe others, stayed over. Ronnie kept our cots side by side. "Here, eat this," he said, cramming something, fingers and all, into my mouth. "Dee fixed it. She said feed you."

Life on the point became that way. "Pinchy!" Ronnie said one day, "Wear something of mine so I can wear your shirt." Afterward we had "the pile" of clothes. There seemed always beer from somewhere, one night a bottle of sherry. Ronnie made a terrible face. "Damned nasty, Pinchy. *Vile!*"

Evenings we pooled our money, piling it in the middle of a table at the Driftwood Inn. We established "our" table at the end opposite Fred's, in front of the Wurlitzer. Kay, always with us, took great delight in her young couple. I never knew what she made of the grins and smiles, our winks and secret looks we thought we were stealing. Laughter sparkled between us, always reason to touch, poke or jab, bump into and rub against one another. It seems to me we were never more than inches apart.

One night Ronnie and I danced at the Driftwood. It wasn't a slow dance. I would've liked holding him close to me as when I danced with Kay. This was a be-bop variation Ronnie and I invented. Kay had told the jukebox man, "put on some new 45's—we need to get the stuffiness outta here." She wanted us to perform. Kay was thrilled, hopping her little jump, patting together her little hands. "Oh, good! Do it again. Good! Good! Let me try!"

We were in love. It was telling; it showed.

A thousand nights, a thousand beds; a thousand words left empty unsaid; a thousand faces, some forgotten, some dead.

Too soon summer days fell short—such halcyon days don't last. Raymond nodded toward the tent, omitting his customary wink. "You boys'll need to take 'er down, summer's 'bout gone." I wanted it to go on, without end. After all, it had been a perfect summer.

Today, as I reflect, the sun yet is shining, days long and hot. It is only a step, from the bait camp to the point, to the tent, to Ronnie. The Driftwood's planks are polished, the old Wurlitzer hot with honky-tonk. There is a sea by day, a moon by night; a sailboat lying at anchor; a pile of clothes, two cots. Always, there is Ronnie—always.

What gauge can I apply? Things once were measured with sticks. This is my stick, against which a lifetime is measured. After all, it was a perfect summer—the most sweet, bittersweet of my life.

———————— Σ ————————

I am gay

Jim sent a couple of letters during the summer. They were short and to the point—covered it all. He hated the job at the mill, he was shunned by his old friends, his father stayed on his ass. Not doing anything much—*You?* He was eager to get back to Austin. Oh, was I familiar with unbleached domestic? He got some from the mill to make curtains for our room, maybe enough for bedspreads, too. What did I think about it? He phoned Mother Ferrell. She said fine with her. His mother offered to trim them with orange rick-rack, nothing too fancy. Sound okay?

"Sounds great, Jim," I answered back. Our summer shared a lot in common; a lot, with one exception—Ronnie. I *may* have mentioned Ronnie in a letter to Jim; maybe I didn't. If so, it was no more than *mention*. One other thing I didn't mention, I didn't want to think about—separation from Ronnie. I didn't know how to face it.

A remedy can be had if one looks hard enough. I found one—I put it off. Stupid I may have been, not dumb. I knew it must come about. If prolonged, I could ease into it. On the right track, pieces fit neatly together. I had a good feeling, confidence high—nothing could go wrong.

Ronnie's classes at Vandal Lake were another week away, the first week at UT set aside for registration and Rush. We could spend a few days together in Austin. Ronnie liked the idea. "Rush what, Pinchy?" he wanted to know. I told him about campus Greeks—I didn't know a damned thing about them. I was a GDI—god-damned independent. I didn't know much more about them than I knew about Greeks. We set out for Austin, Ronnie driving while I played a new role, Big Man On Campus.

I remember a swell feeling I got, knowing I had the answer to a question, certain I'd be called on even before raising my hand. I remember a large feeling bursting inside me when the teacher said, "Very good! You get *two* stars today!" That is the way I was feeling—*proud!*

Jim took care of the room, making all arrangements. I never *looked* at it. He said it was the best room in the place—that was good enough for

——————— Σ ———————

me. I knew we'd have a long porch, not a cramped landing. That's where we spotted Jim, sitting on the railing—Ichabod with his back against a post, outstretched legs crossed at the ankle and ever-present Winston burning between bony fingers. When Jim saw us approach, he frowned. One other thing I hadn't thought to do—alert Jim to Ronnie's coming with me.

"Thought you'd never get here. I came early, been waitin' two whole days. Got the curtains up, wait'll you see 'em. Had enough for matching bedspreads, too. Who's this?" That, he said in one breath, the look on his face, *real* egg. "Glad to meet'cha," Jim tossed at Ronnie. "You didn't mention *him* in your letters—Ronnie, is it?"

"Surely I must've," I said. Ronnie was embarrassed, his face red-hot. I knew he caught the drift of Jim's slur. Jim didn't mean "who's this?" He meant, *"who th' hell's this buttin' in, what th' hell's he doin' here—WHY?"* Did I fail to mention Jim could be rude?

I felt *I* had egg on *my* face. Ronnie managed a grin and a timorous giggle, as though to wonder, "What do I do now?" He slipped me a quick Driftwood-Inn glance, looking to ask, "Still with me, Pinchy?"

Sure, Babe, I love ya'!

Chit-chat and more chit-chat, unloading the car didn't take long. I bragged on the curtains and matching bedspreads—they *were* smart. My attention focused on the single bed destined to become *ours* for the night, Ronnie's and mine. We slept side by side on cots, never in a *real* bed—this bed intended for *one*. I was pleased—I'd never felt more devious!

Jim overcame initial hostility. He probably felt ignored—I wanted Ronnie all to myself. I took him on a walking tour, pointing out what I knew of campus, unaware I'd become an old pro. Campus *did* seem more exciting. I was *sure* having Ronnie at my side made the difference!

We ducked into a campus hangout for burgers before heading to the Cottages. Ronnie wanted to see the town, cruise around. *Cruise* meant drive around, nothing more. It's what we do in Bay Prairie—drive the main street up and down, looking lean and mean; circle through local drive-in hangouts, and *hang out.* I wasn't sure how to entertain Ronnie. Austin, no *small* town, was a *city*, a city downtown at night deserted—*deserted,* for all *I* knew.

I heard a most awful racket as we neared the Cottages. The noise grew louder as we neared the stairway. One foot on the lower step, I looked up to see Jim near the top, dragging behind him a roll-away. I was per-

———————— Σ ————————

plexed. I was stunned—a *roll-away!* Where th' hell did *that* come from!

"Hi, guys," Jim called cheerfully. "I found this downstairs. Thought ya' could use it. They keep one on hand," he paused, "for this reason."

Surely Jim meant "for this purpose." Surely he meant "for use when needed." His pause struck me as incomplete thought—*for this reason, to keep the likes of you apart.* I sensed in Jim jealousy. I wondered if he slyly guessed my intention, suspected Ronnie and me of being queer. Purpose of the hideous roll-away seemed obvious—separate Ronnie from me. This was an arena into which I would not tolerate intrusion. My mouth was too dry to suck shame—*for this reason!* Suddenly I was singled out, struggling inside a narrowing ring, fighting to overcome a pair of wretched shoes.

"Damn you! *Damn* you!" I shouted, stomping my foot on the lower step of the stairway. The balcony shuddered, doors and windows flew open. My wrath belonged to Jim. He earned it, blundering deaf and blind into my private summer. I glared at him, said nothing more. The Winston hung from his lips momentarily, then became airborne. I don't know what Jim may have seen looking down at my face. Color drained from his—thankful at that moment the stairs between us were blocked.

What more could go wrong? I didn't see Ronnie's reaction. I hooked an arm through his and hurried us to the car. I drove into downtown, cruising South Congress. Finally, Ronnie asked, "What was all that about, Pinchy?" The sound of his voice told me the incident made him uncomfortable. "It was—nothing, really," I said, wanting to put it far out of mind. "Jim has a way about him—sometimes he makes me mad."

At Barton Springs Road, Ronnie spotted a miniature golf course. "Hey, Pinchy, beat ya' a game. Loser pays?"

We dropped into Anywhere, Suburbia, amid families, tykes and toddlers—an ordinary, *normal* circumstance. Something about the situation seemed *abnormal*—I felt invisible. I became a Black Hole, unrecognized and unknown; a significant part of me nullified—a fearful thought, unseen and untouched. Where can I find hope? How can I be loved?

I couldn't accept the notion God had disallowed my life. My feeling for Ronnie wasn't *wrong;* what I felt with him, special. I *knew* love wasn't wrong; it, too, special. I'd have said so to anyone that night—even God. Our game was better than any on the course. We played and lost, played and won, played more. I wasn't eager to return to the Cottages—the roll-away

————— Σ —————

awaited. I hated the thought. What more to do on an Austin evening?

Jim appeared asleep—maybe he was. He left the bathroom light burning with the door ajar. A thin crack of light spotlighted the roll-away, gaped open at the foot of what now was doomed to be *my* bed. I would be dishonest not to tell it all. The roll-away was tidy as a tack, white sheets freshly tucked, crisp case on a plump pillow, a coverlet folded to blanket the foot. It was no use to continue fretting; what was done, done. I fell asleep soon, hearing Jim flip-flop and pummel his pillow with a fist.

I didn't ask about the linen, where it came from or where it went, not then, not later. I didn't ask. I knew it was Jim's. He did it all, located the roll-away, dragged it upstairs, laid it neatly out *for this reason*—Jim cared.

A simple word would have been sufficient. That I was unable to tell Jim *Thanks!* was not due to my lack of realization. I wasn't insensitive. I was wrapped in layers of fear and misapprehension. I was embarrassed at my outburst of temper, afraid Jim may have regarded it a childish tantrum. I was humiliated. More truthfully, I felt like a rotten heel.

Jim saw to it our room was never subject to morning sun. His last duty before plunging to bed was one of scurrying about, yanking window blinds as tightly shut as old slats would permit. Our room was kept in still coolness of night and gray light of dawn.

Jim went out early, leaving Ronnie and me to sleep undisturbed. I awoke at ten-thirty, Ronnie yet a tangle woven with the sheet. It draped the length of his body, wistful here, teasing there. Thin cotton briefs casually worn caressed him carelessly—clinging, rounding, protruding. This was the first time I'd seen Ronnie sleeping, *watched* him, that is. The sight of his body is easy, a picture etched in clarity. Comely, proportioned, artful—those words come to mind. The word that came first to my mind was miracle, knowing I touched his body. It does not seem possible love can end in flesh.

Ronnie woke and leaned on an elbow. I tossed a pillow to the foot of my bed and propped myself facing him. We talked, about nothing; spoke, little; said, less. We were languid and dreamy. This, the part I best liked, more so than nights. Looking, that's what counts— seeing. It is like a window, giving glimpse of images greater than can be grasped.

I didn't bother tidying. We left the room as-was. Ronnie wanted breakfast and I was apprehensive at the prospect of facing Jim. The day stagnated in routine. On campus I picked up a registration schedule and we

———— Σ ————

headed for the clock tower. It rises prominent on the Austin skyline, dubbed Penis on the Plains. The observation deck gives a view of Austin nothing short of spectacular. I wanted to give the view to Ronnie—perched on a light pole in Bay Prairie, I knew he'd never see doodle from there. After the roll-away incident, it seemed likely we'd pack up and leave that afternoon. I was grappling for a memorable event, hoping to salvage our special disaster.

That, too, I bungled. Rather, it was bungled *for* me, the Tower not yet open for visitors. It made me wonder if I could ever balance these two worlds I shakily juggled. I shunned the thought, carrying another disappointment back to the Cottages.

Jim sat on the porch, Winston in hand. Ronnie picked up his things and ducked out. "See'ya at the car, Pinchy." The roll-away was neatly made, as was *my* bed. I busied myself shoving aside cartons to unpack later. Jim quietly stepped inside.

"I owe you an apology," he began cautiously, the words coming hard. "I thought—hell, I don't know what I thought. I'm sorry. I offended you in some way. I'm sorry. I *hope* you can forgive me." It isn't bad dialog—it's what Jim said. He didn't make it up—he meant it. There was sadness in his voice, pain in his face.

"I do, Jim," I said slowly. I didn't need to be told, I said it myself—I was shit. I treated Jim badly. I should be the one apologizing. Set to make a fresh start, I began with old baggage. What is this chemistry? I have never understood why Jim put up with me.

"Friends?" Jim extended his hand. I didn't hesitate. "Yes, Jim, friends." Only two times did Jim and I use that masculine greeting—one, the afternoon we first met a year before; the other, this. I never gave Jim an apology. I never again thought of him as Ichabod.

Ronnie was a sleeper on long drives. I took the wheel—I was a thinker, my thoughts as I drove not startling. They made me feel smaller than I felt before. Different from Phil, Jim cared. Between Jim and me, there had been only a simple handshake, no elegant phrases. In its simplicity, that handshake was more complex than Phil's physics. Unlike Phil, Jim did not turn his back on me. I began to see my needs as basic—deep, requiring little. Beside me, Ronnie slept peacefully, his face lovely, his body sublime. I was filled again with awe. Even so, I had to admit, I was eager to return to Austin. The incident with the roll-away put Jim and me on firmer ground.

——————— Σ ———————

We would not speak of it again—not until a later time.

There are times separation comes naturally, follows a subtle course, the moment but an incidental thread in a fabric. Such was that moment with Ronnie and me. Stopped outside his parents' house, we said the usual things. You'll be back on weekends? Yeah, I'll be back. Holidays there'll be more time? Sure, lots of time. Next summer, we'll have all summer? Yeah, all of summer. We said the *usual* things, not the *important* ones. You'll miss me? How about holidays—still love me? Next summer all ours?—I can't wait! A thousand times—*YES! I love you.* Those three words we were not to speak, not to hear, not to think. To dare was to court death.

"I'm not much on letters," Ronnie said, "I'll try—if you write me." A letter is easier to answer than to initiate—the burden shifts. Ronnie's little phrase *if you write me* said what couldn't be said, said what we had no words to say. *"I care about you—please, don't forget me;"* tucked away, folded between I care and don't forget, *"I'll be here—waiting."*

Ronnie held the car door open and touched one foot to the ground. A swimsuit we shared that summer lay between us on the seat where last it had been tossed. He swung back on impulse and picked up the garment. "Can I keep this, Pinchy?"

It pleased me, the whole idea, this little fistful of cloth that had been intimate with each of us by turns. "Wow, Ronnie! Sure!" It was fitting; it suited. I drove away with an erection.

* * * * *

Cozby dropped by the Cottages, "ambled over—I had nothing better to do." That was understatement. He made a point to reestablish contact. It also was pure Cozby—he closely guarded emotion. Anytime it peeked through it did so slipping out in humor.

"Have I given Lecture Two-Twenty-Two-B, summer work in the Midland-Odessa oil patch?" That, also, was Cozby—entertainment. He had a novel way of getting at things. Jim soon had it figured out, the higher Cozby's lecture number, the more insane its content. Cozby could entertain, no question on that. Once going, he fed on attention.

I found it hard to visualize Cozby on an oil derrick, wiry artist with glib tongue. Curly dark hair tufting about the lower edge of a hardhat wasn't my image of roustabout. Jim later said, in his cool and casual manner, "Cozby probably drove a beat-up old pickup truck on dusty back roads

———————— Σ ————————

delivering junk all summer." It was difficult to put anything over on Jim.

The tale Cozby wove had nothing to do with summer work, it being his exposé of which respectable wives, including that of the Baptist preacher, were sleeping with which roughneck. He wound up in a knee-slapping finale, "they're all Bible-beatin' bigots, the biggest bunch in the Belt." Cozby seemed compelled to distance himself from west Texas fundamentalism with which he grew up—I sensed in him embarrassment. I didn't have Jim's acumen. I knew enough to believe Cozby's faith deeper than even he cared to admit. "It isn't faith that bothers Cozby," Jim said. "It's hypocrisy he hates—goody-goody on Sunday, fucky-fucky on Monday."

Gale kept his room next door, locking it for the summer and paying rent to avoid moving his belongings. His new roommate, Scott, was a fresh-man from Turtle Creek, a posh Dallas suburb. Scott was a strawberry blond and Jim said he looked impish—impish, blond and dumb. I said *cute,* meaning, as well as his face, his body. Scott was not the fashion plate Gale aspired to become. Gale could—and usually did—look the part of a G-Q hopeful. Scott's wardrobe was a sports shirt and polished-cotton jeans, his favorite pair no longer so much polished as passively pleasant on him. He carried a six-inch comb in hip pocket alongside a leather wallet, burnished and well-contoured to his buttock. All I said to Jim was that Scott looked *nice.* "Yeah," Jim added, "if you're thirteen and into giggles."

Jim referred to Scott's comb as a Linus Blanket. Scott did become irksome, whipping out his comb, as Jim put it, "to finger through an over-sprayed bush of kinky hair a cyclone couldn't move." Jim, no backbiter, said such things straight to a person's face.

Despite Jim's annoyance, Scott wasn't unattractive. I don't suppose he was a handsome boy. Neither homely nor beautiful, he was, like his jeans, passively pleasant. He possessed a quality that made him hard to define. Later, I'd know that quality—my type.

One afternoon Jim dubbed him Winnie, as in Winnie-the-Pooh. Gale roared and the name stuck. Oddly, Scott *was* Winnie—a life-size, huggy-cuddly, hold-me-tight sleep-with-me-all-night Teddy Bear. That's how he struck me and that's what I called him—Teddy Bear.

Smith, the only other familiar face at the Cottages, kept his third-floor room in the big house. More committed to the serious than to the sublime, we seldom saw much of him. Why we never became acquainted

————— Σ —————

with any of the new guys that year, why none of them ever gyrated to our sphere, didn't seem a concern. It wouldn't have been—ours was *the* group. We were something of a molecular structure, each atom spinning in tension and balance, harmonious to a sharing and exchange of sub-atomic particles.

I despised English Lit with four assigned Dickens novels—none of which I finished reading. Dickens did hold great expectations—Robert. Wearing a brilliant yellow shirt, I noticed him first thing. Slender, with delicate facial features and dark hair; deep blue eyes set against skin the texture of pure vanilla ice-cream—Robert radiated. He was oblivious of the oblivion into which his looks plunged me. Next day, I saw him again, this time in accounting class. Robert was of such beauty I thought it never intended he be touched—certainly not by me. I wouldn't have dared speak to him. I *could* adore him Monday through Friday. I did—from a distance!

I spotted Tim in Greek philosophy. Tim, a husky guy, was solidly built, the cheeks of his face round and rosy, his short-cropped hair sandy. He walked with a hurried bounce I visualized being poetic feet. Tim was not Texas. He was from a colder climate, St. Louis. Despite that, he was a warm person—I saw it in his shining brown eyes.

I was bolder with Tim than I dared be with Robert. I followed Tim across campus after class, keeping distance I thought safely lost me in the crowd. Reality to a philosophy major, I was soon to discover, was no more obscure than I'd been in the crowd.

The second week of class Tim suddenly spun round on the wide plaza at the base of the Tower to confront me directly. He was in my face. "Do you come this way, too?" he bluntly demanded.

Tim's sudden nearness flustered me. I felt like an idiot, my clandestine tailing hadn't fooled him. "Yeah, every day," I stammered.

"Thought so," Tim replied cheerfully. "Always see you. C'mon. We can walk together." I needed no second invitation, quick to realize Tim had also taken notice of me.

Tim bounced away and I had to sprint to catch him, then trot to keep pace. I said Tim was not Texas—he operated in hurry-up-and-get-there gear. Soon we were there, the side entrance to the Tower library. Tim's lecture course was sandwiched somewhere within the stacks between the ground and the sky. He hurried inside, pausing at the door to turn and gaze at me. That's where he left me—somewhere between ground and sky.

——————— Σ ———————

Crossing campus with Tim became routine, even though my next class was far distant. After Tim disappeared into the Tower, I had to break into a wild run, always arriving late. I wasn't going to admit this to Tim and risk losing our trot-dates. I liked the sparkle about him, especially the sparkle of his eyes. His warmth appealed, and so did our trot-talks. Tim was casual, candid and intense, usually in one phrase. The openness he extended captured me—that's what began our relationship.

* * * * *

The glass by which I saw myself was beginning to fog. I discovered theatre and became infected with vision of a wider world. More than one small step beyond magic, theatre touched within me a pit of emptiness I felt gnawing. Due entirely to Jim, new relationships found with other guys gave hope for acceptance beyond Vandal Lake—an arena I bitterly despised. Prospect of finding expression for a sensitive nature made me covet the badge of courage *drama major*. The chasm I crossed from emptiness to Euripides was a broad leap, made so swiftly it seemed only a small step.

I may have leapt before I looked. My parents, practical and thrifty, would hear nothing of such nonsense—the axe dropped fully. I couldn't talk with them about emptiness inside and despicable rejection—notions beyond the utilitarian. Ours was not a relationship open to frank discussion about deep feeling. The business of life was a matter of getting on with it, keeping low and rolling with the punches; along the way, fulfilling requisite basics of home and hearth—assuredly, marriage and family.

I was crushed, or would have been, except I determined to become a drama major anyway. I had to remain in a business degree plan while insinuating myself into drama classes. Registration was a nightmare for my counselors. I conned enrollment in two courses. One was the philosophy course where I met Tim; the other, theatre history.

I wasn't taken with Victoria's London, Dickens no match against Sophocles and Shakespeare, Menander and Marlowe. I was obsessed with Athen's Fifth Century. In epic proportion, I soared tragic and heroic, becoming infatuated and absorbed. Oftentimes Jim would snort, "I know what those books are, *feelthy peectures!*" That absorbing aspect hadn't escaped me either, the male body perfected nude in marble, bronze and glaze. I got a feeling at times, mist back of my eyes clearing, vapor on a window slowly revealing what already is known. I belong to images on those pages, as

———————— Σ ————————

though looking and seeing, somehow is remembering and recollecting.

One evening in the academic center I sat at a table reading an assigned drama. The volume of Euripides lay open. Pages of a book, when left unattended, can flip open or shut, as this one had just done. From the volume's index, a title jumped at me—*Iphigenia in Aulis*. Startled, I myself jumped, pierced by a suddenly remembered image, a bouncing ball of liquid light with a crystal voice. What trickery was this, an extraordinarily fantastic imagination? Where else can ever I have heard those words?

I slammed the book shut and glanced around the library, thinking the disturbance may have called attention. I wanted assurance no one had witnessed the event—as though anything about it *could* have been seen. I slipped from the table and stole hurriedly out, into the Austin night.

I was baffled by this strange occurrence, troubled by uncertainty. I recalled from youth an old woman known locally as Aunty. She wandered in and out of her head, remembering things unknown, thinking she was in some distant place. "Pay her no mind," it was said, "the spell will pass."

Memory may be a trap, sifting and sorting, discarding and recycling bits of useless detail. This bit of detail was an embarrassment to me, more than Cozby's faith to him. The thought of my mind not being right—I could be wandering in and out of my head—was fearsome. Fear I would be accused of concocting so unbelievable a tale is what gripped me. *This* spell I determined assuredly *would* pass. I told no one, not even Jim. I no more wanted to be called liar than I wanted to be ridiculed.

* * * * *

Frequent weekend trips to the coast and to Ronnie continued. Our relationship didn't seem the same. Ronnie didn't talk as much, didn't laugh as before. At times, he was moody and withdrawn. I sensed a distance he placed between us. I could feel a certain point up to which, but not beyond, it was safe to approach. More frequently there was a third guy—not always the same one—who "happened" to come along. Inside, I raged, easy prey for a new emotion—*jealousy*. Ronnie began talking about the navy, thinking to enlist after graduation. At his mention of it, I cringed, afraid if he went away I would lose him—forever.

Saturday nights, dropping Ronnie at his parents' house, I'd drive, drive anywhere, letting the tears go. I hurt—pain I couldn't reach and pain I couldn't remedy swallowing me. The one place for which I longed I could

———————— Σ ————————

not go. Sargent Beach with echoes of our summer became unbearable.

Every weekend my father taunted me. "Are you going to bring that boat back?" I was despondent. "Yeah, sure," I'd mutter. "When? When?" he'd goad. At times, I think I meant to get it—probably I never intended at all. The brain may have all the thinking to do—the heart keeps it going, pumping in those tiny messages reason won't admit. The boat was part of something else. It belongs there, to that time and to that place. It belongs with the sand and the wind and a white-hot moon. It belongs to a summer never to be again—a summer now memory.

I heard a hatchet was taken to her mast. Dee's oldest hacked it down. A chilly afternoon on a late autumn Saturday, I drove down to the bait camp. Raymond was out front mending nets. "She's gone," he said, without looking from his needle. "Couple o' nights ago, in a heavy squall. A barge slammin' th' pilin's down there at th' bridge had a rough time gettin' through." He cut the knot with his teeth, then looked up at me. "Must've sucked 'er under in the wake. Next mornin' she 'as gone," he shook his head and went back to the net, "not a trace." I didn't bother going down to the pier. I didn't want to look. I nodded, turned and drove away. There's truth to be told—the sea claims its own.

Weekends became intense reflections of another year, one I wanted to forget. I was trapped on an unbearably lonely highway. On the return drive to Austin, I would recapture a glimpse of that vivid moment when love glistened. Each time it pulled me back into its glow I cradled in warmth. Then, returning to the coast with renewed expectation, I'd once again be devastated. Each trip on that highway became longer.

I was inconsolable most of the time, miserable all the time. My mind got no rest. It played and replayed details and images, tormenting me with a remembered look, a touch, a certain aroma. I worried with it all. My body got no rest. I began writing about my secret, forbidden love. Seven single-spaced pages later, typewritten top to bottom and edge to edge, I was hopelessly tangled in a web of messy metaphor and snarled simile, cloaked in a pall of dark love—hidden, unspoken, unnamed. It was dreadful! Why I couldn't write about it, was because I didn't know about it—*it didn't exist!*

Autumn fell especially hard on me that November. I lay in bed lost in darkness. There weren't any tears. Hollow emptiness surrounded a gnawing nothing would numb. I screamed into the void. This pain had

———— Σ ————

reached an end. I could bear it no longer. Those are the words I scrawled, at my desk in the dark. *I cannot bear it.*

Jim didn't stir when I quietly pulled shut the bathroom door. He made no sound when I stooped to the small space heater and turned the valve. This was the first quiet moment I'd found. I stood at the window, elbows supported on its ledge, the cheeks of my face wedged between fists. The night was quiet. It was calm. I gazed through the windowpane, gazed up, gazed across the crisp night. It was an almost perfect night, a nearly full moon. I could feel clear silver rays mirrored in my eyes. I was quiet, calm. *The moon is beautiful.* Just that. Nothing more. It slowly rose against the window, drifted beyond sight, fell above the window ledge.

I was cold. I felt my body shivering. I heard my name called, shouted from a far distance. My eyes were dim and foggy, harsh light stark and blinding. I felt my face slapped, harder. A lone figure hovered over me, its long arms flailing. Slowly I recognized a face, that of Jim. I lay on the floor. Window blinds were sky-high. Windows open. Door wide. Jim at the door, fanning it, heavily. "Are you coming out of it? Can you hear me? Answer me! Are you alright?"

My head was feeling split as with an axe and I was groggy. "Yeah, I guess, okay," I at length was able to groan. It was probably more a whisper. Jim pulled me from the floor. He held me tightly against him. We both were nearly naked and I could feel his body trembling against mine. My body trembled also, its tremble a shiver from the cold. Jim dragged me from the room onto the porch. He continued fanning the door while reaching for the blanket from his bed. He wrapped it about me from the shoulder, drawing it snugly at my throat. My grogginess began to clear in the chilly air.

Jim decided the room was safe. He carried me inside and sat me on his bed. "God! You scared holy *shit* outta me!" He pounded the air with both fists. I saw in his hand a piece of crumpled paper. "Don't you know what you did—almost—you could've been—."

"Yeah," I said flatly. "I would've been. It drifted, Jim. The moon, beautiful. It drifted all over me. No pain."

"Why?" Jim demanded. "Tell me why?" He held out the crumpled paper. "What does this mean?" It wasn't a question. I owed him an answer.

I felt finally placid, like the deep, still water of my lagoon. I also carried a deep burden, carried it long and heavy. I welcomed help to unload

———— Σ ————

it. It didn't matter what Jim would think of me, what awful name I'd be called. None of it mattered because Jim cared. Yes, Jim cared. Tears began.

The whole thing spewed out, beginning with the sailboat and the brilliant light in the barn, Ronnie and me, the beach and the tent, every-thing, right through the roll-away and down to my last trip back to Ronnie, everything. All of it—everything. Jim listened. He listened intently, giving his scalp rough knuckles a time or two, fierce ones several times.

"That's all normal," he said. "It happens to guys everywhere one time or another, puppy love, you get over it." Jim wasn't condescending. He spoke to me as I imagined an older brother might have done. I understood what he was saying—I don't think he understood what I meant.

"No, Jim," I told him, the sound of my words breaking, "it's more than that, a lot more."

"You think you're queer," Jim said flatly.

"Yeah, I do. It seems—I am," I said without flinching.

I tried to explain to Jim—it wasn't at all clear to me. I *guessed* it to be something like that—though not exactly. Probably it would have to be called that—so I imagined. I guess that's what it would be called—*queer.*

I told him about the salesman in the green sedan. Jim laughed. He told me about a man he met his first year in high school. Jim said he'd crawl out his second-story bedroom window, clamor down a tree and scale the backyard fence to rendezvous in the alley. The man would drive them to some dark place, give Jim a fast blowjob, then return him to the alley from where Jim would climb back to his window.

"That wasn't love," Jim said unashamedly, "it was just sex. Plain old hot 'n' horny, juicy *sex!*"

At first reluctant, I told him about the blond I dreamed he would be. Jim laughed. "God, was that all! I all but decided you really disliked me," he said. "I couldn't figure for the life of me why."

I told him about Joe almost seducing me. "I knew it!" Jim yelped. "Joe had the hots for you, couldn't you tell? He *always* had a ragin' hard-on when he came to the room, nearly pouncing on you. It poked up like a flagpole in those little jammy bottoms. You never noticed?"

I was stunned. "No! How could I have missed it, Jim?"

That brought us to my naiveté or my stupidity—whichever it was. Jim gave his head a rough knuckling. We talked all night, the sun beginning

———————— Σ ————————

to streak. "My God, the sun's coming up!"Jim said in his perfect way. He switched off the light and drew the blinds tightly shut. Before getting into bed, he grasped me with a hand on each shoulder, clenching hard. His face was near mine, dark brown eyes unquestioning. "Promise me you'll never do anything like this again. *Never!* Promise? *Promise!"*

"Jim, I do. I promise." His hard grip eased into a close, gentle hug. He slid his arms around me, drew my body closely to his. Our heads nestled on one another's shoulder, his cheek warm against my face. Jim held me a long while, a silent hug saying words he couldn't. Afterward, we each went to bed in stillness and gray light.

I promised Jim and I meant it. There would be times yet to come, times in other places when despair so bleakly overwhelmed hope I'd once more feel the edge of oblivion; times when I'd be called on to hear the echo of Jim's words and recall his embrace, to feel again the strength of his love. That morning, Jim's love was nearby. That morning I slept well.

We made some of our afternoon classes. I floated through mine, half dazed, half giddy. It is amazingly therapeutic, that tonic talk. Later in the afternoon, Gale and Winnie wanted to know about the commotion. Jim shocked me—I shouldn't have been. I'd seen him lay back and slam the nail on the head lots of times. At that point, it rolled over me—I was still high, riding the crest of *none of it matters anymore.* Jim said flatly, "Roomie thinks he's queer." Gale, quite deftly, broke his wrist. "Oh, ith that all!" he lisped. Winnie merely giggled.

I said I was shocked. This was only the second time I had heard my name and queer joined in the same breath—that, in less than twenty-four hours. For guys today, it may still take some getting used to, hearing oneself named queer—it did for me, in Austin, Texas, '63. That isn't what shocked me—I was ready for a badge of courage. It was what Jim *hadn't* said, what he *hadn't* told, the *truth* about the commotion—I was glad he hadn't told it.

We heard touted often, *better dead than red.* I'd made up my mind, I wasn't ready to die for an ideology oceans away. This was no different, except *queer* wasn't oceans away. It may not be ideology, may not be ideal. It seems to be a part of who I am, knowing or not knowing it. I *did* know how I felt—my feelings weren't *queer.* My mind was made up on that, too. I wasn't going to die for creeps stalking night streets in green sedans, posing as salesmen—*luckier living than dead or red.*

———————— Σ ————————

"I've got this figured out," Jim continued. "I've got a *real* one coming over, a guy from my Latin America studies. I *know* he's queer. I've had *him* pegged since last year. I bumped into him this afternoon in the Commons, getting coffee. He's bringing assignments I missed this morning."

Gale chirped, "What fun! What fun!" Winnie giggled.

"Here's the plan," Jim went on, "make him think we're *all* queer, put him at ease so he'll 'fess up."

Gale was ecstatic, "What fun! Ooh, great fun!" Winnie giggled.

"Here's my idea," Jim explained, "get him to take Roomie to one of those queer bars where they hang around all over themselves, fondling, groping, whatever it is they do. Roomie," he turned to me, "you'll get nauseated, go outside and puke your guts out. That'll be that. See, you'll be cured!"

"Too-too terrific!" Gale agreed, immediately into it."Who's going to be paired with whom?" he posed.

Jim worked that out, too. "We'll pretend we're together," he told Gale. "Winnie, you can be Roomie's boyfriend. You rub all over him anyway." Scott's face reddened—he giggled all the same.

"Yeah, Winnie," Gale chided, "just don't get all wet and sticky."

Jim gulped and Scott made a face, "Yuk!" Still, he was all giggles. "Shouldn't we practice or something first?"

"Keep a straight face, Winnie!" Jim ordered.

"Not *too* straight, *darling,*" Gale said hysterically. He was beside himself, evidently picking up from Jim's comment nuance I missed.

Scott, sitting beside me on my bed, whispered, "Should we hold hands?" He posed it as a question—I knew he merely wanted affirmation.

"Sure," I told him. Scott took my hand in his, our fingers intertwined. I liked the feeling, Scott's hand clasping mine. I liked the texture of his hand, not quite rough; the gentle firmness with which he held mine.

Scott giggled again, this time tenderly. "I'll put my arm around you," he whispered, lips almost touching my ear. The nearness of his warm breath sent tingly sensations spreading behind my ear, crawling down my neck.

"Okay, sure," I said softly.

Scott took his hand from mine and laid his arm across my shoulders, cradling me to him, snuggling our bodies. His face close to mine, he turned his head slightly to whisper at my ear, "We can still hold hands, use the other." This, he said quietly—he only intended me to hear.

———————— Σ ————————

"Okay, Teddy Bear," I said, and we clasped opposite hands. It was an awkward position, one I didn't mind. Scott, as much as I wanted his hand in mine, wanted mine in his.

After a moment Scott began to squirm, then giggled loudly. "This feels *funny!*" he blurted. "Whadda y'a think?"

No, I thought, not funny at all. "It feels good—really great!"

"Winnie! *Kiss* him and STOP-THAT-GIGGLING!" Jim barked.

Gale was coy. *"We* aren't going to *kiss,* are we, *darling?"* He blew Jim a delicate kiss.

"I'm going to be the *man,"* Jim threw back at him.

"We're both men, *darling,"* Gale capered, "which one will *you* be?"

The scene became something between circus and zoo. Scott kept his arm around my shoulders, I slipped mine around his waist, and we held hands. Then—Joseph arrived.

At first glance, he was short and well-packed into his clothes—"stuffed," Jim later said. Joseph was from Laredo, Mexican-American with creamy copper skin, thick black hair, and large darting eyes the color of rich chocolate. From fully rounded lips he flashed a perfect smile, exposing pearly white teeth. Joseph had a nervous habit, something of an acquired tic. He constantly reached with an exaggerated sweeping motion to smooth his pompadour—whether or not it needed smoothing. Completing his elaborate gesture, he gave the upstanding stack of hair several tiny pats, then reversed the process and un-choreographed himself.

Joseph, unaware, stepped innocently into a situation expected to be ordinary, suddenly confronted with a roomful of guys all but making out. Winnie almost did that, too, setting playful fingers loose to fiddle with hair on the back of my head, letting them trail down the nape of my neck, tease the backs of my ears. Terrific tingles and superb shivers agitated me, head to toe—everywhere in between.

I didn't mind at all, far more entangled with Teddy Bear's fondling than with Jim's scheme. So was Joseph. It was obvious to me he wanted to *watch* us—I suppose he hardly dared. He kept coiffing his hair, shooting darting glances our way, right and left, an out-of-control metronome.

Joseph at first sat primly, knees together, hands fast at rest—except when they flew to his pompadour. Now, he sat with legs crossed at the knee, his foot in a constant swinging motion. He was more fluid, a *lot* more fluid.

————— Σ —————

"Darlings," he articulated to Jim, "I've had *doubts* about you and your *roommate!"* Joseph directed that comment to me.

Scott leaned slightly askew and blew a thin breath in my ear. He was hard. I could feel the hot lump bulging beneath our clasped hands. He had moved them there and held them there, at his crotch. Scott always did that when we held hands, pulled them to his groin. That lump of him, trapped under briefs, was straining against his favorite passive jeans. This wasn't the first time I felt him hard. It wasn't the first time, my hand clasped in his, I rubbed and fondled his bulging hard.

Jim cut an eye our way—Scott paid him no attention. Scott was getting off to it, getting a thrill twice for the price—we usually didn't *play* before an audience. Scott acted as if we were getting away with something, we were *invisible.* It may be tempting to call it exhibitionism; that wasn't Scott. It wasn't altogether that he was daring; he wasn't. What Scott was, Jim all but said so himself, was *mischievous;* mischievous to the point of daring. Mine and Scott's tease may not now seem much; it was then, in '63.

Jim found plenty of opportunity, while Joseph oogled Scott and me, to cast a frowning eye our way. Scott finally giggled. He exploded, erupted.

Joseph seized the moment to address Scott unabashedly. "Darling! What *is* the matter with you?" he coiffed.

"He's horny!" Jim blurted. Jim, of course, minced no words—in this instance, Jim was pissed. "Go in the other room, Winnie!" he ordered.

Joseph chortled. "Winnie," he said with a sigh, "oh, that is *so* cute."

Gale echoed Jim, "Yeah, Winnie, go in the other room. That's embarrassing." I wasn't sure to whom Gale thought it an embarrassment.

"I don't find it embarrassing," Joseph coiffed. "I think it's *cute!"* Joseph was beside himself, his comment made breathlessly.

Scott looked me full in the face. With all the pulpit-sincerity of a church I-do, he said, "Shall we?"

I wasn't about to be left standing at the altar. "Yeah, sure, Teddy Bear—c'mon!" Up we jumped all smiles, fingers meshed in clasped hands; out the door we skipped.

"Teddy Bear," I heard Joseph purr, "it is so *adorably* cute."

Of course we pounced onto Scott's bed next door, stretched on our backs side by side; the lengths of our bodies, side by side touching, crowded to one another. Our hands held the air above us. Palm tested palm, just for

——————— Σ ———————

the feel. Fingers on fingers performed, stretching and bending, lifting and locking, just for the touch; interlacing, clasping and unfolding, clasping again; kneading and pleasing; palms, fingers, kneading, pleasing.

No, this wasn't the first time; I thought our voices quieter, our whispers more intimate. We'd done this before; our fingers now felt more thrilling. Scott and I were not strangers to a single bed; laying beside him now, I felt we shared more—our clothed bodies closer, warmer.

The trap door on the phone ledge flew open and Jim's startled face filled the opening. He gulped. I saw him, I heard him—he gulped. Later he would say, "My God! I thought you and Winnie were *doing* it!" That was later. The face in the little window said, "Come on back. It's all in the open."

"We can't hold hands anymore?" Scott teased—he may only have made it *sound* teasing.

"Darlings, of course you can hold hands," Joseph laughed boldly. "Oh, they *are* so cute!" He gave us, Scott and me, a knowing look. *Knowing look,* one of those phrases we're warned about—what does it mean? I didn't know; I'm sure Scott didn't. Joseph *did* know—*that's* the look he gave us.

Joseph took the prank well in stride. Sexual preference deviating from a strict norm was a fiercely guarded secret. Time-honored, God-given laws legislated a breed of non-breeder outlaw. Consenting Adult and Privacy of Bedroom were legal quirks. The long, hairy arm of the law reached into the bedroom. Other lawful, legal appendages dabbled in toilets. Solicitation was as popular as Entrapment, both routine. Lewd and Lascivious Conduct, another phrase to be warned about, was a blanket charge, covering anything from touching and holding hands to hugging and embracing.

Clubs catering to perverse patrons were subject to no mercy. They were allowed to cower in dark, out-of-the-way places under the loose theory it was better to have perverts in one corral than roaming the streets. That was a double-barrel shotgun—it was also easier to round 'em up 'n' head 'em in. Bold, black headlines announcing *Pervert Sweep, Queers Captured* were the stuff of winning campaigns. That may sound grim—it was grim. That's the way it was in '63. No small wonder queers were queer.

Jim told Joseph all about my *problem*. He over-generalized, graphic with puke and nausea, the *cure* he devised. Joseph was more than willing to accommodate. "Of course, darling, why not?" he responded. "Shall we say, Friday evening? The bars are best on weekends. I warn you," he chuckled,

—————— Σ ——————

"Today's trick, tonight's trade, tomorrow's competition." Joseph said that—no! He *delivered* those lines—*grandly!* In the same regal manner, he gave me another of his *knowing* looks.

I don't know how much of this jargon Jim may have known—I was lost. I asked about the bar and Joseph laughed. "Can I believe this?" he intoned. "Oh, poor thing! Darling, don't you know *anything*?"

"No," I had to admit, "nothing." I felt like a rube. I might have been crushed but for the enthusiasm with which Joseph explained.

"Boys who like boys are gay, attracted to other gay boys—we truly like *all* boys," he corrected. "Gay bars are clubs where gay boys meet. Find one, go with him to have sex—oh, darling! Do I *really* have to tell you all this?" Joseph lamented. "If you're lucky, you find a certain special boy, you fall in love and become lovers—it's simple," he patronized. "The two of you move into a rose-covered cottage and live happily ever after." His chuckle widened to a laugh more mischievous than Scott's could ever have been.

Now, finally, I knew who I was—no, I can't say *who*. "Who" waited, yet to be discovered. "Who" had not been given, only what. I knew *what* I was— clinically, homosexual; socially, pervert; culturally, queer. I had no say in *what* I was, no option for choice. I *could* select category. That, I did.

Clear and brilliant light surrounded me, much like light I saw once before. I sensed warmth and love. I stood alone, surrounded by the others, yet apart from them. I stood in brilliant light, unsure if it was me glowing. I stood on the first day of life, born after nineteen years of labor. I stood alone, in clear light, simply knowing, I am gay—beautifully, stunningly gay.

Things remembered seem curious, my first haircut. Toddling beside my father, I began writhing at the door, struggling to free my small hand in his. Barbershops frightened me, tile floors and ceramic walls, high counters lined in mirror and glass; smell of talcum and lavender, tonic and oil; dead hair quickly broomed from the base of operating chairs. A besmeared shine box loomed, an outdated relic relegated to a corner or wall of prominence, open tins of wax and polish patiently waiting where they teeter or balance. A slick sound, speedy fingers snapping substances slapping smooth leather contrasted with a sharp snip of shiny scissors clicking air. Something about this *men's* place, always made me edgy. I never tarried longer than I could avoid. I'd never again set foot in a barbershop, hair the badge I'd wear.

By Friday, I walked with a bounce, keyed up—though I don't think

——————— Σ ———————

overly anxious. I had no idea what to expect. I sensed something on the brink of happening, something akin electricity in the air, this Friday to be eventful—November 22, 1963.

The Presidential motorcade from Dallas was due at Bergstrom AFB on the outskirts of Austin. The route would bring it up 19th Street, turn onto North Congress and head for the State Capitol four blocks away. It would pass directly below our second-floor windows giving Jim and me unobstructed view—a first-hand, person-to-person glimpse of JFK and Jackie.

I didn't cut my 11 o'clock tennis class, ending at 11:55. A short jaunt from the courts across Intramural Field, across 19th Street and down North Congress to 18th Street took no more than five minutes. Slightly before 12 o'clock, I bounced round the shrubbery onto our sidewalk at the Cottages. I intended to grab a fast shower, then go to lunch with Jim, our regular habit—still with plenty of time to return for the motorcade.

"Hurry!" Jim hollered at me from the porch. "JFK's been shot in Dallas! The President's been assassinated!"

Jim knew I was excited, eagerly looking forward to this event. Did he expect stupid me to fall for that? Stupid, maybe; not *dumb*. I shouted back to him, "C'mon, Jim, this is 1963, that stuff doesn't happen anymore."

"Hurry!" Jim yelled. "It's all on the radio!" I looked into his face and I knew he *wasn't* kidding.

I bounded upstairs. We listened to conflicting reports amid confusion and chaos. I was—what other word?—stunned. How can this be happening in 1963? *How can it be?* Radio reports reached an impasse. In spite of it all, I still expected JFK and Jackie that afternoon. The President of the United States is *not* assassinated in broad daylight in the middle of Dallas, Texas, in front of a huge crowd, in 1963—no, it *can't* happen! I stripped and jumped into the shower, leaving the bathroom door open to hear the radio.

I turned off the water and pushed back the shower curtain, reaching for a towel. Water from the shower head dribbled onto my back. I was wet, head to toe, dripping nude. A voice on the radio sounded with precise clarity. *Ladies and gentlemen, the President of the United States, John Fitzgerald Kennedy—is dead.*

Silence. Dead silence. Stillness. I felt the air itself dissipate. I sensed a pall descending, the community of man paralyzed. I saw, at that moment, everything I had known vanish.

———— Σ ————

———— Σ ————

I may have taken the towel, maybe I didn't. We may have eaten, we may not; the remainder of that afternoon gone, not even a blur. Two impressions fill the space—tears rolling down Jim's cheeks; shroud-like figures, alive before those piercing seconds, aimlessly wandering. Anywhere, everywhere, nowhere. I have a vague notion of us somewhere, trapped on a street amid a hopeless snarl of automobiles and exhaust.

———————— Σ ————————

———— Σ ————

Naked in the grace of heaven

The Cabaret was more crowded than anyone could remember. Everyone said so. "Even Elizondo is out tonight," Joseph commented, *"that* says it all."

"Yeah, sure," I said—I didn't at all know. The small, dark bar was jammed wall to wall with people, all of them male—boys, guys, men. A sea of bodies teemed within itself and swarmed beneath spiraling clouds thick with billowy smoke. The narrow room buzzed electric. A gay bar—it was all I might have imagined, more than I would have dared dream.

JFK's assassination was *the* topic of conversation, threading mouth-to-mouth throughout. Possibly in heightened response, I got a sense of oneness overseeing the crowd, a bond more than camaraderie among males. I felt acceptance, ease of belonging. I had a sense of keen company and conviviality; beyond these, trust. I wouldn't know it right away, I'd have to learn—a queen can't be trusted more than a sequin away.

It wasn't individual trust I felt that night. It was collective trust, a sense of community that binds even disparate outlaws, those trapped in a unity of common fate and shared destiny.

One thing more needs to be set out from the beginning, so that later no dirty laundry is left hanging. A good-looking young guy striding wide-eyed innocent and new-face fresh into a gay bar has one thing going for him, one thing only—he has *everything*. That, too, I'd have to learn later.

Elizondo—a friend of Joseph, one who seldom frequented the bar scene—was friendly and attractive. He was charming and witty, possessed of a quick sense of humor. Elizondo was *extremely* friendly. I mentioned it to Joseph. "Elizondo is *taken* with you. Darling, it's a sure thing!"

All bets down, house takes all—I wasn't sure of Joseph's meaning. I think, "Elizondo's *hot* to take you to bed" is what he intended. I wasn't hot for Elizondo, not even *warm*. I wasn't going to be *taken* by him. I focused on the boy I wanted to meet—standing alone nearby, hair and eyes dark brown, his eyes utterly piercing. Features on his face looked finely chiseled;

——————— Σ ———————

his lips, ripe—sensuously so; lips made and meant, I knew, to kiss.

Joseph laughed loudly, a mischievous laugh. "Darling, you *don't* mean Keith? We *do* want to start at the top, *don't* we! Keith is the *prize!* His is one of the *biggest*—oh, darling, you know—*things*. No one *gets* Keith."

"He's the boy I want," I told Joseph.

"We are going to be hard to please, *aren't* we?" Joseph countered. "Darling, don't call them *boys*. They're *men!*"

"Okay," I relented, *"guy."* To me they were boys—even now, still are.

Keith, not staring at me, was looking. Glances met, eyes connected in furtive courtship. I wasn't being coy—I was plainly shy. This was my first effort at cruising, something I guess that isn't learned. It's an acquired skill in which, then, I had no practice—maybe practice isn't needed to feel from within another's vibration. I felt it throughout my body. I felt it through his eyes—I think he felt vibration through mine.

Keith, himself shy, finally maneuvered to the edge of our circle. I don't know if Joseph dropped it to him that I was interested—I *doubt* Keith needed to be told. He was near enough for me to reach out and touch. Glances, already established, gave way to first full looks. Keith smiled—not just a smile. His eyes fluttered and lowered, his head tilted perceptibly—a gesture of slight embarrassment. Perhaps too much of his feeling shown more quickly than he could control, not yet sure I wouldn't still reject him. The smile he meant for me—I gave him one in return.

Keith was near enough I could have reached out and touched him. I had no idea what to do. Joseph had said, "Be natural—be yourself." What was natural—who, myself? There must be situations requiring no intervention, occasions when chemistry is contagious, times when some thirty-odd thousand years of evolution clicks and no booklet, no instruction is needed.

Joseph captured a coveted cocktail table trapped in the tangle. Keith sat opposite me; I, him; we, one another. That may seem redundant. This was a standing-room-only crowd without standing room. To sit was to be lost within a slender vacuum walled tightly by bodies. Lost we were, in a long, penetrating gaze melting across faces into eyes; his, mine; mine, his; ours, us—not a touch away, lost to the cacophonous din.

I won't wrangle over it. Keith's face was beautiful, a symmetry of molded features with no jagged delineations, no acute angulations; argent skin framed in a tousle of mellow-roast hair; lips a ripe peach sun-split. One

————— Σ —————

who has never plucked a fresh peach from the branch and held it against his own mouth, letting sweet, soft flesh suck at his lips, can only imagine. Keith was desirable, sought-after. Beautiful on Keith came from within.

I was barely nineteen. Keith may have been twenty-four. To me he was without age. Boyish good looks held a clean aura about him, giving hint of something not merely wonderful but of something of wonder. Gender nouns are superfluous. Keith was delicate, not in his person, as a person. He possessed a quality seldom found, one rarely touched tenderly—innocence.

His most compelling feature I've kept till last; it's anomalous, for surely I've kept it longest. Keith's eyes were wide and open, liquid pools streaming as deep lagoons set blazing beneath harvest moons. In his eyes, I touched what lies most deeply within. I touched a child's need—love. To touch that within another is an extreme act of intimacy.

What Keith saw through my eyes I only guess. I felt him intensely inside me, as well—a questioning about his gaze, an uncertainty not yet settled. I reached across the table for his hand. Fingers touched and he smiled. Knees brushed beneath the table. Keith's eyes exploded, *Yes!*

Keith shared quarters on the western edge of campus with Fred, a onetime lover. They shared friendship bonded after passion cooled. A tiny carriage house, too long dilapidated, too long denied, now too old to beg, the little refuge cowered far in the back corner of a vacant lot; cramped against Church Row where bastions of belief as protestant as they were stalwart had rooted. The vacant lot served for parking until something better came along, that something already crowding from the rear—its coming prophesied.

Keith's room was reached from a narrow stairway outside. The group, maybe a half dozen asked after-bar, gathered in Fred's room down-stairs—my first glimpse of bohemia. A simple wooden table with like chair required little floor space, the remainder covered by large, pillow-like cushions. I suppose it was ample—sparse would better describe.

Keith sat on a heap of pillows against the wall, knees pulled upward. He plumped a pillow, plopped it at his feet, then patted it with palm. It was for me. I sat with my back leaning against his legs, his arms draped loosely over my shoulders, hands lightly crossed at my upper chest. The look I got from Joseph was not completely unknown, his face tainted with envy. Elizondo's face was not tainted—it was *filled* with jealousy.

Keith spread wide his feet and drew me between them, pulling me

——————— Σ ———————

closely against him. I felt his legs pressing snugly but not tightly. I knew his body surrounded mine. He clasped folded arms at my throat, an extension of his safety. I could feel his breath whisper above me, a soft touch from his lips barely brush my hair. He drew my body more closely, holding me near. He leaned into me and touched the cheek of his face to mine. I reached with both hands to find his and clasped them. Keith took my hands into his. In a simple pirouette he lifted me and brought lips to lips, mine to his, his to mine. Then—Keith kissed me.

Lips cool and damp touched mine, touched softly and covered mine. I quivered. Lips warm and moist sought mine, sought tenderly and searched mine. I quivered. Lips hot and wet found mine, found fully and fleshed mine. I shivered. Breath from our bodies mingled, one air. My first kiss, Keith. His tongue touched mine, traced and swept across mine; tasted mine, reached and slipped over mine; sucked mine, thirsted and quenched with mine. My first kiss Keith kissed—the party downstairs was over for us.

Chimes from the clock tower joined church bells mourning JFK soon after the assassination. They pealed all afternoon, into evening tolling despair. I hadn't taken full cognizance of the bells until Keith took me upstairs. Perhaps the night air held fewer distractions; perhaps the carriage house nestled so near; perhaps somber voices sang celebration—I became aware of the bells. Four days they chimed, a canopy circumscribing us.

Keith was a Russian studies major. His room, as Fred's had been, was scant, pared to absolute basic. A table with chair and well-used type-writer served as desk; a mattress flopped on the floor, his bed. Assorted books scattered amid papers shielded a partition used for closet. I got an impression the room was once painted gray; time had corrupted pigment. I had no doubt this small sanctuary would continue to hold its space only a brief moment longer, as had the lagoon.

In all the Lone Star, Austin alone can claim the title City of Light. She sits on ancient mountain remnants, sprinkled with reminders of grace and charm, herself lovely rather than old. Moonlight is perpetual, a gift from her distant sister in France. The people of Paris gave Austin their five moon-light towers, preserving them from destruction during Nazi blitz attack. Austin was considered the only suitable recipient—she was the only city that maintained a French Legation. From the original towers, arranged around the Capitol to form the points of a star, others had been copied, giving

———— Σ ————

Austin silver night. Now, we too, Keith and I, bathed in silver of night.

Lips caressed, arms held pressed two bodies seeking shelter in breath, in pulse, in passion. Hands hardly handling detail, definition, delineation; secretly sliding, serenely savoring, sweetly slaving. Bodies sublime; Keith against me against Keith. Skin on skin. Not skin, flesh. Flesh was the word. Made flesh. Made love. Made Keith, me, one.

We drifted from dream to sleep and back again. Keith held me simply, sometimes our bodies side by side; at others, meshed in a cradle of arms. We gazed, eyes searching in silver light, shadows touching. I struck a sense of wonder in streaming silver light—amazement, touching him.

I got a sudden feeling of sadness I wasn't able to understand, one not of grief but of loss; a feeling of fear, more as awareness—what had been could no longer be. The shabby carriage house, crowded by faith; my silent lagoon, crowded by wave; both lost; slipped surreptitiously from sight in a symphony of bells at night. Bells tolling sorrow, bells singing joy.

It's dishonest of me to leave it there. I lied to Jim later. It was expected—the reason, not the lie. I didn't want Jim to think something about me was *lacking.* No one other than Jim asked, "Did y'all come?" He wasn't being gross. That's the way we'd become, Jim and me, nothing held back. Had I not lied to him then, I wouldn't have to step out of sequence now.

We didn't come, not in all of four days, not once. I didn't get a good feeling lying to Jim—lying relieved me of having to explain. I doubt he'd have believed me, anyway. It's too simple, or else too complex.

The truth has already been told. I wouldn't now be so idle as to infer cosmic orgasm—it was nothing like that. I said *simple,* it's what I meant. We shot past sexual orgasm. That's the point where simple borders complex. To touch love within another person is the utmost act of intimacy. Where love dwells, there resides spirit. Perception of essential nature and meaning, the reality grasped through an event sudden, striking and simple is epiphany. Sex for some may be such a path. Orgasm—sudden, striking and simple—is the substance of making love. To borrow from Joseph, that says it all.

I'm tempted to use the word euphoric—a feeling of well-being doesn't satisfy. It had been more than well-being, more than a feeling. It had been a state, profound abstraction and absorption—trance.

The day they murdered JFK, I came out gay.

*   *   *   *   *

————— Σ —————

Jim was seated on his bed in fetal position, Winston lit, as I opened the door. "You had me scared shitless four days," he lurched. "Where th' hell've you been?" He didn't pause for an answer. "I was mad, then I got worried. Not even Joseph knew where th' hell you were." Jim lurched again, "Are you *hearing* me? Where've you been?"

"I hear," I exhaled, falling in a back-dive onto my bed, arms widely flung. I called to him from the bed, "You believe in angels, Jim? I met one. An *angel!* He took me to heaven!"

"Holy *shit!*" Jim shouted, grabbing for his hair. "Are you lyin' to me? You better be lying—you're *not!* Wipe that silly grin off your face—Yipe! Is that *all* you need to wipe off your face?—Did y'all come?—Uugh!"

"Sure, yeah," I lied.

"Tell me you spit it out, you didn't swallow it—Uugh!" he gagged, "You *did!* I may *puke!*"

I lay on the bed, my body stretched as if I were floating somewhere on a distant cloud—I was. "Weren't you *listening* when I told you the plan?" Jim barked. "This wasn't in it, never part of it. Puke your guts out, be cured. Simple. That's all there was to it. You couldn't get *that* straight?"

I sprang upward from my prone position and faced him squarely. "No, Jim, not *straight*. Never again!" I told him, then fell back into rapture.

Jim became angry with himself and *tore* through his hair. "What have I done? *God,* what have I done!" He was more than distressed—he was anguished. "I've *ruined* your life!"

Adrift on my cloud, I bolted upright. "Never say that, Jim, never think it. The night in the bathroom, I thought I was dead—I was dead! Look at me now—*alive!* You saved me, Jim. Look at me! *Beautifully* alive! I'm so happy I don't know what to do—I'll *kiss* you!"

"Hell, no, you won't," Jim barked. "You'll go in the bathroom and scrub your mouth with soap, *that's* what you'll do!" He was emphatic. I'd already taken another back-dive onto the bed, in cloud-nine reverie.

Jim lit another Winston. Finally, he could no longer stand the suspense. "You gonna just lay there with that silly grin all over your face? Can't you see I'm *dyin'* to hear about it? Tell me *everything!*"

I told him all about it, the bar and Keith; the bells and Keith; the bed, Keith. I told him *all* about it. I had to tell it again for Gale and Scott. Gale said, *"Too,* too marvelous! Does this mean you're officially queer?"

—————— Σ ——————

"Not *queer*, silly boy—*gay*," I corrected, feeling a sense of authority.

"Of course, *darling*, how rude of me—*gay!*" Gale delighted in camp, capable of adding his own clip. Gale must be acknowledged for rearranging a breakfast-food slogan. "Kids are for Tricks," he'd chuck.

If Gale thought it was "too, too marvelous," I thought the guys were too, too terrific. Smith yawned and gave his hard-on salute. Cozby took me under his wing, a mother bird helping her nestling fly. He became confidant, of an intellectual sort, with a ready-numbered lecture for anything. Nested in his sardonic wit, no matter how absurd, were to be found sparrows and starlings. I had a feeling about him, this was as near coming out as he could get. In a way, I was correct; overall, not completely.

Daily it was Jim with whom I shared most. He danced with me through heartthrobs, then shouldered me in the wake of heartbreak. He sustained me through the aftermath of romance, in the fall of love's letdown. Scott—let me hold onto Scott a moment longer.

Why this mattered is significant. Guys had no gay identity in '63. Hidden within the secrecy of our own world, we *were* gay, more as genre, the noun being *queen*. Insofar as most of society knew, there weren't any gay people—gay as a concept was not yet an idea, certainly not an attitude. Even among gay people there was no consciousness of pride, no awareness of dignity or worth that comes from inward sense of good. These attributes—if attained at all—were traits bestowed by heterosexual society on that segmented part of pretense, false daytime life. So long as the abominable secret lay hidden, its spiteful facade maintained, the pretender was allowed to clutch delusions of pride, dignity and worth. These truly belonged to a fractional self. The other part of that fractional self went into the night bereft of any dignity, bereft of any worth, stripped bare of all sense of pride.

It may seem unfair to make a sweeping generalization—stereotyping is always slippery ground. Among some of the younger guys, those coming into and reaching their twenties, there was more contentment with their lifestyle. Those I knew were at ease, comfortable with their sexual selves, many of them relatively happy—insofar as happy can be said. During that time, I didn't meet any other male who shared, or could identify with, the enormous pride that came to me by virtue of my gay reckoning. That isn't to say I wore it as a badge—doubtless many others will say differently. It wasn't a badge. It was a medal, ranking of the highest order, to wear it a privilege.

——————— Σ ———————

I accepted that privilege. With feelings of pride, I wore it *proudly*—of all that I can say, that is the best gift I ever gave Jim.

Now, I come to Scott. A couple of afternoons later he came into my room. "Gonna take a nap? Okay if I join you?"

"Sure, Teddy Bear, c'mon" I replied. Until my long weekend with Keith, Scott had never asked permission. He simply came into the room and crawled onto my bed with me. Now, I realized, he must be feeling insecure, unsure of his place in my life.

Scott possessed a quality childlike, though not childish. After Jim dubbed him Winnie, I called Scott Teddy Bear. Scott appealed to me. Teddy Bear began as acceptable show of affection. It also was my distance from Jim's and Gale's mistreatment. Jim regarded him as infantile bordering on adolescent. Gale treated him the same. I never saw Scott in the way they did, never played him as they did. Scott and I did play—let me get to that.

Scott and I began sharing a special feeling for each other—a feeling too elusive for me to recapture. Scott didn't have "tendencies." Jim once said to me, "You outta know—it takes one to know one." He also said, "Scott's too *dumb* to be queer." The best I can do is to say Scott and I *liked* each other. Until males are taught it's okay for guys to show their feeling for one another without using rifles, pool cues or bats, *like* is the only word I have.

Our play did start adolescently. Scott was having difficulty with freshman English. Jim told him I was a whiz. Scott one evening came over to ask for help. I was sitting at my desk, Jim slouched against his bed pillow. Jim's desk was more a place to store things than a working community. Scott stood behind me, back of my chair, as I explained title, thesis sentence and outline. Scott giggled. I felt him seesawing against the back of the chair. He giggled more, seesawing harder. Jim cut a frowning eye. More giggles, harder seesawing. Jim spat out, "Winnie! Are you *rubbing* off?"

Scott giggled, somewhat embarrassed. Rather than continue seesawing, he pressed with his pelvis against the back of my chair. He giggled and began a gyrating motion. Jim cast an *evil,* frowning eye, "Winnie! Are you gettin' a hard-on?"

I thought, but didn't say, "He isn't *gettin'* a hard-on, he *has* a hard-on." I felt it, decidedly warm and efficiently erect, jabbing my backbone.

Such began our playing. Scott continued his amusement—or was it amusement? I *liked* it. It seemed to disturb Jim, whether as embarrassment

—————— Σ ——————

or something else I could never determine. On another evening Jim blurted, "Winnie! That's disgusting! I'm going next door 'til y'all get through."

After Jim left the room, Scott lay down beside me on my bed, our bodies stretched side by side. We clasped hands held high above in the air, playing fingers. That's all there was to it, except we both got erections. Our relationship developed into afternoon naps taken together on my bed, Scott holding my hand clasped to his crotch.

Jim, along with Gale, teased and chided Scott more than they did me. Soon they became accustomed, our playful relationship regarded as no more outrageous than Jim's scratching. What they didn't let go was teasing of Scott. Neither of them resisted opportunity to cast demeaning aspersion. I didn't like it. I was all too aware of those kinds of feelings, the cruelty with which they stung. I began to feel protective toward Scott.

The afternoon he asked about our nap, Scott and I lay together on my bed, two hands playing the air. "Was it really good, with that other guy?" he asked, somewhat timidly. "Yeah, Teddy Bear, *really* good," I told him.

After a moment, Scott asked, "How good was it?" I squeezed his hand in mine. "Wanna find out," I quipped.

Scott was quiet for a moment, kneading my fingers. "Maybe," he said thoughtfully. Then he asked, "Does it have to be now, today?"

"No, not today," I told him. "Good," Scott said. Then, after a pause, "Can I tell you when? I mean, when I'm ready?"

I wasn't sure what my thoughts and feelings were doing—they collided within me. Scott wasn't playing—I wouldn't use him as a plaything. "Sure, Teddy Bear," I said softly at his ear, snuggling warmly to him.

In a moment he asked, "That guy Keith, you gonna see him again?"

"Heck, I don't know, Teddy Bear—I hope so," I said cautiously. Scott nodded, "Yeah, I know you'd like to." He was pensive—quiet little moments just filled this conversation. Then Scott all but whispered, "Hey, does this mean we can't have naps anymore?"

"Don't be silly!" I told him. Scott giggled and clinched my hand. "Can I ask you something, you won't get mad?" He held his grip on my hand. "Sure, Teddy Bear, I won't get mad," I said.

"I've never kissed a guy. Will you kiss me so I can see what it's like?" Scott was *really* holding my hand *tightly*.

"You're not afraid?" I asked him. "No. Not with you," he said.

—————— Σ ——————

"Yeah, Teddy Bear," I said. "Sure, Teddy Bear, I'd like to kiss you."

We rolled our heads face-to-face on the pillow, lips so near I hardly had to lean toward him. I gently touched my lips to his, my mouth firmly on his. I tenderly pressed my lips against his. I kissed him.

I had kept my eyes closed. "How was it?" I asked afterward. "Okay," Scott told me, "kind'a funny feeling, I guess you get used to it. Yeah, okay." He moved my hand to the hard, warm lump in his pants and held it there, clasped in his. I rested my head on the pillow and snuggled at his shoulder, nestled the cheek of my face to his, and fell fast asleep with the beat of his heart pounding against me.

Several times I went back to Keith's—he was never there when I knocked. One night Fred opened his downstairs door and poked his head through the opening. "Keith's not in," he said curtly. "He's out. He doesn't want to see you anymore. Stop bothering him." Then he slammed the door.

I managed to sneak past Fred twice afterward. The first of those times I tapped lightly with a finger on Keith's door, then left him a note with my phone number. Keith never called. The other, the last time I slipped up his stairway, I stood at his door only long enough to hear my heart beating loudly. I touched the palm of my right hand to his door. I don't know why I did this. It may have been a silent good-bye—something I left inside I could not retrieve. I stole quietly down the steps and fled into the Austin night.

Scott usually was gone when I awoke, no doubt to avoid Jim and his comments. The afternoon I kissed him, I know the real reason Scott was gone. We had shared a special moment, one neither of us could ever know again—certainly not beyond where we now stood. Our kiss was the un-touched innocence of childhood, an innocence yet unblemished, one about which is a sense of purity; an innocence lingering on the edge of childhood. Our play, the undisturbed play of two boys a late summer day rambling in the twisting, tangled branches of an old grapevine, one new to them; their lips sucking the last of a season's grapes, juice another day to become wine. Scott trusted me in the way of a child. I, yet a child, also trusted him a child.

Jim once said to me, "There's something that's been bothering me. I want to ask, I know it's none of my business."

"Jim," I reminded him, "no secrets!" A look on his face told me this was an intimate moment. "Have you and Winnie been doing it?" he asked.

"No," I said without hesitation, "we haven't."

————— Σ —————

Jim was perplexed. "I don't understand why not? You know you could get him in bed with his pants off like that," Jim snapped his fingers.

"Heck, yeah! I know for sure I could," I said.

"That's the part I don't understand," Jim knuckled his head roughly, "Isn't *that* what you want?"

"I'm wild about Scott," I tried to explain. "He's my Teddy Bear. I could fall *in* love with him, right now I just *love* him. What I feel isn't all by itself, it's got other things with it. He's not a toy. I respect Teddy Bear too much to take advantage. If I didn't, I couldn't love him. If I had him in that way, just sex, I don't think my love would be worth giving. Don't you see, Jim? It's not what I want him to give me. Our playing is really great. I don't think Teddy Bear wants it any differently either."

If, in later years, Jim went bald I'm afraid he had me to blame. He not only knuckled, he *tore* through his hair. "I've got to stop trying," he said, "when I think I've got you figured out, you come up with something like this, right off the wall. Sometimes I think you're as batty as Mother Ferrell. Then again, maybe you're dangling so far in outer space I'll never catch up."

* * * * *

On one of our morning trots to Tim's next class, his book bag slung over a shoulder, Tim, without missing a step, said, "You're gay." He didn't intend it a question.

Hit by shock and surprise, I didn't hesitate to answer—I did feel a slight stinging sensation to my face. "Yeah, Tim, sure," I said, "I'm gay." I realized Tim wouldn't have known the word gay without knowing gay.

"Ever make your eleven o'clock on time?" He gave me only enough time to know I'd been slapped in the face. "I followed you, just as you've been following me. I'm right about your class?"

I felt I'd been caught with my hand where it didn't belong. "Yeah, Tim, you're right—I'm *always* late," I said.

Tim stopped, dead in my face. "You like me, right?" What a question! I didn't know if Tim was set to pick me up, brush me off, or smash my face. "Yeah, Tim, I like you! Sure, Tim, I do!" I said.

Tim picked up his trot. I picked up my face, still in one piece, and had to jump to catch him. "Thought so," he said.

Again he pulled up short, dead in my face. "You think I like you?"

Uh-oh, I thought, another of *those* questions. What could I lose?

————— Σ —————

"Sure, Tim, yeah! I hope so, Tim!" I said confidently. Off we went again.

"Thought so," Tim said, with another abrupt halt in my face. "You're a beautiful guy, really gorgeous," Tim said. His face, his eyes, his smile beamed all over me. This time he didn't immediately take off in a trot. "Really beautiful," he mused. "I'll bet you drive the other guys wild."

I didn't stammer—I was astonished, dazed. I never thought of my looks as attractive, let alone beautiful. Immersed in looking at other boys, I did not see myself. Truth is, I never looked in the mirror—I was ashamed. Contempt for self was stomped into me, loathing for a body unfit to compete. My looks not celebrated by other boys, beautiful on me was brutalized.

"C'mon," Tim coaxed, "no one's ever told you what effect you have on other guys?" This *was* a question. I *did* stammer. "No," I said, "no one tells me—I don't think—no one looks at me." I felt shamefully embarrassed.

Tim gazed into my face, biting at his upper lip; then away we went. "Hard to believe," Tim said. "I've got a sugar daddy. How many've you got?"

This, another question for which I was unprepared. "None," I said. Tim stopped short again. He looked me straight in the face, eye to eye. I wasn't sure what he expected to discover. At that moment I wondered if he may have thought I lied to him. Off we trotted again.

"Hard to believe," Tim said. "Pick me up at seven tonight?"

Fortunate for me, we arrived at the door to the Tower stacks—*I did a full stop.* "Wow! Sure, Tim!" I shouted, "Wow, Tim, sure!"

"Good!" Tim said, beaming a smile. From the top step he turned round and called to me the name of his dorm. "Good," he said again. "Seven o'clock. I'll be out front, waiting."

Tim disappeared inside as I fumbled to write the name on the inside cover of a book—as though by any chance I might forget! I boldly stroked *7 pm,* complete with period and underscore!

I told Jim about my trot with Tim, our conversation and the date made for later. Jim was excited, more nervous than I. He fussed with my hair, smoothed a wrinkle at my collar. "Roomie," he said, "I feel like Mom, sending her little boy on his first big date!"

Tim directed us to a cabin on the lake. Inside, he switched on lights and mixed drinks. "My sugar daddy's place," he explained. "He keeps this cabin for a place to bring me—when he can get loose." Tim handed me a rum and coke. "I've got my own key—I use the place whenever I want."

———————— Σ ————————

86

Tim continued looking at me; not a stare, a pleased looking. He kept smiling at me, a wonderful smile. His eyes, not exactly soft and neither harsh, sparkled—truly, they sparkled. His face, a rosy glow, was beautiful. Myself? I will believe anything written describing how I looked at that point!

"Hard to believe you don't have even one sugar daddy," Tim said again. I'd been sipping my drink and I asked, "Do I need a sugar daddy, Tim? What I mean is, why?"

"They buy you things," Tim told me. "Gifts. You lay back and enjoy it. Why else do it?"

He mixed us another drink. "You didn't answer my question," he said. "Why do *you* do it?" He handed me the glass and our fingers tangled. Tim did more than look at me. He did more than gaze at me. He became entranced. "You really are—*incredibly* beautiful!" Tim said.

I may have been wrong about Tim's eyes. I saw them sparkle with warm softness as we sat on the edge of the bed.

"Why I do it, Tim, is to meet good-looking guys, nice guys. I want to fall in love with someone special—someone like you, Tim."

"You think *I'm* good-looking?" Tim asked incredulously. It was not simply a question to me but a question of me. My answer was ready. "Wow, Tim, I'm sure! Absolutely good-looking, Tim—I'm sure!"

Tim laughed, not a big laugh. He shook his head, just enough. He set aside his glass and took the one from me. He grasped my hands, pulled me partway from the edge of the bed, held me not exactly in his arms but near enough to him, and he kissed me.

Tim's kiss felt more like one mouth touching another than lips engaged in fondling and foreplay. I thought it likely this was his first time to kiss a guy who turned him on. I wasn't an expert at kissing—so I thought. Tim turned me on. I threw my arms around his neck and *I* kissed *him.*

Tim held me tightly, arms about my waist. I wanted to feel my body near his, his near mine. He grasped me from the shoulder, shoving me backward. We fell onto the bed, me on my back, Tim atop—mouths engaged.

Tim wrestled free, fought with my belt and fly. He jerked at my shirt, pulling it high upon my chest. He yanked my pants, briefs included, below my knees. My hobbled legs hung awkwardly over the side of the bed. I sprang out hard—throbbing, pulsing hard. I grappled with Tim's pants. He held my shoulders pinned, kneeling between my hobbled legs. Tim wasn't

——————— Σ ———————

rough—he was more than clumsy. He was excited—his excitement showed. I don't think he'd done this before.

One hand abandoned a shoulder and slid down my chest. Palm and fingers closed carefully around my hard shaft. It jumped at his touch. Prickly tingles shot upward across my skin to neck, face, ears. My chest heaved, exhaling deep breath. My lips, dry, quivered—I was subdued.

Tim's other hand dropped to my shaft. He pressed lightly, smoothing hair from the base. Outstretched fingers and thumbs made a ring, through which I throbbed and jerked. Tim was captivated by the sight.

"Amazing," he said, *"truly* amazing. Your cock stands up, bending toward me. Hard to believe." My entire body twitched and jerked. Breath came heavy—heavy and very hard. Tim's head moved slowly forward, downward. I could feel warmth from his breath as his lips neared.

Suddenly, he sprang from between my legs and covered his face. "I can't do this, I can't do it!" Tim was sobbing. "I wanted you. I wanted to be with you. I wanted it to be with you—my first. I can't, I can't do it!"

I struggled from the bed onto my feet. I cuddled Tim in my arms. He held me, held his body tightly to mine, and buried his face at my shoulder.

"Tim, it's okay. Really, okay. You don't have to—love is more than sex. I love you, Tim—not just your body. Tim, please! Give us a chance!"

On the street in front of Tim's dorm, in filtered shadow cast by a nearby streetlight, Tim said, "I feel lousy. I messed it up. For you. For us."

"No, Tim. Please, no," I said, the look on Tim's face one of pain. I didn't know what more to say. I smiled; I meant it. I reached out to touch Tim's cheek. He caught my hand midair and clasped it to the seat between us. "I mean what I said—incredibly beautiful!" he said. "Friends?"

"Friends, Tim, yeah," I replied. Tim opened the door and was gone.

Gone, not simply going into the night—gone. Funny, I should know the difference, going and gone. It hung in the air between us, a door closing in darkness. He walked into the night—gone.

* * * * *

Excitement of discovery—new jargon along with a hitherto unseen world—was no different then than now. A young gay male wants to see it all, experience everything at once. Nights at the Cabaret were weekend routine—no other evening I knew coming within shouting distance of the crowd and enthusiasm on November 22. There may have been one—it came later.

———————— Σ ————————

"Darling, slow down!" Joseph cautioned. "Too much, too soon—too little, too late." Queens are adept at giving old saws gay angles. "Mother doesn't want her daughter to end up like *those!*" He flourished a broad gesture toward the rear of the bar. A row of blank, sere faces—some atop paunches, others seemingly hung from coat hooks—maintained vigil outside a narrow passageway that crooked to cramped restrooms.

"Take a good look, darling. They're *hideously* disgusting—Dirty Old Faggots! They follow anything into the tee room, anything wearing pants *and able to walk!* Groping and fondling," Joseph sucked an exaggerated breath, "darling, do I *need* to tell you? *In the piss and the shit!*"

I'd find out they don't have to be dirty, don't have to be old, wrinkled or paunchy and stare from a blank face. *Faggot,* a state of mind sad but shameful, presumes gay males desperately seek sex—abuse and violation welcome. Men whose sense of self is battered, no longer respond emotionally, unable to connect tender feeling with sexuality. Young bodies treated as objects may as well be slabs of warm yearling's liver—vessels used and drained, with no hope for replenishment. It is a suffocating corruption, disease of darkness. Spring's tender flowers must have sunlight. Kept from them, they grow stunted. They yellow and wilt, choked and starving.

I was not immune. I met my share of faggots. Their stories, except for one, aren't worth telling—that, to come in time. Clear, bright light fixed my path. I could not have said as much then. My odyssey was of the heart, its golden fleece, love. Fortunate for me—or fated—those times the spirit of my quest so pitifully failed me, there appeared, from over my shoulder, an unseen Argonaut in full panoply, ready to do battle.

* * * * *

Joseph went with me downtown—I wanted to see the hustlers. A block from the Capitol was the Manhattan Bar & Grill. I wanted to go inside. "Darling, that's the Wrinkle Room!" Joseph groaned. Queens, notoriously, cannot resist temptation. He relented and in we strolled.

Subdued light glinted from glass and chrome, modified and patched art deco—nothing spectacular, just tastefully stale. At most a half dozen men, middle-age, sat perched on stools at the bar. They turned in unison, six little duckies in remarkably similar pose. As we drifted to a table, they followed from behind drooped eyelids, six similar *ho-hum* expressions.

We treated glasses of coke with the dignity of drinks. "Darling, it's

———————— Σ ————————

horrible!" Joseph declared. "Suppose one of those ugly wrinkles falls off and crawls over here. *Eek!"* he shuddered, "I hope the condition isn't contagious!" I was curious. "Won't we be sitting over there some day?"

"Darling! Don't suggest it! We're *much* too young. Poor *dears,"* he chided, "look at them, sitting with rhinestone faces. *Oh, I just couldn't be bothered, could you?"* he mimicked, fluttering his eyelids.

"Sanitation should come mop the bar, those dried-up tongues are hanging so low. That isn't all *dried up and hanging!"* he winced. "Darling, behind Maybelline they're all screaming—*Take one look over there bitches, I'll claw your eyes out!* Let's get out of here—this place makes me *nervous!"*

At the door Joseph threw back his head. With a grand dip he shouted, "Eat your hearts out, *bitches!"* He wasn't called LaTrina Pussylips for nothing—that, of course, was only one of two reasons he earned his title.

The bus stations were downtown, Continental on Congress, Greyhound a block over. Anywhere along a stretch of South Congress, fewer than a dozen blocks from the granite dome, boys could be found. They idled, maybe in pairs, one loitering a few yards from the other; slinking seductively beside streetlamp and leaning suggestively against storefront; legs wide spread, opening to the crotch. Denim jeans were always low-slung, hands stuffed deeply inside front pockets, shirttails loose. It was good for a boy to show skin at the abdomen, better if a thin trail of curly soft hair tufted at the navel, leading down, down, down.

Boys hung out in an area called the meat rack. Certain street corners were favored, considered luckier, more lucrative, easier. It was always expected at least one of the babes would be there, posing to please. Chances were good a scattering of others hung nearby, vying to fill the vacancy if a sedan slowed, stopped long enough for a quick exchange of bids before the boy hopped in and slammed the door.

The boys were young, early to mid-twenties prime—anything much above that, history. Many of them were younger, sixteen, seventeen or thereabouts—one, I know, only fifteen. These boys were no children. They'd been around, were keen to the street. It wasn't uncommon to see one balanced at curbside calling out to prospective potential, not at all uncommon to see him brazenly spread eagle, knees slightly bent and pelvis thrust, courageously cupping crotch or boldly massaging mighty denim-held meat. There was law on the street, their law—unwritten, territorial and rough. The

——————— Σ ———————

boys were fiercely protective of their own, squabble and bicker as they would over who should own the corner or who catch the next john.

"There you have it, darling, the promised land," Joseph gestured epically. "They are simply *too,* too much! Feast your eyes, my dear," he coiffed, "look, but mustn't touch. They're all dirty, probably diseased. Besides," he chortled, "they don't even kiss, only do it for *money!"* Joseph coiffed again in the tedium of finale. "Pardon *me,* darling, I meant to say *they* let *you* do *them* for money. Ah, the trade," he mused, "they do look *fine* this year. Much too dangerous, darling, *much* too dangerous!"

"I'd like a closer look, check out the boys firsthand," I told Joseph. "That skinny blond turns me on."

"Darling! He's in *diapers!"* Joseph protested. "Ooh, so young—at what age do they come now?"

I parked on Congress a block farther and opened the door. "Darling! You really *are* serious! Oh, well," he relented, "the night *is* for danger."

I pulled shirttail from jeans, yanked open the top button of Levis, and shoved hands into hip pockets. I sucked in a deep breath, letting denim slide, swaggering toward the corner. "Darling! *So butch!"* Joseph exclaimed.

The skinny blond was active, what I call animated, twisting, jumping, jerking. He was swinging a loose fist in a circular motion, like cranking a Halloween rattle. "He's swingin', he's hell, let 'im out now!" he chanted as I idled up to him. "How's it hangin', sweetmeat? Any juice tonight?"

A sedan eased to the curb and the boy wheeled on his heels. "Swing on it, Daddy-O?" The car screeched fast away. The boy jumped high into the air throwing a fist above his head. "Stinkin' fuckin' perverts!" he shouted.

He turned to me, "Whatcha called?" He jabbed me on the shoulder with fingers. "Deano," I answered quickly. I jabbed him in return.

Why I suddenly altered my name was a whim, maybe attempt to feign anonymity. I prefer to think of it as effort to construct identity worthy of swaggering posture. The name stuck. I became known simply as Dean.

"I'm Slade," the boy told me . He jabbed my other shoulder. "No tricks?" he demanded to know.

"None," I said, jabbing him on the opposite shoulder.

"Fuckin' perverts goin' straight. You goin' straight?" he jabbed again.

"Me go straight? Nyah, not me," I said, jabbing back.

We got into a finger-jabbing bout. They weren't delicate little jabbies

———————— Σ ————————

I might've expected in, say, the Cabaret. These were shoulder-slouching, torso-twisting, hold-on-to-your-britches *jabs*.

He took a half step backward. Leaning askew, he looked down at my jeans, below the waist, at my basket. "Whee-o! Fuckin' ready, Deano. Fuckin' tight!" He jabbed me and I jabbed him. "That's swingin', man, that's hell, daddy-o!" He jabbed again and so did I. "Whee-o! Let 'im out, he's swingin', let 'im out, he's hell!" Again, we exchanged jabs.

Other hustlers standing nearby, hanging not far from us, kept watch on our jabbing match. Slade got pretty loud. Several boys began moving toward us. One of them, an older boy, twenty, twenty-one—a good-looking boy, tall and handsome with dark hair and a real stud body—came between us as I was throwing a return jab. He caught my wrist hard with a fist and carried my arm high into the air. He not only was tall, he was strong.

Slade drew back and laid a first-degree jab into tall boy's handsome shoulder, damn near spinning him. "He's swingin', he's hell—fuckin' let 'im go!" Slade hollered.

Stud boy wasn't expecting this. He gripped my wrist harder in the air. "Fuckin' let 'im go!" Slade hollered again, throwing another first-rater into Stud, who finally let go my wrist to intercept it. "I said, he's swingin'!" Slade shouted to Stud. He jabbed me again, "Tell 'im, Deano, you're hell."

"Yeah, I'm hell," I said. I jabbed handsome stud to prove it.

This began another fracas, the three of us throwing random jabs, knocking one another about. Slade whooped and hollered, "Let 'im out, let 'im out!" Several other hustler boys rushed into the scene. I guess they thought I was making trouble. A police cruiser that same moment wheeled alongside at the curb. We three were within arm's reach of a nightstick brandished through open window. "Okay, sweet boys, move those pretty asses!" the cop called out. "Daddy means *NOW!*" He slammed the nightstick *WHOP!* against the side of the cruiser.

The other hustlers moved back from us. They scattered, leaving the three of us alone on the sidewalk. I idled along between Slade and Stud until the police car cruised on, headed up the block. "That knocks it," Slade said. "Perverts not out anyhow. You goin'?" he asked me.

"Yeah, sure, I guess I'm going," I said. Seized by reckless abandon, I thought, what th' hell. "Wanna take a ride?" I asked.

"Fuckin' swingin', Deano!" Slade cheered. "Wait!" He clutched me

———————— Σ ————————

by the arm, gripping hard."You got a buddy? My buddy goes, too, okay?"

"Sure, Slade, heck, yeah," I said, suddenly remembering Joseph at the car. "Fuckin' hell!" Slade cheered again. He called ahead to handsome, dark-haired Stud, "Hey, Pacer, say hi to Deano—we're goin' ridin'! Ain't it swingin', ain't it hell? Whee-o! Let 'im out, let 'im out, boys, he's hell!" Slade whooped and hollered, swinging his fist round and round through the air. The three of us turned and galloped down Congress Avenue toward my car.

"Pacer. That's an unusual name," Joseph commented. "Does it *mean* anything?" We drove to the top of Mount Bonnell, one of Austin's mountaintop mesas. It was west of downtown, overlooking affluent suburbs. There were many such scenic spots around the city, Mount Bonnell, being the tallest, favored by lovers for parking. I pulled off the winding roadway behind a low curtain of red cedar. We were isolated on the brink of space, twinkling stars above, tiny lights far below glowing in the distance.

I didn't say much, Pacer less. Joseph was never at a loss for words. Slade—Slade, for all his rough and jagged edges, was as busy as a bee in a buttercup, buzzing, buzzing, buzzing.

Pacer had to piss. He'd been in Greyhound earlier, sipping long necks, watching and waiting. Joseph didn't get out of the car with Slade, Pacer and me. The three of us pissed. Across the top of the car Slade called, "Hey, Deano! Stay in the back with me. We'll get along. Pacer can listen to your buddy—he don't say a lot nohow." Pacer sat up front in the driver's seat and I got into the back, behind him, with Slade.

Slade was already inside the car when I crawled in. He slouched on the seat its full length, his back awkwardly leaning against the closed door, his neck uncomfortably bent on the lower edge of the window opening. It precariously framed his head.

He folded his left leg at the knee to make room for me. It rested on the seat, his right leg sprawled on the floor. His shirt was unbuttoned, hanging open to the armpit. He neglected to buckle his belt—it splayed wide where flesh skinned into denim. The waistband of his jeans was undone—it gaped. The zipper tab of his fly stood upward, casting a glint of dull brass. One arm stretched along the back of the seat, the other balanced on elbow atop the rear of the front seat. Slade was wide open, giving himself to me.

There was something delicate to his act of surrender; a surrender not for conquest, more than of giving; an offering, the best and the most

—————— Σ ——————

empty hands and empty pockets could summon. Slade had been silent. His young face, already displaying distress of the street, scraped a sadness within me. His young face, calm not yet broken by tomorrow and days after, melted into mine. For a very long while, we, neither of us, moved or spoke.

Sounds from the front seat became sloppy. Slade rolled his right leg on the floor against mine. He gestured with eyes toward the front of the car. Only the tops of heads could be seen. Slade grinned. On the seat he wedged his left leg behind me and gently nudged me with his knee. He cast his eyes down across his body. "He's swingin'. He's hell. Let 'im out." Slade said this to me slowly, slowly and softly—very softly.

I pulled the zipper, opening his fly, and tugged at his jeans. My fingers felt softness of skin at his hips. He thrust them upward to free denim and my hands peeled it down his legs. His boyhood stood before me strong and slender, shafting from a nest of golden down shadowing a tight bag. It had the appearance of a rounded sack holding a pair of heavy-ripe figs. I took both hands, one above the other, to completely hold him.

Slade's skin was silk stretched smoothly over hard muscle. There was no waste or slack. It hardly softened the juncture of bones supporting. His ribs, sinewy fingers enfolding pounding heart and heaving lungs. Chest, stomach, abdomen swept down, down, past the cleft of navel, down across the gentle crest, down the apex of veins and nerves where tissue flushes and blood boils, where sense and significance are snagged by sensation.

Slade's cock parted my lips. They readily gave way, intrusion welcome. My tongue teased and fondled, playing skin on skin. Hands, fingers; mind, mouth, muscle—blended. Slade tried to wrap his legs around me; denim constricted. Joseph, bent over the front fender, was getting his brains fucked silly from the ass up. Slade jerked his ankles from twisted denim and laid back on the seat. I crawled between his legs held open for me, held open until my mouth again reached his cock; then, closed over me. I sucked him until his balls pulled up tight, convulsed in jerks with his body. Thick, warm, salty-sweet liquid spurted and streamed and spewed inside my mouth.

Slade didn't grin at me—he *smiled.* Before Joseph and Pacer were done, while neither was watching, Slade collared me with both hands. Puppylike, he slid my body upward over his naked skin till we met face-to-face. He whispered softly, breathlessly, "You're hell, Deano." Then, quickly and tenderly, he puckered his lips against mine and kissed me—a child's

——————— Σ ———————

kiss; the kiss of a child moving from distant childhood into—what? "You can have me again," he said. I never did. Since that night, many times over, I've wished I had done so. I've wondered, had I done so, perhaps Slade—*what?*

Slade wanted to drive the car back into town. It was wild—we were reckless. What th' hell, we were swingin'—the night *is* for danger.

*   *   *   *   *

I went downtown often after that, alone. Slade was always there. He'd come running to me, swinging his fist, "Let 'im out, boys, he's hell!" Slade danced round and round me while we lolled and loitered. At some point he'd zero in on one of the lumbering sedans. "There's my mark, gotta go," he'd call to me over a shoulder, making fast for the corner. He never failed to make a quick turn mid-dance and look squarely back at me, "Later, okay?" Slade was always busy, always on the move—except the one night in the rear seat of my car. "Later, yeah, sure," I'd answer back to him.

The boys on the street accepted me. For awhile I was one of them, one among them—I think Slade fixed it. The boys were a carefree bunch, sweet boys who had no name other than names the street gave them, pretty boys who had no yesterday, no tomorrow—only nights the street gave them.

There was horsing around, grab-ass and slaps on the butt, an arm strung loosely on another's shoulder—only for a moment. It was law, written on the street. One night an older sedan the color of pale green slime cruised Slade's corner. It reminded me of one, slimy and green. A night or two earlier, the john in this sedan shafted his boy, dumped him in the dark alley behind the bus depot, then tossed a wadded one-dollar-bill through the window. The boy gave good—he earned the twenty he'd been promised.

The hustlers were laying for the prick. They had him primed, would've gotten him that night. He suddenly spied the boy he owed and chickened. When the puke-green car came round again, two of the studs, both of them butch and studly, stood almost to the curb—hips touching, jeans bulging. Each had an arm hung snugly on the other's shoulder. While the john was getting an eyeful, they turned face-to-face—their mouths met full and hard. Tires screeched on the pavement as the sedan slimed away. "They don't like it slapped in their ugly face, sure as hell not on the street," one of the kissing studs declared.

Slade had been priming a mark, prancing and dancing, arching on tiptoe to thrust his pelvis each time the car cruised him by. It was his score;

——————— Σ ———————

the next pass he'd make it. Before the john came round again, Slade left the corner and raced to the doorway where I idled. "He's yours," Slade said to me, "I'm givin' you the score."

Slade was hastening me to the corner. Another hustler had taken his position, trying to cut in. Slade didn't like it. He rushed forward, dragging me along. "Fuckin' get back!" Slade yelled, kicking and shoving the other boy from the curb as the car approached. "Take 'im, Deano," Slade said to me, "I want you to have 'im. You're hell!"

There was little time to argue. This was not for me, certainly not for money. The few dollars in my pocket would have been wealth to Slade—I doubt he'd have accepted money from me. He needed the score—it was the only way he knew to survive. "No," I told him. "It's yours. I c'n do without."

"Next time," Slade called as he jumped into the car, taking a quick look back at me as he sped into the night. "Yeah, sure, next time," I called to him. There would be no next time. I never saw Slade again.

I returned to the street again and again. "Seen Slade?" I'd ask Pacer. "Not tonight," he'd say. Then, "Not yet." Finally, he just answered, "Nope."

It wasn't the same on the street. The luster was gone, the thrill empty without Slade's crude vitality. Little by little Pacer drifted up Congress, toward the Capitol, a stretch of blocks considered a dead end, no scores. He was withdrawing from the other hustlers. I trailed along behind him, hoping I'd be able to lure cruising traffic his way.

It bothered me, what had become of Slade. Jim said, "He let you have his prick for free, what more do you want?" Joseph reminded me, "Darling, you didn't listen. Mustn't love them, it's only for money." What Gale said stung the most. "What's the difference, one hustler more or less."

They knew it bothered me. They never understood why. I couldn't make them understand I loved Slade. I don't think I fell in love. I knew, from the night we touched, I knew I loved him. It bothered me, something had happened to Slade. It bothered Scott, too—he wasn't giggling. I never told, even Scott, how hard I was hurting.

On a night much like the one when Slade said "Say hi to Deano," I slipped beside Pacer, hands pushed deeply inside my pockets. Pacer was silent. In a moment he said, "Your friend, he your buddy?"

"Nyah, just pal," I told him.

"Slade 'n' me, we'as buddies," Pacer told me. "You'as good for 'im.

———————— Σ ————————

Slade said it, 'n' after, he'd not pick a mark 'til first he'd seen you."

Then it hit me—I can be so *stupid!* Buddy wasn't just buddy. It was *buddy.* That may be the strongest word they could handle. It was then I realized their hunger, their need, isn't only for tens and twenties they hurriedly stuff into their jeans, not for that alone. In their own way, perhaps the only way they know, they reach out to grasp affection. They reach out to hold, if only for a moment, love.

I wanted to say something, anything. Words at that moment failed, my own voice deceived, "Slade'll be back."

"Nope," Pacer shook his head. "Somethin's come to 'im. Slade'ud not've cut out. Not on you either—you'as hell for 'im."

We both knew, said nothing. Pacer turned aimlessly up the street, moving into the night. I stood silently watching as he drifted away. Suddenly it became very real—the night *is* for danger. Whatever it was had come to Slade, I hope for him that it was—*God! Let it have been!*—something good.

I didn't go back to the streets. Pacer, I knew, would be gone, too.

* * * * *

Robert was all the more beautiful when I saw him up close. Two things baffle me. Joseph said of the hustlers, look but mustn't touch. Sound reason dictated his advice. Joseph was fearful of hustlers, threatened by their sexual nature—meat on the open market, pay to play. He preferred to play, not pay. I didn't see hustlers that way. That their sex habits and mine didn't exactly parallel meant little to me. Queens weren't as apt to pay for sex as homosexuals hiding in closets, posing as men. That isn't to say sex didn't have its cost—queens often paid a price.

Place in my path someone like Robert and look but mustn't touch glows neon. I feel threatened in a way different than Joseph—no price too high, any price too great. Robert was beautiful—not merely handsome or good-looking, not even just pretty. He was *beautiful,* possessed of *beauty.* To attempt description is useless, serving only to limit and detract—I'm not able to distance myself from Robert with enough sufficiency to be objective.

Robert belongs to a time when gods were not above making love to men, and men were not above accepting love from gods. Gods gather to themselves beauty, which they alone are privileged to touch. Robert belongs to gods—his, a beauty that sustains them. Through his image, they endure. To gaze on Robert is to remember and behold. Joseph would've pranced in

——————— Σ ———————

without regard for angels. I feared to tread—look, but mustn't touch.

The other thing baffling me, "Who," I wonder, "is eavesdropping?" I never *dared* dream Robert would walk straight up to me and place his hand *upon* my shoulder. I never *dared* dream he would lean so near I would smell freshness at his face, that he would look *upon* me with enormous, clear blue eyes—whom the gods would destroy, they first make mad!

Thunderbolts at that point would not have been necessary. Madness—who decides that? I had one saving grace the afternoon Robert walked up to me—I was still seated at my desk. Jim said, "What on god's earth did you do to him? All semester it's been *Robert-Robert-Robert.* You burned a hole in your yearbook staring at his picture. Suddenly, out of the blue, this goddamn Greek, this friggin' Fiji—who yesterday didn't know you were alive, much less give a flyin' fuck—now, you tell me, he gets in your face *smooching* before class is over and asks you—*tonight!*—for a date. To top that," Jim exasperated, knuckling his head, "you have the balls to ask me, '*what if he's gay?*' All I want to know—how th' hell did you do it?"

Distance—I'm still too close to Robert. I couldn't now put it more succinctly than Jim was able then.

"Jim," I protested, "I only said Robert was *close* enough to kiss. It really *is* a date—to study."

"Uh-huh, uh-huh," Jim countered, "big luxury apartment on the lake, a bunch of frat guys—have a few drinks, stay all night. Hey!" he knock-knocked on my skull, "anybody at home in there?"

"Well," I wondered, "what if?"

It wasn't on the lake, just nearby. It wasn't a luxury apartment, only one for which Jim would've killed. There were Fijis, there were drinks, it did last all night. It began after class that afternoon.

Robert walked up to my desk, leaned down to me and said, "Hi, my name's Robert. Are you doing anything tonight? I'd like you to meet me and some of the other Fijis to help us with accounting. You seem to know what it's all about."

I *did* know what it was all about—the *accounting.* I explained it, over and again. Not that I minded, Robert was very beautiful. I can't recall anything of the other Fijis, not even how many there were. Drinks flowed, whatever I wanted. Robert may remember what he kept bringing me. I don't. He was very beautiful. I didn't take my eyes off him once.

—————— Σ ——————

Finally there comes a point where whisky and accounts receivable part. Robert said, "Liss go it over all again, you won't mine?"

I thought, "Oh, Robert, yes, I do want *mine!*" I said, "No, Robert, I don't mind."

One of the Fijis said, "I gotta get outta these clothes." It must've been a good idea—all of them stripped to underwear. Robert wore boxers, glen plaid. He was breathtakingly beautiful! I don't remember if I removed my clothes. I didn't take my eyes off Robert.

After awhile another of the Fijis shouted, "Accounting sucks!"

"Yeah?" another demanded. "Would you let prof suck you to pass?"

"Hell, yes!" the first boy replied, "Wait—do you mean this exam or the whole course?"

"What's the difference?" the other asked. "You'd let him suck you?"

"Hell, yes!" the first boy returned. "I'd let 'im suck hell outta me for a goddamn A!"

"For a goddamn A you'd have to suck hell outta him!"

"Nyah," the first boy replied, "Not me, hell no."

"You wouldn't suck him for an A?" the other goaded. "Robert would. Isn't that so, Robert?"

"For a goddam A, I'd suck anybody—anybody could suck hell outta me!" *Robert* said that. I guess, to borrow a phrase, that says it all.

Fijis were crashing all around the apartment. Lastly, it was only Robert and me, maybe one other stumbling somewhere far in the background. I remember Robert's face, his eyes, his mouth. I remember his body. I remember him, so very beautiful. He, too, was crashing. He told me he was sorry he was drunk. "Why don't you stay?" he asked. "I'll find us a place."

I remember his face, I remember him looking into mine. We looked; we looked. My eyes never left him all night. Finally we stood, the two of us, alone together, looking—looking into each other's eyes.

How long we may have held this moment I am uncertain. It is imprinted indelibly in my memory, forever present. Robert and I were the moment—timeless, eternal, divine. Robert first appeared to me a god. He approached a man. Now, in his presence, I stood with him, naked in the grace of heaven. We were the moment.

Robert walked me to the door. We stood in dim light. In stillness, the silent early hour before dawn, I slipped from his eyes. I had no illusions.

——————— Σ ———————

I would have stayed with Robert a lifetime—I did not stay the night.

Some stories can end this way; ours didn't. Soon after, Robert asked me to pledge Fiji. He pleaded with me; I declined. I had no illusions. After the semester ended, we no longer had class together. I didn't see Robert again. I phoned him from time to time, keeping in touch. I followed his picture yearbook to yearbook. Throughout following semesters, I phoned him on special occasions—times when I was unbearably lonely and times when I was drunk. I needed to hear his voice. Some calls to Fiji House were rudely late or unacceptably early, depending upon how the clock is viewed.

Robert never refused my call. He never brushed me off, he wasn't condescending. He spoke warmly, at times tenderly. We always made a promise to meet for drinks—we never did. I had no illusions.

The last time I phoned Robert, after we talked awhile, he asked, "Are you okay? Is everything alright? You don't sound like it."

I told him, "I just need to hear your voice, Robert."

He asked me, "Does hearing my voice make it better?" I said, "Yes, it does. Hearing your voice, Robert—*you* make me feel better."

"Good," he said, "I'm glad you called. Get some sleep. Call me tomorrow. We'll make a date—let's have that drink."

"Wow, Robert, sure," I said.

Maybe someday or the middle of some night we'll have our drink together. I'm glad it's waiting. It's altogether likely, with cunning and expertise, I'd have gotten Robert into bed or into the bushes or into a dark lonely place. I had no illusions. Robert knew I was gay. He gave me his trust. He gave me something more than trust. I saw it in his face one early morning near the lake, in the hour of stillness before dawn—respect.

The taste and sensation of Robert's body may have lasted minutes. The touch of his hand upon my shoulder has remained a lifetime. Yes, there is love between us—trust and respect don't stray far. It's telling; it shows.

* * * * *

UT homecoming brought an overflow crowd to town. The Cabaret was packed, as crowded as anyone could remember—almost as crowded as the night of the assassination. Everyone said so, even I. "Darling! So many men!" Joseph exclaimed. "I'll be sore for days!" His comment was uncanny.

The mind must will bits of information, pieces of the picture, into lost recesses. Two faces are clearly etched, amid the bluish haze of Cabaret

——————— Σ ———————

light, and later, within dim light in my cold room. Once they had names; no longer. There is only one face, one body, one feeling. I wanted the smaller of the two. His face was impish, pixie-like—cute, until later. It was the larger of them whose body I'd serve; between them, a feeling mine alone.

Jim came into the room collecting blankets and pillows. He was having a girl that night, camped in the rear seat of his Chrysler parked downstairs on Congress. "I'm beginning to see the advantage of turning queer," he said, helping me push our twin beds together to ensure plenty of mattress for my two tricks and me. "You can bring cock to the room—I can't cunt." He called over a shoulder from the doorway, "Hey, guys, take good care of my babe tonight, y'hear?" He flipped the light switch off and closed the door behind him, leaving us in filtered light from artificial moon.

At the Cabaret, the smaller of them told me it was okay with his lover, the larger, for the two of us to trick. His lover wanted to be with us, to watch—afterward, the two of them could be together.

I admit, the arrangement strikes oddly. Accommodation and malleability became daily companions in this world of night. Underlying belief in the good of humanity, faith in people, was large—still very much intact.

Before Jim closed the door, the smaller of the two began kissing me, manipulating me toward the bed. During his spider-tango, my clothes were skillfully separated from me by the larger of the two. An enticing web baited, deceit is unsuspected until the snare inescapable.

The smaller one kept my attention with puckering lips, had me on the bed, prone, atop him. I was vaguely aware of his lover near the foot of the bed, methodically shedding his outer skin. Big lover straddled my thighs. Cute imp slithered from beneath me, coiling at the head of the bed. Knees clenched, he pinned my arms from the shoulder. Big lover, big thighs astraddle, held my legs in a vise, large hands bearing rough against the small of my back. He was rod-hard, his long, thick cock forcing at the space between my buttocks, rending intrusion, tearing. Driving hard, driving deep; slamming against my body, ramming deeper inside. Each powerful thrust plunging farther, higher within me, sending wave after wave of intense pain so thorough, so agonizing it rendered me numb. Nerves no longer responded, no longer transferred to conscious brain.

Throughout the assault, I was forced to look into that impish face, now with eyes of fire and a devil's grin, tongue slashing from bared teeth,

———————— Σ ————————

hissing. I know that my face was drawn in pain, begging. I had to squeeze my eyes tightly shut to hold back tears. I felt them, stinging. I heard a cry, a terrible scream. I was unaware it came from me.

It ended—not at last, not finally, not ever. It was over. Big lover, drained, withdrew his long cock in a sudden jerk. He dismounted, spent. Leering impish devil laughed as he released his knee grip; laughed, grasped my head and shoved my body away; laughed, puckered his lips and popped a kiss onto mine. My eyes flashed a fire different from the blaze that lit his, a fire so intense it smoldered the blaze in his. I know that it did so. I felt it rise from within, a single surge that swiftly shot from me, striking his face with a splatter of spit. I don't know if it's possible to do—at that moment, I damned them to the fires they chose.

Through the years since, I've been shouted at and heckled, called names; abused verbally, mentally and emotionally. I've been mugged and bashed by queer-fearing savages. I've had my scalp slashed open, my ribs kicked in, my face smashed. I've been beaten with fists, clubs and bats. None cling with the dreadful clarity of which I remember that night—none.

The two of them lay tangled on one bed. I don't know what they did. I huddled, curled on a tiny corner of the other, lost in hollow emptiness—a feeling other rape victims know. Sleep was refuge. Quite simply, I moved—or was moved—out of existence, to a place having no existence, no conscious-ness. It's a place that can't be fully known; a place of infusion, healing; one of whatever is most essential. It's a place some years later I'd again be taken, not because of pain, because there was need.

It happened in Manhattan in my ground-floor efficiency on West 23rd. I walked back from Greenwich Village just past midnight and sat down on the edge of the sofa. I lit a cigarette, holding it between index and first finger of my right hand, the cigarette in mid-air slightly away from my lips. A figure clad in a white garment floated before me, suspended. Its arms were extended upward, hands palm out. Words I heard spoken were unfamiliar to me, seeming to be *ekky haumy.*

Four hours later I was sitting in the same position, right arm and hand suspended in mid-air just away from my face. Between index and first finger was an ash skeleton of the cigarette I had *just* lighted. It was totally intact, straight square end where I placed the fire, tiny rings embedding the paper clearly visible, not an ash dropped—the cigarette entirely burned.

——————— Σ ———————

Later, in my office at Time Inc., I asked a co-worker, Howard, if he knew such words. He pondered letters I scribbled on a pad, deciphering the words as *ecce homo*. "It's Latin," he said. "It roughly translates, 'Listen, man, behold! Hear, man, hark!' Why do you ask?" he wanted to know.

"No reason," I told him, nodding my head as though in understanding. "Just wondering." Howard handed me in return a blank, quizzical look.

I had only a vague sense of awareness I'd been to a place, and the vacancy between one instant of awareness and the next, it following after the elapse of a large gap of time. That there is such a place is all that can be told.

* * * * *

"One thing I've discovered," Jim said as he bounced into the room, bringing with him the heap of blankets and pillows, "hair on a girl's tits turns me off!" It was past mid-morning, the other two gone. I hadn't been aware of their leaving. "C'mon, get up," Jim ordered. He began stripping the bed. "Something the matter—God! You're bleeding!"

"I didn't want him to, Jim, I begged him not to—hurt me! Kept on, kept on—he wouldn't stop—forcing!" I broke into tears.

"Goddamn son-of-a-bitch, the bastard!" Jim slammed into the wall, hard, with a fist. "C'mon," he gently coaxed, helping me into the bathroom, then the shower. Jim's jaw was set, muscles of his face tight. I thought his lip trembled. He patched me as best as could be done using vaseline.

Jim didn't knuckle his head. He winced and shuddered as I told him the episode in gruesome detail. "That makes me mad," he said. His jaw trembled. "It boils my blood. You're just a little guy—I saw the size on him. Look at you—God! I'm not even queer—it makes me mad!"

Jim looked to me as though he might cry. "Where does an asshole get off?" he demanded. "Because a guy is gay, what gives him the right to hop on and split the boy's butt wide open? It makes me mad!"

"What's the difference," he raged, "this and raping a woman? Hell, what more was left? Blow your fuckin' head off, smear brains all over the wall? I'm not even queer—it makes me mad!"

"What makes me madder," he went on, "you guys don't have a fair chance. Hell, the bastards'ud lock you up and throw away the key—nobody'd give a rat's-ass damn—you're not worth shit! I'm not queer—it makes me mad, the whole goddamn, ass-backward-'s-hell, fuckin' mess!"

* * * * *

————— Σ —————

That Cozby has been noticeably absent is no oversight. That he's been all but silent through these pages is typical Cozby. That isn't quite true. Cozby commanded center stage whenever he was with us—basically, three of every four days.

Cozby was a deeply personal, private human being. His humor, a brand his own—sometimes borrowed, always built upon; refined, polished, perfected—rolled from him with the spontaneity of Austin's springs. Cozby's humor could do well in stand-up delivery. In a pure sense, it would fall short for those of us fortunate to have been allowed close to him. His was a living humor, weaving new fabric from old threads. What he might say a given moment, funny to outsiders, conveyed a full range to those of us with him yesterday, the day before, the week preceding. Nuance scrambled about us with the chaos of spilled marbles. I think through this continuum of humor Cozby was to be discovered.

He was gentle and generous. Gentle, he possessed a richness of compassion for what he termed—in Lecture 43.b—the muck of humanity. Irreverent as outwardly he could appear, compassion kept him laughing, kept at bay his dogs of despair. His generosity was not of nickels and dimes. He gave, not through himself, of himself—his time, his understanding, his talent. We were enriched through the artist's perception. He gave words of encouragement, slight nudges that moved us to upper plateaus. His sharp words enabled us to make the climb.

I'd like to say Cozby was our conscience. In some respects, he may have been. That is less than accurate; he was our mirror. "A place where light is sharp and bright, where color doesn't wash—that's where to paint," Cozby told us. We must have come near. Reflected through him, we were able to see ourselves in clearer light.

A time somewhat later in Manhattan, the afternoon of my birthday, 1970, Cozby did a pencil portrait of me. The flow of artist's hands was indistinguishable from pencil and paper, images appearing from fluid fingers. I saw and believed again—Cozby is gifted. In the finished piece a billowy mane cascades the perimeter of my face, still boyishly pretty; lips round and full barely part to accentuate a mood sensuous; large, open eyes penetrate from a depth of innocence. Above all is caught a feeling of great sadness at a point on the brink of suddenness. Cozby inscribed it *To Hamilton, Who sees less clearly than he wishes—And more than he should.*

————— Σ —————

Cozby taught me men are pretty—Lecture 3.a. "Pretty, pretty men," he said. "Women can be *beautiful* creatures, or merely *creatures*. A woman is never pretty; plain, never pretty. Men are pretty, not beautiful. Beautiful is feminine; pretty, masculine. Masculine without being rugged or effeminate. Pretty, pretty men." Oddly, there is logic to his diatribe—men *are* pretty.

I remember an earlier time, before Jim and Cozby left Texas to join me in New York, I had a letter from Jim. "Cozby isn't the same," he cautioned. "Vietnam did something to him, things he saw—I'm not sure. He doesn't seem able to open up. Can't let it out, even to me—I don't push. I'm a little afraid. Thought you ought to know beforehand. Give him time."

I saw painfully etched on his face, scarred across his eyes—Cozby had lost his humanity. It saddened me his faith hadn't been strong enough; too fragile, it failed him. His portrait of me is all the more dear.

* * * * *

Jim told me not to do it. "No," he said, "not just *no*—n-o, NO!" Jim, could read me aloud. "You're going to do it anyway, right?"

"Not necessarily—maybe," I said. I meant, I wanted to tell Ronnie about me being gay—I mightn't do it after all.

"Do one little thing for me, this one little time," Jim begged. "For once in your life *listen to me!* Don't blurt it out to him. Suckin' dick is one thing—Ronnie may not be able to stick those words in his mouth."

I nodded. I thought I understood Jim's point. "Okay," he said, "if it feels right, do it. Don't come back shit-faced and say I didn't warn you."

I thought I understood his point. I didn't think Ronnie could do less than welcome news of liberation. Gay, I discovered, was not bizarre manifestations conjured by phobia and ignorance. Gay, I found to be a healthy expression of sexual identity, more normal for me than heterosexuality. My sentiment, my feeling, is richly varied—as deep as that of heterosexuals.

I recognize a decided disadvantage. Individuals, much like myself, are stifled emotionally and sexually. Persons thus traumatized remain hideously scarred, many never able to recover. Ignorance and social intolerance are real cases truly deserving of being called "arrested development."

I hoped my telling Ronnie, my coming out to him, would legitimatize our relationship, lend a degree of credence and respectability, perhaps prompt him toward easier acceptance. I was hopeful of a full, loving relationship with my beautiful blond. I thought I'd considered the threat. I

———————— Σ ————————

doubt in the delirium of my bliss I was capable of realizing the extent fear gripped—neither could I plumb the depths of hatred.

This was my first time to pull on that double-weight, half-life suit. It didn't fit at all well. I altered it to something more a loosely flowing robe. My parents were perplexed at lilting voice and light-headed step. I bounced. What of it—a break from the books accounted for that. This was Christmas!

My best box wasn't tied in foil and ribbon, hidden under a tree. It was waiting up the road, Christmas written all over it—*Open Me First*. Any remnant of nagging anxiety evaporated the moment I saw his face. Ronnie was still my sweetheart, the love of my life. It was telling; it showed.

Christmas Eve, traditionally the most silent night of the year, everything shuts down. I'd gone to Ronnie's—his folks were having Christmas cheer. His Mom said, "Ronnie, honey, mix you boys something tall and sweet. 'Tis the season!"

I smiled. Ronnie grinned at me, scrunching his nose. He mixed us rum and coke, then another. Soon, the pint was dry. The younger children had long since been sent to bed. The two of us were Santa's helpers, assembling toys to delight bright eyes Christmas Morning.

Ronnie began mixing Vodka and coke—splashing coke over Vodka. His dad, sitting in a chair to one side, was sedentary. His Mom carpeted the floor with Christmas cartons. We opened most of the boxes, spreading contents helter-skelter. The floor was a jumble of instruction leaflets, packets of fasteners, peculiar parts. Suddenly everything was funny. The more Ronnie looked at me, the more he giggled. He glowed. His face was Christmas, red rosy cheeks, dimpled grin, sparkling blue eyes—he glowed at me.

Ronnie whispered, "Ssh! I'll mix another!" He attempted to stand, his equilibrium didn't—Ronnie stumbled backward. I lurched forward to catch him. He caught his balance, falling face first into me. The two of us crashed to the floor atop what now was looking like Christmas rubble. We made a clattering racket—his Mom came running.

"Ronnie, honey, you boys are drunk! Dad, look, aren't they so cute? Ronnie, sweetheart, I'm putting you boys both to bed."

She settled us on Ronnie's bed and closed the door, neglecting the light. Ronnie tossed back the covers and leaped on me. He hastily tore away my clothes. I lay naked before him. He hunkered at my pelvis and grabbed my cock, fisting me to arousal. I didn't get extremely hard—we drank a lot

——————— Σ ———————

of booze. Ronnie went down on me, taking me into his mouth.

I began wrestling with his clothes. As I gazed down my body, the sight of him eager for me humbled and inspired. As I watched him physically taking me, I wanted—I desired—to give myself totally, intimately, to him. I became less than I was individually, more than we were together.

Our passion caused a commotion. Ronnie's Mom called through the door, "Ronnie, honey, are you boys alright? What's going on in there?"

Ronnie answered her through my megaphone, "Nuttin', Mom!" He reached behind for a corner of the bedcover and hurled his body toward me, plunging us into a darkness filled with warmth and security. I hunched in its belly, incapable of imagining more.

Was it just *no* Jim said? I thought I understood.

New Year's Eve seemed the perfect time. Ronnie and I parked on a quiet country lane. We finished a pint of Orange Vodka. The winter night was crisp. A bold moon glowed dark amber. I suddenly decided, *love is orange.* Later, Cozby coolly told me, "Orange is the color of madness." Sure," I thought. "Love *is* madness, *sheer* madness—*such* madness!"

I did a *mad* thing. I said, "Ronnie, I'm gay."

"Yeah, Pinchy, me, too," he replied. "I'm feeling good."

"I 'm *gay,"* I said to him. "I like boys. I like you, Ronnie—I'm in love with you!" I did something *more* mad. I reached to embrace him.

Ronnie bolted. He flung both arms defensively between us, his blue eyes, always sparkling, suddenly cold steel cutting against me; in his eyes, fear. I was wounded, I hurt him. "Ronnie, you're afraid of me! Don't be afraid!" What then I said was the *most* mad thing, "I wanted to *kiss* you!"

I had done it. There was no turning back. I had, in one quantum leap of orange, catapulted us from ho-ho-ho to no-no-no. There's nothing more I can say. Words are too pitifully inadequate to span a starlit night stretched from shining sea to moon gone mad—the color of love.

Ronnie said, "We c'n still be friends. Don't make love to me. Okay?"

His voice was icy. *Friends* was the coldest word I could've heard. "Sure, Ronnie, okay," I said. My heart plummeted—I knew it was over.

I drove to land's end beyond Sargent that night, alone, empty. I stood for a long while, north wind to my back, gazing across an angry sea forced against its will, pounding in a struggle to survive. I felt the turbulence within, felt the anger, the struggle. Not for myself alone; after all, I'd reached

—————— Σ ——————

a sandy shore where waves in frothy spew expend, spreading foam. It was for Ronnie I grieved, for my own stupidity. Sadness was the color orange.

I saw Ronnie only one time more. It was later, at his high-school graduation. A bus thronged by crowding well-wishers waited to ferry the grads away for a night's frolic. I hadn't previously gotten Ronnie anything for the occasion—I hoped he was expecting something from me. Nothing seemed right—after all, it had to be a perfect gift.

At the last minute I scooped three coins, real silver, from a small box atop the bureau in my old room. I held them clenched in my hand. As Ronnie stepped into the bus, I pressed forward and folded his palm onto the coins. I said, "Keep these, you'll never be hungry." What I wanted to say I didn't. I couldn't say it—I wasn't allowed. *Hold these close, keep me near.*

I clasped his hand, palm folded with silver, in both mine. Our eyes met, strange in the way they lingered, strange in what they almost said. For the most brief, most thrilling moment, I thought Ronnie might leap from that ferry, leap that night into my arms and run with me, into the night.

Of course, it didn't happen. Ronnie beamed at me, his old grin, his old sparkle, his old love, then disappeared into the bus—gone.

* * * * *

The world would never be the same. It had changed forever.

———————— Σ ————————

I am with you

Sing me an old song, something I can remember. A feeling in the air, in restlessness, in a mood almost felt—it was in the music. Folk music, ballads and lyrics plucked inner strings not yet resonant. Old words and tunes, ancient rituals and celebrations, long lost under shards and debris, haphazardly stumbled into the Twentieth Century. Sleeping pylon colossi at Stonehenge began to vibrate. The first vibration rocked through breaking stillness —*I Want To Hold Your Hand!*

Spring unfolded from leaf to bloom—everyone wanted to hold someone's hand. I was touching and being touched as often as anyone—with the probable exception of Joseph. Jim wondered how Joseph managed to fit classes between toilets. "There's not a tee room on campus where that queen hasn't spread cheeks." I was on the lookout for someone special. He didn't need to be special in an extraordinary way, not special in the eyes of anyone else—he needed be special only to me.

My view was pristine. I was after TAD—The American Dream. TAD fell neatly into three parts—fall in love, get married, live happily ever after. Joseph facetiously referred to it as a rose-covered cottage, nicely summed up, "It's simple!" TAD's parts can be described—prepare thyself, work hard, share the good life. Simple, the reward for being an American.

There was one problem, a bumpy area, a tiny obstacle—TAD carried a large qualification requirement. It was no different than the sheepskin I pursued. Once in hand, it provided credentials accessing the key to open America's wealth. Without credentials, no key; no key, no wealth. My problem was one of credentials. Credentials weren't a matter of being gay or non-gay—that was no problem. I learned as much from Koestler on Communism. If a system is wrong, dead wrong, one changes it. America is about Freedoms and Guarantees, isms memorized verbatim, spat back on exam day—isn't that what America is about? Change—it's as American as greed,

——————— Σ ———————

certainly no problem. The problem, the key; that key, love. With it, every-thing; without it, nothing. That much was clear to me. What wasn't clear, what was hazy, were credentials. How can I *qualify* for love?

Sooner or later it had to happen. Jim and Gale went to the Cabaret. Scott pondered. "Whaddya think—should I go?" he wondered aloud.

Jim was at no loss, "Hell, no, Winnie, you've got to have pubic hair!"

I said, "Teddy Bear, I'd *adore* having you on my arm—*you* decide."

He decided. "Nyah, I've got you, Babe. What else do I need? B'sides, we've still got a date, 'member?" Scott grinned and giggled.

"Sure, Teddy Bear, I remember," I said, "you tell me when!"

Inside the Cabaret, Joseph performed a grand dip. "Sparkle, bitches, your mother's here!" His entry line was delivered, never spoken. I also was a-sparkle. Showing off new faces gained esteem. Showing off new faces from a private table gained envy. I was still a new face—one was until he'd been *had* around. I wasn't above wallowing in attention. I got a feeling somewhat like that of a schoolboy bringing his folks to open house. *Mom! Dad! These are some of the guys. What'd I tell you? Aren't they neat!*

We claimed a table down front, at the foot of the Cabaret's low stage, where Charles and his ebony grand emerged in spotlight. Charles, glib on the ivories, could tinkle out delightful romance melodies as though they just occurred to him. His voice was half as mellow as Johnny Mathis with a tenth the molasses of Liberace. Ambience was decadent or superlative—or both at once—when Charles, in white dinner jacket and black bow tie, commanded the keys. He often was lost in reverie, magic drifting in hazy swirls of smoke and shafts of bluish light, converging amber-to-red on black.

Black was the motif—walls, floor, ceiling. A few forty-watt standard reds clung closely against the high ceiling, providing at best dim illumina-tion. A small—intimate should be the word—cocktail bar spun a half circle at the front of the club, shielding the inside from outside view. A fake wall created a narrow vestibule necessary for queens to adjust themselves—clothing as well—before staging entry. The small bar had an expected array of glassware, none of the accustomed neon—only a clock face with a bright caption *JAX*. Backlit bars indicating hours floated in a black panorama, twinkling star-dots surrounded by a pin-light border. I wouldn't describe the bar as intimate—I never saw intimacy on stools surrounding it. It had the potential, two guys caught in one another's eyes, drinks waiting, cigarettes

——————— Σ ———————

burning, the night young and beckoning—the night steamy, burning.

The Cabaret possessed two distinctions. One, its murals lining long walls facing intimacy and decadence. Stories are told, truth fabricated to legend and passed word-of-mouth by sequined Homers. This Iliad had no Homer, hence no saga. There wasn't so much as a story I could discover, how the murals came about, when or why, by whom—no Trojan Horse, no Hektor, no Pericles. That was odd. The four-foot-tall panels depicted the stuff of just that—heroism. Male bodies nude in chiaroscuro struggled against, with, for one another. Their unsung epic molded the Cabaret in a herald of light and dark, tension and stress, agony and ecstasy.

The Cabaret's other distinction lay next door, identical space created by partition of a once-spacious store building. It had been cut through the center and walled solid. That sister space, the Jesters, was no sister to the Cabaret. It was the most popular macho-jock, beer-drinking, whisky-swigging, tit-grabbing parlor near campus. Come to think of it, the Jesters couldn't have been sister to the Cabaret—it may have qualified as brother. Both siblings held court on The Drag, a stretch of Guadalupe Street bounding the west side of campus. Jesters lay within shouting distance of St. Peter's Gate, the northwestern-most entrance to UT—St. Peter' Gate shot a beeline straight to co-ed dorms.

Joseph wasn't alerted I was bringing Jim and Gale. He was beside himself. "Is it in the air? Something added to the water? Darlings," he purred, "I *knew* the two of you liked to play with dollies—*boy* dollies!" I'd been around Joseph long enough to know a little something. He wasn't smug simply because they were in the Cabaret. Joseph *wanted* Gale, in a wild way. I knew a little something more—he wasn't going to *get* Gale, not that night. I *lived* with these guys. Stupid me was smart enough to know both were imbued with more *tendencies* than Teddy Bear could count.

Jim could've been had, probably that night, if circumstance a right mix of guy and gonad. Gale—Gale was hung up on Gale; *much* too hung up; *too,* too hung up. He relished the sudden rush of Gale worship. It whipped him into a frenzy of flirtatious feeding that was all feast—feast for him, famine for would-be hopefuls. Joseph had his hands full, so to speak. He was only a face in the crowd among those fighting for a piece of Gale tail.

It wasn't mysterious. Gale was a looker. He had exceptional looks, handsome looks—a lean, trim body to go with those looks. Gale may have

——————— Σ ———————

been prime-cut G-Q, he never could have made it on the street. He wasn't typical meat rack, too smooth and squeaky-clean, cosmopolitan. Not that he didn't have or couldn't summon coarseness, he couldn't reach out in the way of a hustler. I *lived* with these guys. I knew Gale was a prostitute. He prostituted not for beads and baubles and not for pleasure. He prostituted for the cheapest of all reasons—vanity.

Jim eyed me a number of times, finally seized an opportunity to bluster into my ear, "Gale's *eating* it up. Too bad *he's* not going to be *eaten!*"

I met Brett that night. He'd been looking my way sometime. I wasn't sure his looking my way was looking at me. I knew who he was. Queens *always* maintain an underground to supplement their rumor mill. Brett leaned down to me as he passed my table. "Don't hide your light under a bushel," he whispered. Returning from the tee room, he hesitated easily in view and laughed. I guess he intended that a come-on. It didn't take much gesturing from me to coax him to the table.

"Did you hear what I said?" he asked.

"Sure, I heard you," I said. "I don't understand. What light? Under what bushel? Do you mean a bushel of something or just a bushel?"

I amused Brett. He reared his head to give a laugh. Brett didn't simply laugh—he cackled. The two, ignorance and stupidity, may go hand-in-hand. Jim didn't believe I could be stupid; Brett didn't believe I could be ignorant. I amused him—he maintained his aura of mystery.

I asked Jim about the meaning of Brett's comment. "That's something he pulled from the Bible," Jim said. "It doesn't mean a bushel of anything. It means, don't cover up your light."

He saw from my puzzled expression I didn't know *what* light. *"Your* light," Jim fumbled, "don't stick it under a bushel. Hell, that's the same thing! I don't know what it means—if you've got it, flaunt it!"

Flaunt it—Gale was flaunting it. Maybe he had the light. If that was Brett's meaning, I thought I'd just stay under the bushel.

Put to me more succinctly another time by another do-gooder, "Why do you run around with the Laredo bunch? They're whores. They'll never be anything more than whores. You're cut off. It puts you in the same light—a nellie bitch grabbing crotch on anybody, anytime, anyplace."

Some may have been true, not all. Joseph gave new dimension to sex with heights he scaled. That's no figure of speech. Jim and I gave out

——————— Σ ———————

waiting for him one evening. We'd gotten hard-to-get tickets to a screening of *Black Orpheus* in Romance Languages—Joseph never showed.

He trailed a campus jock into a tee room in the English Building Annex. The two of them lolled at the mirror, dawdling in the lavatory until everyone else had gone. Then, they got it on. Neither of them knew it would be, that building was locked following afternoon classes. It was only used for overflow—appropriately enough. They found they had no escape—no escape in the usual manner. There was no doorway out, no window they could open. The jock at last kicked out a ventilator on the top floor. With athletic posture, he cajoled and pushed Joseph onto a ledge. They shinnied down a drainpipe and jumped onto the lower roof of a neighboring building, then clamored through a parapet window, walking out the front doors "as casually as anyone else," Joseph later extolled, "my ass so *loose* I had to step with toes to prevent it *sloshing!* Darling, you *know* I worry about my hair!"

Joseph was more envied than despised for doing what others wanted to do—have sex, and have it more abundantly. He learned it in Catholic School from older boys—I guess sex was sacred to him. Joseph wasn't prim about it; not prim doing it, not prim talking about it. I don't presume to insinuate all the Laredo boys were rampantly sexed. They all were honest about themselves, as Joseph. More than honesty, they felt good about themselves. It was that about them which made me stick.

There was a bar party that night, an *after*-bar party. Word circulated through the Cabaret, setting tension higher. Bar parties did that. It meant a chance to get close, *really* close to that guy on whom one had his eye. Dancing was the thing, slow dancing, holding close, *really* close, touching and handling, feeling that other body with one's own body. The kiss was another thing, mouth-to-mouth, tongue-to-tongue, spit-to-spit.

My comment may earn me a hard-on salute. In '63 kissing *was* a big fucking deal. Public display of affection between males was taboo, forbidden, outlawed— enforcement strictly regulated. No act between two males—public or private—was worse than kissing. Even today, here in Bay Prairie it's yet little different. Were I greeted on the courthouse steps by a kiss, my balls'd be hung from the nearest tree—that's where we were in '63.

Word about the party spread in the glare of bright light during a customary scramble, Last Call For Alcohol. For some, the scramble was a last-ditch effort to grab a guy while the grabbing was good and head for the

——————— Σ ———————

bunk. For others, it was head out before scars and blemishes of hard wear and tear were seen too clearly. Not far behind them were those who'd first rather die than be seen in a queer bar. We all had reasons—tonight it was the party at Chez Le Nelle.

Chez Le Nelle, Stanley's, Albert's and Joe Angel's house, hosted the Nellie Awards. They weren't bar regulars, tonight an occasion for which they ventured out to extend invitation to the Oscar-upstaging event. Albert and Joe Angel were Laredoans, and many queens considered the awards too trivial for them to be bothered—those whose noses weren't already too high to sniff the air weren't bothered turning them higher. That's one reason parties at Chez Le Nelle turned out well—no cheap, tacky queens.

Jim and Gale danced, not with one another, although each of them first danced with me. Jim said, "Once you get the hang of this, who's going to lead and who follow, it all becomes fairly natural."

Jim was a good dancer, graceful, easy to follow. We had rhythm together, the two of us. He held my body closer than he held any other guys dancing with him that night. "I know you won't grab for somethin' not in your own pocket!" Jim *giggled* at my ear.

Even Jim's giggle felt *nice;* like his body, sliding and gliding against mine; his hand, holding firmly but not forcefully; his arm about my waist, safely but not securely; his face against mine, warm and steady; his heart beating near my own. The sensation of Jim felt—nice. We had rhythm.

I went with Brett home that night. We didn't make love, kissed hardly, barely touched. He wanted sex—sex without love. Let me qualify. How can I know if I want sex with a guy without first knowing he can love—sex without love turned me off. I pretended to be asleep, little dreaming this sleeping dragon on a later night would awaken to slay me.

It now seems peculiar I'd ever have done so, for awhile I emulated Brett. His cackle was a snap to duplicate. Slender and a bit taller than me, it wasn't hard to affect his demeanor. His mannerisms are what can be called affected—I easily affected them. It wasn't caricature; imitation is also called flattery. Brett wasn't flattered—that travesty waited.

It is more scary thinking about it now than it was scary then when not knowing about it. We had no role models—no heroes, no champions; none to emulate, none to inspire. We had none in real life, none in make-believe, none in between. Roy Rogers had Dale Evans, Popeye had Olive Oyl.

——————— Σ ———————

Superman was pursued by Lois Lane, and Robin Hood, Maid Marian. Buck Rogers probably had a space-cadet—I don't remember the name.

The nearest to gay sentiment I recall is the movie *Shane*. I became emotional at the ending—Shane drifting away, young Joey calling to him across a hurting gulf. *Shane! Come back!* It's the one movie to which I'd like a sequel, Shane a little younger, Joey a little older. *Shane, Too* picks up where the original left off, cold and lonely, empty and hurting, then—fast-frame forward. *That* would be a slice of real American Pie.

So much for make-believe moments in movies. Later, I'd have my own Shane with original ending—my own slice of real American Pie.

Books written during the last flowering of gay sentiment, the 'Twenties, may as well have been among those that fired Nazi zeal—burned. They were inaccessible to a general reader. By mid-century, anything written and published shared a common ending—death, with dishonor and disgust. Notable is Gore Vidal's *The City and The Pillar*. Until death at the end, I could identify with the suffering hero, his agony and torment in a search for love, the despair of his loneliness and rejection. When later re-published as *The City and The Pillar Revised,* it was too late. I was unable to *believe* the book. Its hero suffered too deeply and too grievously to admonish compassion in the brutal buddy-rape scene. As an example of self-esteem, I thought one character as pathetic as the other.

Andre Gide's *Corydon* was the only book I found that offered, beyond a positive attitude, the one thing I so abundantly didn't have—hope. *Corydon* wasn't a story. It was academic without being pedantic, intellectual and philosophical in its argument favoring homosexuality as a natural counterpart to heterosexuality. The book wasn't for a casual reader, evidently not intended for anyone. It was renegade—banned and censored. I was given my copy by a guy I met. I never knew how or from where he got it. He told me, "I believe you'll like reading this. I want you to have it."

Another dim light finally glimmered. Jackie's reading list began making sense. What couldn't be said directly could be said delicately without being at all said. That didn't satisfy. I still felt a dry craving. At least I knew somewhere out there others were framing the frustration I was finding. It was a message from the farthest reaches of space—*You Are Not Alone!*

Brett heard about my imitation of him. He arranged an afternoon "tea" where I could perform. I don't remember whom of all "invited" were

———————— Σ ————————

present. I'm glad I took Jim. I did my best-ever Brett before a salon gathering. Brett never cracked a smile. I noticed a corner of his lip twitch—or curl.

Afterward, Brett took the floor. He coldly announced to his guests, "Here's an interesting anecdote. Queen Victoria once invited to court a comic who made his reputation imitating her. After he was done, court awaited the Queen's response—protocol, you know. Finally, the Queen spoke, '*We* are *not* amused.'" Brett stood before me as stony-faced as he described Queen Vicky. "*We* are *not* amused," he said icily.

I felt embarrassment and humiliation. Jim—it was plastered on his face—was pissed. Boiling with anger, he didn't care that he was rude. "We're gettin' outta here," he announced dryly. "This damn tea's bitter'n hell!"

That also enraged Brett. At a still later time he exacted revenge. The Plantation, a 24-hour greasy spoon near campus, was *the* place, invaded by queens after-bar *when* there was no party and *if* there was no trick. Ill-fortune stalked me—there'd been neither that night and I was seated at a large round table with Brett and company.

Brett at such times conceived of himself holding court . He said loudly, "I know a wonderful story. A perfectly delightful trick I once picked up was rather cute but a terrible disappointment. I expected sex. I said to him, 'I'm fluff, I want to get fucked.' The little trick pretended to pass out, though I knew better." Brett leered at me, knowing fully I was familiar with the story. I felt my face redden. I had no idea what he intended to tell— neither could I see acceptable escape.

Brett relished my misery, thoroughly enjoying himself as he continued his tale. "I was horny. I slipped my hard little weenie against his cute little butt and humped myself off. He lay rigid and stiff, as cold as a corpse—I never dreamed the cute little trick was *frigid!*"

Gales of laughter followed. I sat in silence, crushed and humiliated, relieved it was over—he'd had his moment. Brett *wasn't* done. "The best part of the story is seated at our table tonight—the cute little *frigid* trick is Dean!" Jim wasn't there to shuffle me away, all that needs be said.

We were all queens, nellie or butch. We had no access to sense of self, effeminate wimp the stereotypical image. With no alternative, we felt obliged to fit the caricature, borrowing and stealing from one another's handbag. Some became Legend-for-a-Day—one idol, truly legendary.

"Darling, the P-E's have gone into hiding!" Joseph exclaimed.

———— Σ ————

"Joseph, what th' hell are *P-E's?*" Jim bluntly demanded.

"Darling, where *have* you been? Absolutely *everyone* knows about the Piss-Elegants—*too,* too grand, my dear, none of them having a pot—*piss* and *elegance* running down *both* legs!" Joseph gave style to flamboyance.

"It means one thing, darling," he added. "Rock Hudson's in town!"

Jim choked, *"Who?"*

Shock delighted Joseph. "Darling," he relished, "did I stutter?"

"Not *Rock* Hudson?" Jim gasped.

"I'm afraid so, darling," Joseph coiffed religiously. "I know the feeling, I too hate disappointment—we *are* everywhere."

"The Rock Hudson?" Jim persisted.

"A three-dollar bill, darling," Joseph assured.

Jim said, "If he's queer—nyah, all those kissy-kissy love scenes."

"Darling, it's *only* kissing," Joseph said flatly, "sucking on a tube nine feet long with *shit* in the *bottom!"*

Jim said, "Joseph, you queens are as perverse as J. Edgar Hoover, seeing a queer behind ever' tree 'n' ever' shrub 'n' ever' bush!"

What shocked Jim was image—Rock didn't fit the stereotype. He was probably a decent guy—none of us ever knew. We were not "permitted" to meet him—the P-E's made sure of that. One thing is certain. The P-E's didn't need a bushel, which they didn't have, to go with the pot, which they also didn't have—they had nothing to hide under a bushel.

Sense of self didn't seem of concern at Chez Le Nelle. They spun a cocoon to keep the outside world out—and the inside world in. Stanley's phrasing always struck me oddly, "Yes, my dears, we *have* ventured out."

The three of them were quiet guys. Joe Angel was delicately pretty—not nellie, effeminate in a modest way most becoming a man. Albert didn't drink often. When he did, he was all thumbs, never obnoxious but effervescently bubbly—tipsy on him, endearing. Stanley spun the cocoon. He was cool and calculating—not in a malicious sense. He was a poet, his poetry a poet's poetry, cool and calculating. It was euphonious, never earthy; impassioned, never passionate. Stanley was afraid of a world outside his control.

A time later, I paid Joe Angel's share of rent and moved in with Stanley and Albert for the summer. They had moved from Chez Le Nelle to Mrs. Jenning's House, occupying the penthouse floor above Brett's apartment. Stanley should've written a poem about me. He could've let the poem

——————— Σ ———————

come by itself. He should've stayed and watched, while the moon was hot.

I slipped onto the sunroof one night drenched in Austin moon, bathed in balmy breeze. The Cabaret was dead. The night wasn't. Neither was I—stretched long on the chaise, hard in the hot night, nude against the moon, finger flesh fantasy drenched, bathed balmy.

Stanley stepped out onto the roof, saw me and stepped hurriedly back in. Just as quickly, he stepped out of in and back into out. He told me it wasn't working out, me being in. I should find another inn—I was out.

Barbara, a girl I palled with that summer, said it was a silly reason, him forcing me to move. She laughed when I told her I had a thrilling jack off—a totally *absorbent* jack off. This comes a bit later.

The Nellie Awards finally came and then they went. As they came, both Jim and Gale went—Jim, because he figured it'd be fun; Gale, because his name, at the last minute, was added to the category Debutante of the Year. I was nominated to that category weeks before, along with another guy, JC. Both of us had come out; Gale merely stood out. We were gay; the vote went his way.

Jim was pissed. He said, "It really sucks. Guess that's why, it just sucks." Jim never made *why* clear. I knew why. The award wasn't important, winning not at all important—after all, it was done for fun. Jim was disappointed with Gale. "Gale's a thief. He stole the night. It belonged to you and JC. I expected better of Gale—he hasn't got the *balls* to suck dick!"

I did get two things from the Nellie Awards that night. One was number—I owe Stanley for that. He took a stand-back second look at my outfit—white tennis shorts and shirt under white dinner jacket—and said, "My dear, what a *snappy* little number!" It had to it a certain ring I liked.

A few days later, Jim and I were strolling on the Drag. I said, "My dear, what a *gorgeous* little number!" Jim looked about to find a street sign or something printed with numbers. "Where? What?" he insisted.

"My dear, right here," I told him, practically poking my finger in the face of a guy walking beside us, *"this* little number, isn't he a *gorgeous* little number!" After that, boy, to me, became number. It signified more than boy. A number is gorgeous, beautiful; cute, adorable, attractive; desirable, sexy, lovable and havable—though havable, mostly in my mind.

The other thing I got that night was a friend, JC, who's outlasted thousands of miles, thousands of words—and countless numbers.

——————— Σ ———————

Joseph said, "Darling, you've *got* to meet Harvey." Joseph phoned, appropriately, Sunday afternoon. He *insisted* I come to his rooming house on Nueces. "Harvey—the man I told you about—is *dying* to meet you." Joseph led me a block down the street to a parked car, a big, black sedan. Harvey was also a big man—big in stature, big in size, big in standing.

"Darling," Joseph maneuvered, "do get in, sit down. You're *much* too obvious, *standing* on the street. I'll leave you two alone," he laughed devilishly, "to *get* acquainted!"

I didn't like Joseph leaving me. I only agreed to meet his older friend—the man *dying* to meet me—after Joseph promised to *stay* with us—*not* leave *me* alone with *him*.

Harvey was pleasant enough. His voice was quiet, in control, slick. "So," he smoothed, "you're Dean. I've heard a lot about you."

"Yeah? What?" I asked.

"Oh, Joseph's told me all about you," he furthered.

"Yeah? What?" I repeated.

"I'm sure everything. You should know Joseph by now, he can't keep secrets, especially from me. I've said many times, queens are fickle."

I thought I'd try sophomoric psychology, steer him into talking about himself—I wanted to get *him* off *me*. "I don't remember seeing you at the bar. Get around much?"

Harvey's laugh was glib. "Oh, I'm sure Joseph has told you all about me. What he hasn't told, you don't need to know. You'll learn something of me, I give you as much as you need—only as I determine you need it."

Harvey was methodical, very methodical; not only methodical, Methodist. *In* the hierarchy, *headed* for the echelon, *upper*. Methodical, Methodist, and Married. He suggested a drink. "I'll buy," he said.

A drink sounded like a good idea—I didn't feel at all comfortable alone with Harvey. To me, the image *bar* conjured the image *people*. Instead of a bar, Harvey drove us to his Methodical, Methodist, Married Home, the Family being away. He handed me a very tall and slender, very chilled glass of something very sweet, very red and very potent—*very* potent.

I, too, was potent—*very* potent. The drink was good. He handed me another. Still another. Yet another. Harvey was glib, methodical. He was slick, smooth. So slick, so smooth I stood nude before him barely aware. Barely aware how long and lean, how slight my naked body on his parlor

——————— Σ ———————

floor stretched—arms flung with ankles crossed, scorching flesh between; back arched, head thrust onto carpet; butt tight, suspended on a supple sea of nylon. So slick, so smooth I barely was aware how high my cock reached; how fully it rose; how broad, how flooded, how red the head; barely aware how it jumped and jerked, how it drew my balls tightly in a rising sack, throbbing and pulsing; pulling me, writhing on the floor; lifting me, squirming from the floor; sucking me, into the air; sucking me, through the air; sucking me higher, higher, higher—only the Mighty Line can come higher!

You stars that reigned at my nativity, Whose influence hath allotted death and hell, Now draw up Dean like a foggy mist Into the entrails of yon laboring clouds, That when they vomit forth into the air My limbs may issue from their smoky mouths And my soul, ascend, to Heaven!

I may not have mentioned, Harvey was holy. Believe me, holier than thou. According to entry in Webster, chastity belt is over chasuble. Either way, over chaste or under, I took care my chasuble stayed chaste; it did—until I thought it no longer chased.

Harvey never regarded me above the rank of fickle queen. I suppose he became overly confident, less cautious. Soon afterward, his wife caught him with another guy flagrante delicto. The scandal was hushed, her divorce squashed—does one *ever* know details? Harvey was moved from Austin, moved methodically up Methodist rank. We corresponded at length over distance for many years. I spit on more stamps for him than for a dozen others combined. My letters were love letters—I'd better stop. I'd rather not sell either myself or him completely short. My letters weren't letters *of* love; they were letters *about* love.

Harvey was a man of intelligence, a man of learning, widely traveled both by jet and armchair. He was a man capable of deep thought and introspection—more, I'm afraid, when the mood suited him as means to other purpose. I spilled my blood in feeling inked over those pages, dotting i's and crossing t's in reverence, in awe and in despair. If anyone can know my love, can know it as well as, if not better than me, it is Harvey. Philosophically and intellectually, passionately and plainly—honestly. There wasn't ever, had never, been doubt—I wasn't interested in either a romantic affair with Harvey or a sexual one with his body.

Some years later while living in New York I saw Harvey on three separate occasions, times when upper echelon business brought him into the

———————— Σ ————————

city. The first was soon after I met Billy and we'd been seeing one another. The second was after Billy and I became lovers and set up our apartment together. That was during our first year when things between us, Billy and me, were great. The third time was near the end of my second year with Billy, near the end of our relationship, near the end of us as lovers. It strikes me strangely, more as coincidence than as occurrence, Harvey would've been there beginning, middle and end.

At the time of his second visit, I wanted to talk with Harvey about something that happened to me before I met Billy. It happened during a time when I had Frank sleeping with me, and Jim and Cozby living with me in my fourth-floor alcove apartment overlooking West 23rd Street in Chelsea. I'd given Jim and Cozby the bed in the alcove; Frank and I used the hide-a-bed. Frank is of no consequence, except for me thinking I was in love with him, him knowing how to keep me thinking so. Frank was a devotee of Scientology. He attempted to use that as a wedge to drive Jim away. He had no chance of prying Jim and me apart, though he almost cost me friendship with Jimmy, with whom I'd been close since Austin.

Jimmy and Carter, the boy who gave me Andre Gide's book, were lovers in Austin and for awhile in New York. After separation as lovers, they hadn't broken up friends. Jimmy called Carter *Nibby*—I cannot think of him simply as Carter. Jim saved me from Frank and Frank's Scientology. Jim also helped me save friendship with Jimmy.

None of this I wanted to tell Harvey, the actors and their roles incidental. I wanted to talk with Harvey about something that happened one night. I was then very much enthralled with Frank. We were on the hide-a-bed, him on one side, me on the other. Frank never held me at night. He insisted on "air" space. I was near asleep, maybe asleep, when it happened, coming through the wall from West 23rd Street. A dove sailing on white wings descended and hovered above me in a silvery gray haze; hovered momentarily, only long enough for me to hear the words *I am with you.* Then, the white wings sailed through the wall opposite—and beyond.

I didn't get to tell Harvey about the night of White Wings. I began telling him—he cut me off. "Stop right there. I won't listen to a word more. Miracles and appearances don't happen—never did. It's a figment of your imagination. I said before, you queens are fickle. You delude yourselves into believing whatever pleases you."

————— Σ —————

Harvey made a believer of me—that's what crystallized. This Methodical Methodist Minister Married of Upper Echelon Eminence had no vision, no faith. For all his religious crust, Harvey did not *believe!*

I'd been wandering in and out of my head again! Our correspondence continued, irreligiously so—I felt disinclined to pour my soul to him on paper. My feelings about love were delicate, unable to withstand rough treatment. I had grown weary, struggling to fit into pre-molded concepts.

Years beyond, after I split with Billy and moved back to Texas, I saw Harvey twice more. We arranged to meet in Houston, once at the Warwick and, the last time, at the Shamrock, the year before it was razed. At the time, I was living near the coast, Bay Prairie environs. I drove into Houston for the purpose of meeting him. He had written in advance, "The room will be quite spacious. You're welcome to stay over." It seemed a social gesture.

The evening I arrived, we went to the Ranch, a sprawling Country-and-Western gay bar on Buffalo Speedway, near the Astrodome. The Houston Rodeo was in town, playing the Astrodome. That meant lots more cowboy hats, lots more cowboy boots—and lots more cowboys! Pardner, that's Texas, Houston anyway.

I fashioned my eye on the little number waiting our table. He was duded-up and looked just good enough to eat. I said that to Harvey, and Harvey said to me, "Why don't we see if we can get him for you tonight?"

It occurred to me, more *we's* than *you's* and *him's* bucked in that stampede. I fashioned another thought—*methodical* couldn't turn this trick. It truly didn't matter to me. I felt I'd already had the boy—in my mind.

A certain amount of reason was left in brain cells not yet alcohol-deadened—enough, anyway, before a new rush—for me to realize I didn't want the boy's body. I had to have all the boy—his heart with him.

Harvey bought drinks as fast as I could drink them in order to keep the waiter coming in hope that later the waiter'd come. I drank them almost as fast as they were set before me and the waiter gone. I knew that's where later he'd be—gone. An out-and-out proposition proved methodically what I'd known intuitively. At that point it didn't matter—I was drunk.

Later that night at the Shamrock I was roused from stupor sufficiently to become aware I was being manhandled by Harvey. I didn't want sex, not in the way of hunger. I fought my aggressor. It wasn't much of a fight, no real fight at all—that's the word to convey my meaning.

——————— Σ ———————

Next day over Chinese, Harvey said, "I offer this by way of apology. Quite simply, I'm accustomed to bed favors from those sharing my bed."

What I heard was the word apology. I said, "Accepted and forgotten." I leave it here. Chips can fall where they may.

The next night was repeat of much the same scene. In the morning, I woke to find a note. "I expect you'll be gone before I return. It's disappointing to see you're still the fickle queen I met in Austin. You've changed little, other than becoming a drunk. I *expect* you'll be gone when I return."

The words were cold and sobering. I was uncertain how to respond. Sometime previous Harvey sent me a volume of Cavafy, a modern-day Greek poet. Cavafy eloquently set to verse love of a depth and magnitude he could envision, one he was never able to realize in his own life. Harvey said the poetry gave voice to my lament. On the backside of his note I penciled, *I've Read Cavafy—I've Cried.* Then, I, too, was gone.

It was difficult to make my way through the lobby of the Shamrock, across its parking lot. Tears streamed from my eyes, flowing down cheek and face. My vision blurred. The words of Harvey's note were cruel, unkind. They contained small shreds and large hanks of truth, my life reduced. I had changed *little;* my need for affection and love, *deeper;* my pain, *greater.* I *drank* to escape loneliness. What hurt most—Harvey was, after all, a faggot.

*   *   *   *   *

John Rechy published *The City of Night* in '63 and a paperback circulated the following spring, '64. His book made the cover of *Life*—the *entire* cover. Black-and-white photo, a guy standing on a city-street sidewalk at night in front of a plate glass window looks not at the camera but into the store window. Even in *Life,* no face. The guy didn't need a face. Levis well-fit at narrow waist, denim jacket across broad shoulders; trim hips; arms thrust back to slide palms deep into hip pockets accentuating the overall look, enticing the eye to that nice, *nice* butt. He didn't need a face. I *knew* he was hot, prime meat, all stud—ready. Sure, the scene was lonely and dark, may have been wet—it was steamy and seductive. Like my scenes. Like my streets. Like my nights—steamy, seductive.

"Darling, I feel so *naked* and *visible!* Am I wearing Saran Wrap?" Joseph asked. "Queens on *Life!* Exposed up and down the Drag, on *every* counter. Oh, I *hope* it doesn't *ruin* cruising. Now everyone will want a *queen* of their own! Oh, I wish I'd brought my raincoat—I feel so *naked!*"

————— Σ —————

I bought the book. Garner & Smith, a bookshop on the street floor of Goodall-Wooten Dorm, had a large display conspicuously stacked on a table inside. Joseph wouldn't go into the shop after he'd seen the window-poster arrangement. Once inside, Jim *browsed*—cookbooks!

"Miss *Goody-Woo* can lift her skirts now!" Joseph shrieked, looking upward at the balconied dorm, "Every man up there has a copy *tucked* in his pants—pages *stuck* together!"

Jim said, "Joseph, do you think *everyone* is queer?"

"Darling, of course not!" Joseph blurted. "Who'd want *all* of them? Men *know* what they *like*. Men up there," he pointed upward, toward the balconies of Goodall-Wooten, "*like* what *I've got!*"

Joseph wouldn't go with us—"he wants to sniff a new toilet some-where," Jim said. Jim and I cut classes the remainder of the day and drove to Lake Travis. He spotted a place we'd be able to get the car off the road partway down a rough trail. It wasn't difficult going the rest of the way on foot. Across a sharp bank, we found large flat boulders, more like slabs of stone, extending from granite cliffs to gently slapping water.

We read the book there, most of it, anyway; taking turns reading aloud, barefoot with cuffs turned up, shirts discarded. It was a secluded place open to sun and air beside placid water. It gave us distance from the scenes Rechy described, the queens he portrayed and the hustlers whose bodies had slapped against theirs, much like the lake against these granite slabs. I guess the slapping, both of water and flesh, cleansed and purified a sense of feeling known only to the most wretched—despair.

Jim asked me, "Tell me how you feel, what's it like."

I tried to explain my feeling of love—that's what it is for me, love. Sex is part of feeling love, inside; one way to touch love, outside.

"It's all sex with Joseph," Jim said, "find 'em, fuck 'em, forget 'em. He's never in love—you always are."

"He doesn't know the feeling being left behind, forgotten." I'm not sure why I said that—I didn't have an answer for his question.

Jim told me about Don Quixote, battling windmills in the air. "It may be no different for you," he said. "No one saw them except Don Quixote. He fought because he believed." Jim fell silent a moment, his eyes penetrat-ing mine. "Are you sure about love?" he asked.

"Jim, I'm sure," I told him. That was all, no whys or wherefores. I

———————— Σ ————————

had none. I had only a feeling and my belief in that feeling. I began to realize believing alone is not enough. To sustain belief, for it to endure, it must also have vision—faith. I know I gained the vision, faith in my belief. Later, when I had nothing to cling to, love was my only strength.

* * * * *

One morning in early spring, Jim said, "I've found a place down-town, 6th Street. Le's drive down, do some browsing—I'm sick of this room."

The area was way downtown, down downtown, east of South Congress, old Austin that had stayed old. Run-down and shoddy. Junk stores. Salvage and reclaim dealers. Trade-in refrigerator and appliance merchandisers. *Used Furniture.* That's what Jim was looking to find.

We loaded an oak corner table and a maple coffee table into the back of my car. I discovered a tall, frosted light globe, octagon-shape and stepped like an enormous quartz crystal.

"I knew that damned geology would ruin your mind," Jim said. "So it *looks* like a big drippy crystal—beats hell outta me what you'll do with it."

Back at the Cottages Jim said, "This'll take no time at all. I've got it figured out. It's all in my head." The corner table went into the corner, our beds headed into its two open sides, and the coffee table landed within the new perimeter. "There," Jim said. "Like I told you, no place for crystals."

He went with me anyway to find a hardware store, where I bought a few feet of twist-link chain, some lamp cord and a couple of electrical parts. Near the checkout I picked up a red light bulb. "Nyah," Jim said, "too whorish. Get the blue."

Voila! A hanging *crystal* dripping blue over our new corner table. Joseph said, "Darlings! It's so very—*gay!*"

Restless is a good word—uneasy, disquiet, discontent; the feeling was there. Beatnik was beat. Coffee houses and folk were brewing while ballads and Beatles battled. Rock 'n' Roll rocked out and Rock rolled in. Hair was a new idea, taking root from Liverpool. Paisley prints and Madras plaids replaced pale pinks and muted pastels. The mood was serendipitous—no one knew it. Serendipity was still around the corner. Restless is a good word.

Gale was restless. He leaped into Modern Dance middle of the semester. Jim said he was light on his toes. Said also, "Good, it'll keep him busy. He's still on my shit list."

Cozby may or may not have been restless. He signed up for a

—————— Σ ——————

summer of seminars with the artist Georgia O'Keeffe in Taos, New Mexico.

Jim was restless. He applied to the Peace Corps. Said, "I'm in a rut. I need to be doing something."

I was restless. Said, "I want to switch my major to Drama." My folks wrote back, *Like Hell You Will!*

Scott didn't seem to be restless, though he decided we'd have our date. Jim was gone to Dallas for Peace Corps exams—Scott and I had the place to ourselves. "Should I take my pants off, or what?" he asked.

"No," I told him, "let me do it, that's part of it." We were terribly clumsy, me stripping him and him, me. Scott was giggly and so was I. We jumped into bed skinned to our briefs and I contoured my body to his.

"Should I do anything?" Scott questioned.

"Nyah," I told him, "not unless you want to."

"I don't do anything?" he wondered.

"Nyah, just lay back and enjoy it," I assured him.

I began touching his abdomen, rubbing and caressing in a systematic fondle to fancy. Scott cupped my shoulders lightly and said quietly, "Hey, can I tell you something? I've thought it over—I think I've changed my mind. Is that alright?"

"Sure, Teddy Bear," I told him, "but I'll do it if you want me to."

"Nyah," he said, "if I didn't know you it'd be okay—I wouldn't have to face you again."

I lay close beside him, an arm stretched across his chest. He cradled my head at his shoulder. "How about if I just love you," Scott asked softly, "would that be okay?"

"Yeah, Teddy Bear," I said, "you can love me even a little bit."

Then Scott said, "I've thought it over. Okay if I love you a bunch?"

"Well, sure, Teddy Bear," I said. "You can love me all you want. That's all there is anyhow, all there is in this whole wide world—just love." I snuggled my body to his and closed my eyes.

"Hey," he said again, "you forgot something. Kiss me goodnight?"

"Wow! Sure, Teddy Bear," I said, rolling the cheek of my face slightly against his; him, rolling the cheek of his face slightly against mine. Our mouths met, and I planted a big, wet kiss on his puckering lips. It was a sweet, sweet sleep that night.

*   *   *   *   *

———————— Σ ————————

I don't remember where or how we met Don—Jim would recall. He fell in love with Don. Yes, it was telling, a bounce to the step, a lilt to the voice, a sparkle in the eye. "It's a one-night stand," Jim told me. Then Don phoned. "We're just sleeping together," Jim told me. Don called again. "I thought at first it was only sex," Jim told me, "now Don's my lover." Jim looked at me, not funny, not strangely, not oddly. "Guess that's why, I'm beginning to see. Guess that's why."

Remarkable—a little thing between a guy's legs stretches into his mind, changing his life. Jim figured it out, he didn't want to go to the Peace Corps after all. How not to go is what he couldn't figure. "I'll never get picked anyway," he concluded. With that, he put the matter out of mind. Jim found an apartment on the west side of campus, a one-bedroom upstairs duplex, a '30s house conversion. He bounced in one day and hollered, "Hey, grab your skirt—le's go!" That was how Jim did things. He poked around until something poked back—*Wham!*

"Jim!" I said, "It's great! You and Don are going to live here?"

"Nyah, me and you—Don's got a place. I'll be staying with him most of the time—we need a place, you and me."

"We do?" I said. "If this is it, what'a we need to do?"

"Nothing," Jim told me. "Get packed. I've already rented it!"

A couple of things need to be said. For one, the semester had about six weeks remaining. Jim and I, sophomores, weren't eligible to live in unapproved housing. The other, neither of us had any money. What little money we had was so pathetic it was worse than no money at all. Jim said, "Piss on it. I'm broke, I'll worry about that later." Later, what happened later, was innocent and harmless. It should never have happened at all.

Near midnight, we returned from a caffeine junket at the Night Hawk on the Drag—both of us giddy. Workmen installing evaporative coolers earlier in the day left a tall ladder extended to Smith's third-floor window. They set the cooler in place and left for the day. Smith's light was on. I said, "Wouldn't Smith think it funny if someone *tapped* on his window?" I climbed the ladder and reached across the cooler to do just that. Smith *did* think it funny. He came to the window to see who it might be tap-tap-tapping so late at night. He raised the window. The cooler not fastened, tumbled down, atop my head. It fell across my shoulder, knocking me from the ladder as it flew to the ground—*smashing to smithereens.*

—————— Σ ——————

There wasn't much blood but the ivy was crushed. That's the way the affair wound up—not much blood, Jim and I pretty well crushed. Someone *had* to pay for the cooler. Word was sent, re-sent and sent again. Smith saluted himself out of the deal. Jim said, *"We* shouldn't have to pay, *they* left the damned ladder out—*they* never finished the job." It was major business, major enough to bring out Mother Ferrell in a major business suit.

"Yipe! I heard the old bat was dead!" Jim groaned. We were trapped. She was already up the stairs.

"Oh, ho," she began, "what other mischief have you little hoodlums been up to? Why, look at this room—you've ruined it!"

"We think it's *gay!"* Jim replied smartly—he *adored* himself!

"Gay my rear end, you little hoodlum, it's nothing at all what a nice man's college room oughtta be. It's a floozy bordello, if ever I saw one! Mother Ferrell should've known better—a nice boy wanting to hang curtains. Nice boy my rear end! Nice boys don't hang curtains and tell Mother Ferrell one of her rooms is gay!" She did an exaggerated bump-and-grind to illustrate *gay.* "I'd say hmmn, hmmn, hmmn to that!"

Jim said, "We think it's *very* gay!" He hardly kept a *straight* face.

"Hmmn, hmmn, hmmn," she said again, in Jim's face, "a little *queer* if you ask me—hanging curtains and making bed covers!"

Suddenly she noticed our packed belongings. "Why! What's this, all these boxes? You little hoodlums are moving out, planning to skip! We'll see about that. Mother Ferrell will go to Dean Arno. Mother Ferrell knows the law. You two little hoodlums will be outta this University so quick it'll make your hmmn, hmmn, hmmn ache."

She *shook* her finger in Jim's face, not merely to scold—to under-score power behind her threat. Then, she simmered from a rolling boil to a moderate stew. "Mother Ferrell's a fair person. If you boys pay up, Mother Ferrell will shut up."

She demanded our final month's rent in addition to the hundred-and-fifty on the cooler. Jim and I scraped and dug and we paid. It took the very last of the money we had, all except a quart Mason-jar filled with pennies I collected, weeding them from my pockets daily. Jim said, "The old bitch blackmailed us! Guess Phil was right about her all along." We were free to move into our apartment—the same afternoon.

Jim said, "Know what I think? We've come full circle. Yup, full

———————— Σ ————————

circle." Then his Mom *come* through. She sent a check and Jim took us shopping on East 6th again. He bought an old Duncan Phyfe dining table complete with six chairs. He also bought a mattress for his bedroom. He'd have bought me one, too. "Nyah, I'll make out," I told him. I used seventy-nine of the pennies to buy an inflatable swim-floaty at a surplus store and we stopped to buy "groceries." My folks didn't come through. They weren't about to see their son a drama major. Their son, determined to become one, said he'd not come home for the summer. They said, with Final, Ultimate, Authority—*No More Money!*

Change was everywhere—none of us surmised it. Change, somewhat like life, creeps up with such cunning one isn't aware until in the thick of it. Then it doesn't matter—he's already sunken into it, circumstance hard to conceive otherwise. Change, in that way, is like life. Change in another way is like life. It sometimes *BANGS!* before one, doesn't give him time to react. He's in the thick of it, carried on its current—swept along or swept away.

Attitude's the word, the one I want. It's what was there, attitude. We changed ours. We took genre and made of it a Proper Noun. We took *gay* out of the closet, gave it a good dusting, and with it clothed our bodies. Why? Our bodies are all we have, our bodies and what's in them. What's in them is GAY, all the way. What we are, we are totally, completely. We aren't shells moving about till dark playing hide-and-seek. These are our lives. We determine to live them totally, completely, in the wholeness and in the oneness of what we are—*GAY!*

There's another part, a part I'm going to tackle. Gay also embodies love. Many of us came to gay by way of love—fall in love with a guy, make love with him, discover our gay self. We all saw it happen, coming to gay by way of love. There was a *but* none of us saw—coming to love by way of gay. It's much the same—it works from the opposite end.

I often wonder if that may be the answer I couldn't give Jim the afternoon we talked, while standing on flat granite slabs. I wonder if Joseph has discovered the answer. Two concepts mirror image must be one and the same, the commonality they share, the oneness in this instance, love.

Attitude is what we had. We found it and we embraced it. We carried gay with us, into Mother Ferrell's Cottages, into classrooms, onto streets; carried it to Chicago, to Kent State, to the Stonewall Inn; to Attica, to Atlanta and Amarillo. We swept the nation—we carried attitude into the

———————— Σ ————————

homes of Middle America. We reached inside to find pride. We held pride before America, displaying dignity and worth, demanding to be people, first and foremost—*we are people!*

It strikes me as backward, crumbs garnered over bodies of so many fallen, we've come to Queer Nation. There's anger in that and it's degrading—the name and the anger. Let me not neglect the upsurge of queer-bashing, or the onslaught of AIDS, and the reason behind both—hatred.

God doesn't love queers! America knows this, from pulpit to embalming room—*it's IN the Bible!* I may be the one reading between the lines—Sodom and Gomorrah *is* a tale often misquoted. Perfection of physical beauty divinely inspired is assertive—*Angels of the Lord are Beautiful!*

It is to me a source of wonder the new covenant is overlooked. I had to discover it for myself, beginning with Matthew. Jeremiah had mentioned it—*that's* in the Bible. I doubt God minds queers *reading* about it. It's different here in Bay Prairie, me preaching Gay Gospel from the courthouse steps. They still have trees—high and nigh!

*   *   *   *   *

The finish of that semester brought things to pretty much an end. With no money, summer school was out for me. Jim was accepted into the Peace Corps. He left me the apartment, saying "Take care of yourself. Whatever you think to do with all the stuff is okay, I'm leaving it with you." Don left for Mexico. I was stuck with his visiting Mexican charge, the Flamenco Queen Dominguez—Domino, I called *her*.

Domino was more broke than me. He peddled his ass—it's more honest to say he *tried* to peddle it. What small pocket change that brought in he drank. I had the good sense to hide my jar of pennies or I'd never have made it. College jobs in a college town are nil to none. Despite appearance, Austin *was* still a town.

Domino didn't like the apartment, didn't like the "straights," a young couple occupying the floor below. He created disturbance all hours of night—cops at our door became more than habit. His scheme succeeded, the owners relieved to finally break our lease and return Jim's security. Domino also had Jim's utility deposits refunded—to him. That's how he managed to rent another apartment.

Th apartment was south of campus, an area that was old Austin. Not ancient Austin, Austin of a more gentle time when genteel people reflected

———————— Σ ————————

their means in sturdy residence constructed near town. Near town had become mid-town, and there was little doubt mid would be gobbled by bureaucracy—that "little doubt" merely the question "when."

A widow split her home through the center to create shotgun quarters. The apartment went for less money, bills paid. Domino kept money in his pocket by keeping the old lady conned and primed—she was a soft touch. I still had no job.

Actually, I had less than that. I didn't realize it until I returned one afternoon to find Jim's Duncan Phyfe missing. Domino tried to convince me of robbery—he was the thief. I discovered he sold most of my clothes, too, including the black-lens sunglasses I referred to as gay deceivers. I felt relieved he hadn't taken my books. I borrowed twenty dollars from JC to repurchase Jim's table. I was angry, more with myself for having been so trusting. "Once I killed a bird," I told Domino. "It hurt me more than the bird." Domino was silent. I felt we communicated.

Lenzo's Italian Restaurant on North Interregional seemed a likely job prospect. Max, authentically Italian, was Mr. Lenzo's manager-partner. He told me, "Sorry, kid, we don't need nobody now. No jobs." Sitting at a rear table in the main dining room, he hardly paid me any attention, having never moved from his chair.

I was letdown. I doubt Max saw my disappointment. He may have thought I looked hungry—I was skinny. He called to me as I reached the door. "Kid! Hold it! C'mon back, over here." He nodded me to the table where he was sitting. "Look, kid, this ain't much. We got this party tonight, out at Old Man Lenzo's. It'll be a few hours, understand that's it. Just tonight. We got the kid from our other place 'cross town, maybe you know it, Pizza-To-Go? Tonight, you help out serving, there's twenty in it. Like I said, it ain't much—it's all I got. Whaddya say, kid, deal?"

"Wow, sure!" I shouted. "By God, Max, sure!" It's worth repetition, Argonauts and Angels!

Max was the Argonaut; Ron, the kid from Pizza, the Angel. I knew it right away, in the kitchen at Old Man Lenzo's. I was so excited about the forest—a twenty-dollar forest!—I hadn't thought about the trees. This kid was a tree still growing—solid trunk, not too branchy; well proportioned with good limbs; maybe get a little more height, no need for pruning or topping. Ron was seventeen. He had short, sandy hair and grayish-green

——————— Σ ———————

131

eyes, a round face and a pretty smile. I got a feeling something was about to happen, something good—*all* good. It began when Max introduced me to Ron in Mr. Lenzo's kitchen.

"Kid, this is that other kid. He's gonna help. The boths you kids take care of it, whatever looks good. Eat's much's you want. The boths you kids—Hey! No booze, okay? Youc'n call me, Max, kid," he said to me.

As afterthought he turned back to me and said, "I forgot that other kid's name. Youc'n aks him. Another thing, kid, don't aks me no more questions tonight. Aks that other kid when you aks his name. He's been around Pizza long enough. Oh, yeah, another thing, kid, when you get that other kid's name, come and tell me—I hate to keep aksing."

Max suddenly noticed the other kid standing near my side. "Hey," he said, "I'm just seeing, the boths you kids look good together, good-looking kids. I didn't aks, maybe the boths you kids already know each other. Hey, that's okay. Keep looking good, kids, keep looking good—Max is happy."

After he left us, the other kid said, "Some trip, old Max, huh? Aah, he's okay. I goof on 'im. Don't bother me, long's they keep him outta payroll. Name's Ron, swee'heart. Le's see how good the boths us kids look together."

Ron didn't do anything ordinary like shake hands, although we stood facing one another in pretty much a shake-hand position. He laid a loose fist on each of my shoulders and leaned his forehead into mine. He stuck out his tongue and wiped it upward across my lips, tipping the end of my nose. "Hmn, not bad, swee'heart. Yeah, I'd say we'll make it."

With that, he turned back to the stove. "How about I cook, you serve, okay?" He pulled a large tray of oysters something-cheesy-looking-on-the-half-shell from the oven and swung round toward me. "I'm not really queer, swee'heart. Just tryin' to be gay."

At least we began on a first-name basis! Ron was a good worker. He kept the trays of oysters-whatever and pizza coming, and I kept them going. The party was in back of the house on the lawn. It was transformed into a bistro of tables and chairs. Colorful paper lanterns glowed in crisscross strips, jigsawing on strings overhead. The lawn filled with guests—couples, marrieds, singles; those attached, those unattached; those waiting and looking, those waiting and watching, those simply waiting. They were of all ages, all of one stance—successful.

Successful easily describes the party as well. I stayed busy, keeping

——————— Σ ———————

full trays out and empty ones in; along with that, pumping pitchers of draft.

Beer was the most difficult to organize. I'd empty a pitcher by the mugful long before I could maneuver it to a thirsty table. I had to juggle two pitchers at once to make a single round. Between beer rounds, I took empty trays back to the kitchen to exchange for full ones. Ron was equally busy. All I saw of him the first few hours was his ass, turned up in front of the oven.

I came in with an empty tray as Ron took one steaming from the oven—we almost collided. "Watch this one, swee'heart, it's hotter'n blazes. Same's this kitchen. Oven's a scorcher. How 'bout it, swee'heart, bring in a bucket o' cold suds next trip?" Ron didn't give me time to protest. "Aah, Max don't even listen to Max. He's a wipe-out."

"Sure, why not," I said. The trays were tangled between us, Ron tugginng on the hot one I now held. "Hey, swee'heart," he said, leaning across oysters, cheese and shells to lick from my chin upward across my lips to the tip of my nose where his tongue lapped a saliva finale. "Hmmn, tha's what I thought, tas'e better'n 'em ahstures."

I haven't mentioned the kitchen was at the back of the house. A large window looked out onto—and into from—the backyard festival. Max caught my arm. "Ever get that other kid's name? Never mind, I'd forget it again. Hey, kid, hey-hey-hey. Y'a doing a *swell* job. *Ter-rific!* This's ol' Max you're talking to. I know how you kids are, a little of this, a little of that. Hey, what's a stick of bread without wine? *Ter-rific,* kid! Forget what ol' Max said. Take the boths you kids some beer. Hey, kid, just keep it clean, okay?"

Juggling pitchers became a major challenge. Ron could empty one in less time than I could fill another. I thought the party-goers would satiate and slow down—they gained momentum. I hardly got any beer at all. In the kitchen Ron was beginning to struggle—with pans and trays, with the oven, with himself and his body. "Swee'heart, this's bitchin, real bitchin'! Tas'e my ahstures!" He scooped one from a shell, grabbed my hair and tilted my head backward. With fingers holding a cheesy oyster, he pried my lips and mouth wide, wider, to stuff the moist mass inside. He plopped it at the back of my throat, then clamped my mouth. With fingers and palm, he massaged at my throat until the prize went down.

Ron supported my head with both hands and leaned into me. He brought his mouth to mine, full mouth on mine, sending tongue across lips into my mouth. His tongue thrashed and flogged, scraped in broad darting

——————— Σ ———————

circles. Ron sucked at my mouth from a deeply inhaled breath. His tongue slowed, retreated. He pulled his mouth from mine with a loud *Smack!*

It was a wet kiss. Ron licked his lips and mouth, still holding my head, looking into my face. "Hmmn, swee'heart, bitchin'. I wouldn't trade ahstures for that!" His tongue shot out again, *washed* my chin and mouth.

Max came hurtling through the door. "Hey-hey-hey, the twos you kids. We need food! We need drink! Ol' Max don't aks for a lot. Whaddya say, huh? Keep him happy, keep him happy. Okay? Okay."

I've never been able to figure whether or not Max saw Ron kissing me. When I think, "No, he didn't," I figure Max must've been blind. When I think, "Yes, he did," it doesn't figure at all. What I finally figured Ron had already said—you can't *figure* Max.

I made a round of tables and returned to the kitchen with a stack of empties. At the same moment, Ron lost footing in front of the oven, sprawling head-over-heels into a gooey mess. Max came in behind me. "Hey-hey-hey! Kid, how can I run a kitchen? I turn my back, maybe a minute I'm gone, and what happens? It all goes on the floor. Whaddya say? C'mon, kid," he said to me, "le's take care of it, huh?"

I helped and we carried Ron into a bedroom off the kitchen. After we got him onto the bed, Max said, "Do me a favor, kid, see to that floor. Hey, get the mess outta way so nobody falls, huh?"

I told Max it was my fault, I was the one who brought him the beer. "You won't fire Ron, will you, Max?" I pleaded.

"Who's talkin' fire, kid? Hey, I got mouths to feed, bread to bake. Let ol' Max take care of the details, whaddya say, okay? Look, kid, watch out for him, huh?" he gestured toward Ron. "Do this for ol' Max, kid—keep an eye on him, see he's okay. Whaddya say, huh?"

Soon afterward the party began thinning. Max said, "Hey, kid, the party's goin' out for a swim. Don't worry about the mess. Here's the twenty, kid. I'm throwin' in five more. You done *ter-rific*, kid."

He replaced his wallet in his pocket, then wheeled back at me, "Wait up, kid, do this one thing more for ol' Max—see to that other kid, whaddya say, okay? Hey, I knew right off, the twos you's good kids. Kid, take another five. You done *ter-rific!*" He gave me a slap on the side of my face. Then, halfway across the back lawn, he turned and came back to the kitchen. "Kid, I like you. You want a job, come by Monday. We'll talk. Okay?"

————— Σ —————

I was jubilant. "Wow, Max, sure! By God, Max, sure!"

Ron couldn't stand on his own. His body was heavy, dead weight. I carried him to my car. "S'em ahstures, swee'heart, s'em ahstures," he kept saying, "din't I say, you tas'e berre'n 'em ahstures?"

Ron wouldn't go with me to my apartment. He told me he had to go home "to my ol' la'y, shees, my mom." He said, "wri'it down, you num'mer. I'll cawl. *You!*" He poked me in the ribs with a finger. I wanted to walk him to the door, but Ron insisted he be let out at the curb. "Tas'e berre'n ahstures, swee'heart. Bitchin', berre'n, ahstures!"

I wasn't sure I'd hear from Ron. It was an outrageous evening—I knew I'd gotten attached to him. I also knew that scraps of paper with hastily written phone numbers are easily discarded. Jim said once, "People are like buses—miss one, catch another."

It may have been as well Ron *din't* stay at the apartment. Domino was bad news—sure as anything, he'd have screwed *something* up. I was trying to get out of that situation—with a job, maybe I could. I didn't want Domino onto it—I didn't intend to support him. I *did* want to give JC back the twenty—that was my problem. I couldn't call JC—he lived at home and didn't give out a phone number. I couldn't wait for him on campus—I *din't* want to miss Ron's call. *I* couldn't call *Ron*—I was so excited I *din't* think to get *his* number. My life suddenly became very complicated!

I thought of Carl, a friend of JC whom I'd met. JC had said, "Try calling me at Carl's. I'm often there." He gave me Carl's number—where did I put it? Into the middle of this mess my folks drove up. They'd taken a Sunday drive to Austin "in order to track you down and talk sense to you."

Mom! Dad!

They tracked me down and they talked sense to me. I guess I must've talked nonsense back to them—we were worse off than before. My dad became angry and stomped from the apartment. Mom tried to smooth things over. I walked with her to their car. I noticed, for the first time, they both seemed much smaller than what I remember them being.

During our parting the phone from inside rang. *Mom! Dad! The phone! Gotta go, it's Ron! I might* have said it that way! I *did* run back to the apartment, hoping it would be Ron calling. It was. He was wiped-out, hung-over, goofed-on. His old lady din't like it none he came home drunk. She was glad he came home and din't pass out somewhere. He was supposed to tell

———————— Σ ————————

that nice man Thank You for getting him home, "so thanks, swee'heart. Now we got all that outta the way, when'm I gonna see you?"

I told Ron about Max—maybe I'd get a job. He said, "Swing by Pizza after you see ol' Max?" I said, "Yeah, on North Lamar, I know where it is—Oh, closed on Monday? Sure, I can pick you up at the house. Yeah, I remember where. Yeah, I can find it. Yeah, soon's I see Max."

Then he said, "Swee'heart, remember that ahsture? Bitchin', babe, real bitchin', din't you think?"

I *din't* have to think—"Wow, Ron, sure!"

Carl at first said, "We can put your things in the garage. I never use it." I'd told him about Domino. I never knew why he offered. Carl said, "You can stay here with me if you like. With things stored, it won't be overcrowd. I'll help you get on your feet, no rent to pay. I know how it is, summer jobs." For me, it was really a godsend—Argonauts and Angels!

Max gave me a job, dishwasher, buck-fifty an hour, at the restaurant on North Interregional. It doesn't sound like much. That's what the job paid and that's what I made—I was *proud* to get it. Sometimes Max slipped me an extra five. Waitresses piled my hand with quarters and fifty-cent pieces on busy weekend nights—I'd leave dirty dishes till later to bus their tables. After a month on my quart of pennies, a few half dollars was *real* money!

After he hired me that Monday morning, Max said, "Hey, kid, how 'bout it, run me an errand on your way home? These crates got dropped here and they go to Pizza. That other kid—what's his name?—he's out there cleaning today. How about it, kid, run these by on your way?"

North Lamar wasn't on my way—it was far out of my way. If that other kid, what's-his-name, was there, it most definitely was the way I wanted to go. "Sure, Max! Why not?"

Ron said, "I tried to call, swee'heart. Let you know I had to work. Wiped out our date, huh?"

"Heck, no," I told him, "look who's standing here—*din't* I tell you, I'm working, too?"

"No goof? Babe, that's gotta be the bitchin'est bitch of all!"

I told him about Carl's apartment. "No goof? Can I help you move?"

"Sure, sweetheart—except I've already moved! Here's the phone."

Ron simply beamed. "Din't I tell you, soon's I saw you, din't I say, swee'heart, we'll make it? Bitchin'!"

———————— Σ ————————

Carl's apartment, on 18th Street near Red River, was part of what was called the Compound—a horseshoe arrangement of six chalet-style cottages built in the '30s, a project of the UT school of architecture. There didn't seem any reason for its name other than it *looked* like a compound—an arrangement resulting from union of separate similar elements, especially of a kind usually independent. That *was* the Compound.

The six Compound units weren't run-down, weren't in disrepair, though neither were they spiffy and polished. The owner kept the buildings structural—it was the tenants who *cared* for them. Those who occupied the Compound weren't so much tenants as shareholders, sharing in the unique distinction of the Compound and holding onto their unit—forever, it was said. That also was a distinction—those who occupied the Compound weren't transitory in the way of roomers and renters. They *lived* in the Compound. It had that mask of stability, a sense of being, belonging to a larger picture moving into history. In one way it was a Pompeiian fresco. We knew, with individual understanding, the Compound was very much like my lagoon, it's season, too, numbered.

I should mention as well that shareholders of the Compound weren't standard. There wasn't anything ordinary or run-of-the-mill about them. Those who sought—and found—shelter there were every bit as unique and distinct as the shelter they compounded.

Carl's cottage was one of the mid-size houses. It was open floor-to-ceiling, as were the others. A stairway climbed upward by landings and finally led to the uppermost level. It was somewhat a balconied alcove, the balcony overlooking everything below and the alcove tucked into a dormer nook that was mostly window. That's where Carl had his bed and, on the floor beside, where I tossed my floaty.

I said serendipity was just around the corner. Carl's garage held eclectic the house no longer could. What about Carl do I remember? That he was handsome in a classical way? Had steady, piercing eyes? A dark shag of wonderfully thick salt-and-pepper hair? That his smile had permanently dimpled his cheeks? His voice was mellow and liquid quiet? That occasionally I'd glimpse in him a playful Peter Pan posing as Pinocchio?

Mostly, I remember Carl mornings, reaching through sunlight from his dormer-alcove as the phone from between us jangled on the balcony floor, Carl on his bed, me on my floaty. It was Ron who called. It was always

——————— Σ ———————

Ron. He called my first morning at Carl's. Carl said, "I think it's your little boyfriend," handing me the phone. He propped on elbow watching as I talked with Ron, listening perhaps. Probably there was sound—what did we say? Not a word comes to mind, except for little things and nothings so terribly, terribly significant. It was a voice and an image forming across a charged line, the focus of remembering following a night of dreaming. It was seeing Ron on his back, knees up and head thrown back; rolling onto his belly, tangling with the cord twisting halfway round. It was knowing he, too, was seeing me. We were forming features against contours, finding sense beyond reason and feeling beyond that. They were the first words of the day, days that began in the warmth of Carl's eclectic, serendipitous sunlight.

Carl would say, "It's your little boyfriend," and then, cupping the mouthpiece, "He *sounds* cute!" Carl began to phrase it musically *before* picking up the phone, "It's your *cute* little boyfriend." Early on, Carl said, "Do you want to get that, you know who it is?" I told him, "No, you answer, Carl." I liked hearing aloud—*it's Ron, your boyfriend.* Another time Carl said, "Shall I answer that, tell him you're not here?" *"Yes, Carl!—No!"* Carl soon stopped asking which of us would answer. He always did, sometimes Peter Pan, sometimes Pinocchio. I *din't* mind; I rather liked it. That summer in sunlight, Carl shared with Ron and me, shared with us in a love we had.

The most I saw of Carl that summer was during my "cute little boyfriend's wake-up call." It may seem juvenile—it may have been juvenile. It *din't* feel juvenile. Carl said, "I think it's *very* sweet. It shows he cares." Even today I can think of no words any better with which to describe.

Ron and I both worked long hours, 11 mornings till 11 nights, but it was more like midnight before we'd finish. Pizza and Lenzo's weren't easily accessible to one another. North Lamar and North Interregional were separated by fenced expanse of state mental and VA facility. I'd pick Ron up mornings at his Mom's. He'd drop me at Lenzo's, take my car and return after Pizza closed, usually having to wait—it took me longer to close the restaurant than it did him carry-out pizza.

Lenzo's seemed always to have a large table of diners who ran up a large tab and still had a large bottle of vino going round after the doors were closed. Ron'd say, "Swee'heart, they got two ways to go—up and out. You got only one—in the car with me. That's where I'll be."

He called it goofing. We'd drive somewhere, anywhere. We always

——————— Σ ———————

ended up parked on the street in front of his mom's house. Ron liked to touch just for the feel of touching—he touched me often. Parked on the street, he'd slouch on the seat and pull me closely to him, his arms slung over my shoulders and clasped loosely at my throat. Sometimes he'd press his chin atop my head, smooth his face against my hair, sniffing about my neck. He always held me for a long while, parked on the street, spreading hands about my chest, clenching and squeezing my body to his, his to mine. He seemed to purr, whispering about my ear, nibbling and licking, until, finally, his mouth with biting lips sucked mine to his.

Ron wasn't rough, not in anything he did. Cramming the oyster down my throat wasn't delicate. From his hands it wasn't rough, not coarse. He was gentle without being tender. His kiss was that way—gentle without being delicate. His kiss, like the oyster, full and moist, warm, with lots of juice, was succulent, to the point of sinful—licked and sucked clean of sin.

There was tenderness in the way Ron held me, a gentle tenderness that wasn't delicate. My body wasn't fragile, needing to be handled carefully. Ron's care was his handling, his gentle and his tender. When he held me, when he kissed me, it was always the first time. There weren't a lot of words. They didn't seem needed. What was needed was there—it was us.

Ron said, "Know why I kissed you at Lenzo's party, swee'heart? 'Cause I'as scared you wouldn't kiss me."

"That's the only reason?" I asked.

"Nope, swee'heart. I figured you'd taste good!" He squeezed me and tasted again. "Bitchin'!"

Six twelves didn't leave extra time. The seventh day wasn't altogether ours either. Half of it belonged to Lenzo, set aside for cleaning. I guess that's why our sunlit calls and moonlight parks were so valuable. I'm glad there was no urgency. It gave us a chance to explore one another. Without that, I don't think we could've become as we did.

August days in Austin come one way—hot. If one of them isn't, it's only because it's hotter. Ron said, "Swee'heart, tomorrow outta be ours. Le's make it bitchin'!" I told him about a place with flat slabs on Lake Travis, the one where Jim and I had once gone. Ron said, "Gotta be it, babe."

He helped me with the floors and then he helped us to several buckets of Michelob draft. Waxed-paper champagne icers Lenzo seldom used were all we could find for the beer. Ron fabricated foil covers and

—————— Σ ——————

wedged the buckets into shipping crates, stashed in the car alongside pizzas he made. "Hope youc'n find th' place, swee'heart, 'cause all I want with this hot beer's some cool water. Know why?" Ron licked the air as though it were me and poked my ribs with a finger, "'Cause with you, babe, I got it all!"

The beer *was* hot and the water cool; the edge of Lake Travis, no beach. The granite slabs on which we staged rested atop others below the water, reinforcing the bank. Precarious feet found unsure footing before deep water. Ron shucked his clothes first thing. "C'mon, swee'heart, it's wipe-out. Goof on it." He hurriedly peeled my clothes—I wasn't doing it fast enough to suit him. He stood back to admire, my body naked before him, "Bitchin', babe. You *are* one bitchin' babe."

We drank beer and played in the water. Ron was a better swimmer, stronger; he helped me. We weren't actually swimming, more floating. "C'mon, swee'heart, I won't let go." He took me with him to water so deep, cold currents shafted from below. "Easy, swee'heart, le'me hold." He used his body as a raft, cradling me astraddle one leg, my torso partly resting on his. One arm balanced against the water, the other held me. There was little current. We floated for what seemed a long while, Ron holding me, fingers lazy at my shoulder. It was an effortless buoyancy, body suspended weight-less on body, skin sensing skin in liquid movement. I felt serene, somewhat surreal, as though time were dripping from one of Dali's melting timepieces.

Ron lifted his head from the water to lick-kiss me. We flipped. I went under and came up flailing. He encircled my body, his holding mine. I could feel his feet treading in water below. He brought us together, mouth-to-mouth, one bitch of a kiss; then, sealed it with a lick. "That's no goof, babe—I love you." Supporting my body on his, Ron ferried us to shore.

On the flat slabs we drank the beer, sprawled on our bellies opposite one another, propped face-to-face on elbow. Ron set down only one cup from our Lenzo's carry-out; we shared from it. We rolled onto our sides, first one way, then the other and back again, sun slapping bare skin. I guess we must've finished the buckets of beer. We fell asleep, sprawled on our bellies opposite one another, head-to-head, faces on folded arms.

There was *real* moonlight when we woke. Ron said, "Swee'heart, stay with me tonight. At my mom's." We parked in our regular place at the curb. At the door Ron said, "Ssh, try not to make noise so we don't wake my mom." He led the way in darkness, through the living room and down a

———————— Σ ————————

hallway that took us to his room. I clutched his Levis from the waistband at back while he led us through a maze of obstacles. Along the way he haltingly paused to whisper, "Ssh, ssh, no noise—wake my mom."

Once inside the room he closed the door and flipped the light switch. It wasn't a large room, though neither was it small. There just wasn't much to it. An old armchair sagged against one wall, a square table pushed into the corner beyond. Short planks atop mail-order catalogs effected bookcases. They gave appearance of railings in the corner opposite the table. In front of that, opposing the armchair, was Ron's bed. It was only a mattress, a twin single, hugging low to the floor. I thought it rested on paving bricks. Most everything was a place for piles—not stacks—of clothing.

Ron scooped from the bed an armload of shirt-sleeves and pant-legs tangled with socks and briefs. He tried to balance it atop the armchair pile, but the entire mess tumbled. "Ssh, my mom!"

He scooped up another pile. Seeing no likely place to put it, he plopped it on the floor beside the table. "Ssh, swee'heart. Your clothes, take off—I'll help."

He stripped from his jeans and made a broad-sweep effort with spreading hands to smooth rumpled bedding. "Ssh, swee'heart, I'm gettin' out the light. See ya'in bed."

Ron flipped back the coverlet. He lunged into bed beside me and flipped the coverlet over us all the way to our ears. He scooted one arm under my neck and rocked me to him, was in the process of latching his legs to mine and snuggling our bodies when the overhead light glared.

"Ron! Are you drunk again?"

Ron rolled his torso far enough to peek from beneath the coverlet, holding a shushing finger to his lips. *"Mom! Ssh! I got company!"*

"You got WHAT? Ron! WHO?

"Mom! He's okay!"

A STRANGER? Ron, you brought a STRANGER into this house! MY house? Young man—Let me see, Ron, let me see just WHAT you've done!"

"Mom!"

I *felt* her approach the bed, *felt* her take a step back, *felt* her lean forward toward me, and, gingerly as one might warily approach a hidden menace, I felt her *lift* a corner of the coverlet to expose my *sleeping* face.

"Mom!"

——————— Σ ———————

"Well, I suppose it's alright—just this once, young man! Yes, I suppose it's alright—he does have a kind face."

"Mom! Din't I tell you? Din't I say—Mom, he's okay? Mom!"

Ron leaped from bed and slammed the door behind her. He switched out the light and lunged back into bed with me. He *din't* bother pulling up the coverlet, just adjusted it so there'd be no space between us. He wrapped my upper body in his arms and latched me to him with his legs. He huddled near, cuddling me to him; bodies close, flesh stinging. Our foreheads pressed, noses touching. Ron kissed me, gulping at my lips, gulping at my breath, gulping saliva from my mouth. "Hmmn," was all he said before we slept. "Hmmn, swee'heart."

Next morning Mom had coffee waiting for us. She was also waiting. Gran'ma, too. It was a plain house; once fashionable, still comfortable; not exactly cozy. There weren't usual appointments I might've expected, framed photos, ceramic doo-daddery and the like. Except for an old rug in the living-room, the house had about it an austerity.

Mom sat reading a morning newspaper from another sagging armchair—it appeared to match the one in Ron's room. She seemed a typical Mom, clad in pink-chenille housecoat, wearing scratchy-brush rollers capped to her head. The newspaper was camouflage, allowing not-so-discreet surveillance. Gran'ma was just Gran'ma sitting in a small rocking chair. She didn't often speak; when she did, it was to parrot. "Ron, Gran'ma needs more coffee, don't you Gra'm?" *Uhm-hmn.* "Ron, Gran'ma also thinks your friend has a nice face, don't you, Gra'm?" *Uhm-hmn.*

The rug didn't seem to belong—maybe it belonged, the other stuff didn't. It was a rug of the sort before carpeting—tight, heavy loom laying flat to the floor on horsehair matting. Pale blue background supported leafy floral executed in tones not so much autumnal as earthy. It's what made the room not quite austere, almost cozy. Flattened through wear, its tightly loomed nap felt tempting under Levi denim. I wondered how it would feel against bare skin. Ron and I lay on it, twisting and rolling, swinging, balancing cups of coffee. I liked the aroma of his body, the morning smell of him.

"Ron, are you rubbing on your company? Don't crowd on top of him. Ron, for heaven's sake, get off the boy. Do you think he likes that?"

My thought jumped, *Sure, Mom, dint you know—we're in love!*

I guess Mom may have thought it was late growth-spurt catching up.

————— Σ —————

It was something more, a statement to be made, touching and feeling. A statement, not of identity—a statement of being.

"Ron, there's more coffee."

"Nyah, Mom, gotta go!"

"I can make another pot, Ron."

"Nyah, Mom, Dean's waitin'. Gotta go!"

"Shall I hold supper?"

"Nyah, Mom, we'll be a'right!"

"Are you bringing your friend back? Tell him, Ron, he's welcome!"

"Sure, Mom! Thanks!"

"Ron!"

"Later, Mom!"

"Invite him back, Ron! Do you have to rush? Ron—*come back!*"

"Yeah, Mom. Love you, too!"

I hadn't fully understood why we waited, why there was no urgency to make love, until I understood why Carl's sunlight was so brilliant then and is now still so vivid. All the body's needs can't be serviced by the body; some needs can only be met through the body, with the body.

Summer was ending. Soon, Ron would have to leave. Ron and I talked about it. We never dwelt on it. It was one other thing we shared. The most I remember Ron saying about it, "I wouldn't have to wish I could take you with me if I *din't* have to go."

Ron's dad was in LA and Ron's mom got him summers. Ron said, "Aah, LA's okay. I c'n hang out there. I *din't* want to be here this summer, either. He's got no place for me, not there. My Mom's got Gra'm—she's got no room. I'as always scared, when I called you, I'as scared you'd be gone, too. You're th' bitchin'est, swee'heart!"

Ron and I shared our last evening, our last night together, at Chez Le Nelle—Stanley's and Albert's "Farewell-Summer, Welcome-Back-Joe-Angel" party. They invited lots of people—lots more showed up uninvited. It was a good party, the best of the season. Chez Le Nelle was legend for parties. Stanley said, "Make them wait—then, give them something worth the wait." I'm sure it was a good party, everything I later heard it gossiped. Really, I don't know. Ron and I slipped into the back. We found a bedroom and bolted the door. The one cold beer we took with us grew warm, then hot. I suppose later it was thrown out, during morning cleanup.

—————— Σ ——————

We had sex that night. There are other words to use—sex is okay. We had sex. I don't know how it happened. I don't know if we intended or didn't. It wasn't planned, lights never turned out. Clothing was peeled, stripped, discarded. We lay on the bed, bodies naked with one another, an extension of lip and tongue, kiss and mouth—oyster and juice.

Afterward, we lay side by side in the light, bodies skin-on-skin, flesh-to-flesh. No hands, no arms, no other motion. No tension, no urgency. Faces to one another, forehead and nose touching, mouth and tongue meeting and engaging, holding and dwindling. Eyes focused into eyes, feeling; not looking or seeing; not gazing, not staring—feeling. Keeping these images for other moments we'd be long-distance. Holding for this moment, now, that which was between us, that which could be held in no other way; through that, without awareness, embracing in our presence vital nature— God. It's as much as most of us, here in this dust, can know.

We parked in our place at the curb one last time. Ron held me in his arms, held me closely against him once more. We kissed—*we tasted*—again. "Hmmn, swee'heart. Hmmn, bitchin', swee'heart!"

Ron walked toward the house and I called softly. He paused, turned to me, silent in silver light. I *din't* have to tell him. I know I *din't* need to tell him. I *din't* want him leaving without me telling him, *"Ron, I love you!"*

———————— Σ ————————

Sleep, my lamb

"Queen, will you look at that? It's Miss Dean—*with the whole U.S. Army!*"
I heard the comment but paid it no attention. My rating at the Cabaret
jumped straight to the top of the charts some weeks earlier—Paul and Gerry
ventured in from not-too-distant Killeen and Fort Hood. It's what I needed
that spring. The rating scale doesn't drop low enough to register the dip
mine had taken. Carter told me, "Bar queens are shallow. You'll find love."

Through fall and winter I held in safekeeping the special feeling Ron
and I shared. I truly missed him, the caring for each other we found together. I also found there was little I could do to alter circumstance. "Consider it a lovely summer romance," Carl said, "something to cherish—they
don't always blossom into love."

That's what it was all about for me, love. I was *too* serious. Jimmy
said, "You aren't serious enough." It was a hung jury. I was so confused as
to wonder, "Can I be too serious but not serious enough?" I knew one thing
—sex as pastime didn't fill my need. Once I tasted something berre'n
ahstures, ahstures din't tas'e berre good.

It wasn't love that generated Cabaret enthusiasm—desire did that.
Once word got about I wasn't a fast lay, my popularity tumbled. Status at the
Cabaret was a nefarious commodity. It may have boiled down to diplomacy.
That's the way JC had it pegged—he should've known, government major.

Likely, had it not been for Carl, JC and I wouldn't have become
more than casual acquaintance. Carl helped JC get one of the Compound
units. Before fall semester, as I was packing to leave his apartment, Carl
called the owner and helped me get the cottage opposite that of JC. Between
us, JC and I had the two larger units, both at the rear of the Compound.

I occupied my cottage alone. JC shared with two roommates, Lester,
a queen he'd sometime earlier met, and James, a friend of Lester whom JC
hadn't known. Lester and JC persistently warned me to be careful what I
said in James' presence. "Don't wreck your beads," Lester told me, "James

——————— Σ ———————

is straight." "Straight and *nellie*," JC added, "definitely *not* gay." JC called him Jane Ann—of course, he didn't do so to James' face.

James was effeminate in mannerism, in speech, and in the way he carried himself. I wouldn't characterize him as nellie. He didn't have about him a characteristic swish I associate with nellie. It wasn't a great matter to me anyway. Softness has about it a quality I find delicate, appealing in a guy. Besides, I wasn't out to seduce James.

One afternoon sometime before Christmas James strolled over to my apartment. He wanted to see my holiday tree. Somehow we wound up on the mattress in my third-level alcove, seduction having been an affair of mutual engagement. We enjoyed my tree a number of times during the festive season—I didn't tell JC or Lester we did so from the mattress. James hadn't then come out as a gay individual. He may never have summoned the conviction to enable him to do so. Within, James was *definitely* gay. It saddened me, he was fearful of reaching out, fearing even to touch or caress my body. As he lay motionless, stretched rigidly before me, I realized how easily I could use his body for gratification. He evoked within me pathos and I approached him with tenderness, hoping he'd come to care for himself enough to care for another.

Politics was in JC's blood, Austin, born and bred. One needn't worry about failing to notice JC's breeding—he was sure to make it known himself. I don't want to be misunderstood. JC, often accused of conceit, was no braggart. He did have something none the others of us had—heritage. He was *proud* of his heritage. Heritage was something we all were lacking. That fact was nowhere evident—it was bound up in history, our gay history. That's not to say we were living in the past. We had the present. Little did we know, we *were* history, history in the making. Détente, rather like gay, was a word not yet out of the closet—tact, I suppose, the stuff of politics.

That fall, 1964, we went downtown for LBJ's final campaign speech the night before votes were cast. Lyndon spoke from a podium that carried the Presidential Seal. He stood curbside near the pavement at South Congress, flanked by well-groomed trees. Behind him a wide, granite-paved avenue led up the hill to the Capitol.

We elbowed our way to the front of the crowd, the *absolute* front. LBJ stood within spitting distance of me, shielded only by bullet-proof panels rising near-invisible above the Great Seal. Campaign excitement

——————— Σ ———————

146

swiftly moved into election excitement at Austin's Civic Center. Inside the stately Driskill Hotel, where the Johnson contingent headquartered, Carl and his boyfriend, a good-looking guy named Ronnie, found themselves standing in an elevator alongside LBJ. As the elevator doors opened onto the lobby, the threesome, Secret Service surrounding, were caught by a *Life* photographer. *Life* ran the photo next issue in "Speaking of Pictures," LBJ on election night at the Driskill, flanked by unidentified Carl and Ronnie. Joseph, who said it first, said it best, "Darling, we're everywhere!"

The matter of diplomacy arose over Jane Ann, my holiday tree and me. James wearied of JC's innuendos and told him so in words to the effect, "Fuck off, bitch!" They tangled, near to the point of pulling hair, over which of them was the bigger of bitch. JC at last said, "I may be a bitch, Jane Ann, but grab your own skirt—you've left toenail polish scratched on the ceiling!" Lester flipped out and screamed, "JC! Get over yourself!"

Despite blood behind breeding, JC was irate. "Imagine!" he said to Carl, "that bitch telling *me* to get over *my* self! I have news for her. I'm *over* it—her and him both!" Carl said, "Don't let it bother you," to which JC said, "Bother me! My dear, I *couldn't* be bothered. I'm *totally* over it!" That became my Cabaret Diplomacy—I'm *totally* over it, I *can't* be bothered!

One thing about queens, especially jealous queens, there's nothing—*nothing!*—that gets under their skin more than knowing they can't get under another's. Assuredly they were after skin the night Paul and Gerry walked in. It was to me they were attracted—I have to say triple attraction. Partly, diplomacy prompted me to approach them, thus enraging the other queens. Rage is one matter, jealousy quite another. It was quite that second matter when the two of them, Paul and Gerry, left the bar leaving with me.

More honestly, I did approach soon after first seeing them. I made eye contact with Paul. The first thing I see in a guy is his eyes. Usually I know if we're going to connect. That's what happened. Paul and Gerry were lovers with somewhat an open relationship, one on the verge of remaining open. I took advantage of the Cabaret queens—I knew Paul and Gerry *weren't* on the make. They got away from Killeen and the army base to relax among other gay people outside the confines of homophobia—another word yet to be coined. More directly, they needed lodging overnight in Austin. That fell into place. I had the big unit in the Compound, they had little money, none among the three of us felt threatened.

——————— Σ ———————

It wasn't mysterious, it's what I saw in Paul's eyes; really, what I hadn't seen—coldness. That told me they weren't on the make. I'm sure Paul saw much the same in my eyes. He told Gerry before we left the Cabaret, "I had a feeling tonight, down here in Austin we'd meet someone nice."

Paul called me hun, his term of endearment for everyone. Paul liked me and I fell for him. We shared my third-level mattress, the three of us. Gerry allowed Paul and me to share. I'd like not to leave this as it seems. Paul and Gerry were from New York, Queens and Brooklyn—to me, exotic. They were also nice guys. On a scale one to everyone-I've-ever-met, they're still near the top. I did fall for Paul; Paul did like me; Paul didn't fall for me. Paul didn't let me fall; he let me down easy; in the end I, too, liked Paul.

The three of us became something of a ménage à trois so far as Cabaret politics were concerned. It wasn't anything we did other than being our gay selves. Where there's a spark of the electric to relationships it doesn't for long go unnoticed. High-voltage has its own danger, sparking stray static electricity—jealousy. That's what happened. The bar crowd thought I latched onto something they couldn't have. I knew what I had with Paul and Gerry was better than sex—certainly every bit as much fun. Truth be told, it was something the bar crowd could never have had.

Paul told me about other guys on the post who felt isolated. "What would you think if I tell them about you?" he asked. "I'd think, *Wow!*" I told him. Once back at Fort Hood, he and Gerry began giving my name and address to other guys who would come to Austin for a weekend. Soon it reached a point I just left my door unlocked and the boys would be there, at times as many as ten or twelve. They were from places scattered all across the U.S. The Compound was more freedom than they'd had since induction. Those nights when I walked into the Cabaret *with the whole U.S. Army,* it was diplomacy—sheer diplomacy!

Of all the soldiers who came to me from Fort Hood that spring, there was only one boy among them I knew to be gay. He was stunning, a blond beauty, Bob, from LA. JC fell in love with him. JC had a black Impala convertible with red interior. Weekends the two of them, laid back, blond and hidden behind dark glasses, sailed through the sun. It brought a touch of Beverly Hills to the hilly streets of Austin.

Paul and Gerry would sometimes alert the guys beforehand to my being gay—most often they didn't. The boys were left to discover that *salient*

——————— Σ ———————

fact once they arrived. For most of the soldiers, I was their first close encounter of the gay kind. It was never a big deal with any of the guys, largely, I think, because I was open with them. My being at ease with myself allowed them to feel more comfortable. I've come to believe my being gay posed no threat as much because it was not hidden—it wasn't lurking, unseen.

All the boys were great guys. I made no concession and they fell into step—that was life at the Compound. We made do with what we had, bedrolls being standard issue—the boys had to bring their own. The second level was one large bivouac. I had to post my barracks off limits—queens wouldn't leave the boys alone. These guys didn't come to me for sex. They were far from home, lonely, homesick and sick of the army. What they needed and what they wanted, I gave them—a place to *feel* at home.

My painting of *The Last Supper* became famous. Actually, it wasn't my painting and it really wasn't The Last Supper —it did bear resemblance. The painting, impressionistic, was striking, hung on my second level. It was painted by an artist, Martin, one of the Laredo boys. He loaned me the painting—a large, rectangular rendering done in vivid color oil-on-masonite, Martin's impression of a night at the Cabaret.

One of the boys admired it and asked, "Is this *The Last Supper?*" JC was there with Bob because we were taking several of the boys that night to the Cabaret for their first time. He looked at me and grinned. "In a way, you can call it that," he said. "Yeah," I added, "The Last *One's-a-Meal!*" Later, at the Cabaret, less than a minute inside, the boys understood my joke. Back on base at Fort Hood, they told recruits they were sending to Austin to be sure, while there, and not miss *The Last Supper!*

Crowded weekend nights at the Cabaret were often dangerous. To put it bluntly, a handsome young guy might find himself having his hands full keeping away hands having a handful of him. Early on I realized I needlessly worried over the privates' privates. Even at the Cabaret, the guys conducted themselves beautifully. No doubt they felt vulnerable—it was for them a new twist to an old tease. They may have realized it was only a version of the same skin game. What kept their cool was the boys' ability to laugh with us rather than at us—I think that had to do with *The Last Supper*.

At times some of the boys remained with us at the bar, at least for awhile. Most stayed only long enough for a beer. One of the boys told me, "Whew! You guys got a lot of *balls* to dig this scene—I'd rather dig one

——————— Σ ———————

without balls!" Most often I steered them next door to Jesters. I figured once on their own they'd be alright—I never felt they needed my hand.

It was deceitful of me. With the exception of our Compound circle, the bar crowd thought I was having a frenzy of orgiastic sex with the soldiers— I let them keep thinking so. It wasn't merely a matter of jealousy. They were *angry,* angry because I wouldn't *share* the boys with them. They were correct about that—I *was* sharing with the boys. The reason they weren't sharing with them is because they were unable to share.

Vick is the boy I remember most clearly. He wasn't the most beautiful, the most handsome, the most sexy. He's the soldier boy with whom I fell in love—Vick, too, was in love with me. He came to Austin one weekend when I had *the whole U.S. Army.* I think, on the last spur of a moment, he jumped into the car with the other guys—he didn't seem well acquainted. Vick was a big guy. I don't mean large. He was big, big frame, big guy. He was hunk—all man. Vick didn't bring a bedroll. That night the second level was wall-to-wall male bodies, spillover extending onto the lower level.

I said, "Vick, c'mon up here, you can sleep with me." The other guys hooted at him, whistling and clucking. "Yeah, Vick, that's th' honeymoon suite!" "Hey, Vick, if ya' need any help, don't call me!" "When the lights go out, Vick, it's all pink on the inside!" "Go ahead, Vick, what th' hell, long's you don't kiss!" "Think you're man enough, Vick?"

Vick was a shy boy. For all his size, he was embarrassed. I said *C'mon up here, you can sleep with me* from the railing overlooking both second and lower levels. Vick was standing on the second level, among the other guys stretched already in bedrolls. He gave the appearance of a lost little boy who didn't know what to do. I said, "C'mon, Vick, I'm waitin'."

That set off a new wave of catcalls accompanied by sounds from puckered mouths. Vick steeled himself and stomped across their bodies. From the steps leading upward to the third level, he hollered over a shoulder, "Beats th' hell outta anything you nuts got rolled up in th' sack youc'n get your hands on!" The other guys hushed. They'd had their fun. I think it may have surprised them Vick went up the stairs. Maybe they wondered if he had the balls to sleep with me. Then again, they may have realized it did beat hell out of what they had rolled up in their sack.

Vick was nervous—I *knew* the guy'd have to be nervous! I said, "Vick, you don't kick, do you?" He said, "Nobody's ever complained."

——————— Σ ———————

150

"Good," I said, standing with him face-to-face, "'I don't bite."

I didn't get kicked that night and Vick wasn't bitten. I know he lost his trepidation. Our bodies touched, resting one against the other at different times during the night. Trepidation was all Vick lost. I guess it was a good thing to lose. After that, whenever Vick came to Austin, and he came more often than anyone else, he never brought with him a bedroll. He didn't need one—he had a place on the third level.

Somewhat later, after Vick had gotten his discharge, he phoned and asked me to meet him in Houston. Before leaving Texas he wanted to see the Gulf of Mexico at Galveston. I drove to Houston one weekend to meet him at the O'Brien twins' home where he was staying. He told me I'd also be able to stay there, with him. I was unacquainted with the O"Brien twins, who at the time were out of own. The house bespoke major league. "Vick," I asked, stunned, "how did you manage this?" He said, "Don'cha think I learned anything from ya'? There's *always* connections to be made!"

The O'Briens were receiving shipments of crates they bought in lot from auction at San Simeon. Vick was prying them open, having himself one hell of a time discovering what wonders and treasures lay hidden inside. I shared Vick's bed that night—he had no trepidation. We slept closely with one another. He was a big guy, a real hunk. I knew then he was all man because, inside, he was all tender and gentle. Trepidation was all he lost. The two of us may have lost more than that.

The next morning Vick didn't get up before I awoke. He lay quietly beside me as I slept. After I awakened, he told me he'd been awake for sometime. We lay on our backs beside one another, bodies touching full length. We talked.

Vick asked me about my being gay, my feelings. "What's it like to *love* another guy," he wanted to know. "How does it feel to be *with* a guy?"

I couldn't think what to say. I don't know that I gave him an answer. If so, I don't remember what I told him. I'm sure I said many things. I know I didn't say what should've been said. We lay together for a considerable time afterward, saying nothing. Finally Vick blurted, "I gotta get up and *do* somethin'!" He pulled on pants and stomped out barefoot. I followed, pouring myself a cup of coffee on the way. Out back, he wielded a large hammer, slamming against tough, wooden crates.

I've often wondered about that morning. In my wanderings of

——————— Σ ———————

thought, I'm bothered to have found a tattered notion hanging, a loose thread I haven't been able to neatly tuck. Vick wouldn't touch me, not that he didn't want to touch me, but because I didn't first touch him. I would've liked touching Vick—I loved him. It was because of love I felt for him I wouldn't touch him. I wouldn't betray his trust—I couldn't betray him.

We found ourselves in a reversal of roles. Ordinarily it's expected the male will be aggressor. We both were male, and Vick was unsure how to respond—the inadequacy of his traditional male model suddenly confronted him. I was gay. Misconceived thinking then-popular presumed I'd be aggressor. It held a misguided notion—queer seduces straight.

What I've come to recognize, Vick wouldn't betray me that morning either. He trusted me. He'd come to understand I regarded him as more than a piece of meat. He was at ease with me. Vick knew I wouldn't try to seduce him. He wouldn't make use of me in that way, either—Vick refused, also, to regard me a piece of meat.

It may seem I've overlooked the obvious. I've never been blind to feeling Vick held for me. We likely could've become engaged in an affair. Vick wasn't gay. He'd never become gay because his sexual personality wasn't oriented gay. Vick hadn't fallen in love with me—Vick did love me. I'm sure he'd have been willing for intimacy. Love is no excuse for sexual play. If through one's sexuality he's able to grasp love, his sexuality is viable. If through his love he's only able to grip sexuality, his love is not viable.

After he returned home to the San Fernando Valley, Vick kept in touch by letter for a number of years. I shared with him in his marriage and, later, in the birth of his first child. I think it was me who stopped answering the letters. It may have simply been time. We shared—I have little doubt what Vick shared with me he's given to no other man.

In a last letter, Vick spoke of the night we spent together in Houston. "I'm not good like you in putting my feeling on paper. I thought a lot about you and I wasn't sure about myself. We could've got it on that morning in bed. When we didn't I figured you didn't want me. I don't think that way anymore. I know you cared one hell of a lot about me, as I did for you—I still do. That's what I want to tell you. And also to say how damned glad I am it was you I met and not someone else who would've just fucked up my head. I know now what I wanted was out here all along. Sleeping with you is about as good as I've ever had, even without us doing anything. For that,

——————— Σ ———————

about all I can say is thanks. Also, thanks for taking care of me."

Reading his letter, I knew, for me also, sleeping beside Vick, sleeping *with* him, is about the best I've had with another man, even though we'd not done anything. I guess what may have been part of it is absence of feeling pressure to perform. With Vick, I find another part as well—*I* didn't felt threatened by *my* sexuality.

* * * * *

Jim returned to Austin that winter, '64. In the final winnowing after summer training, he was sifted from Peace Corps—too late for him to enroll in the University for fall semester. He worked awhile back home in north Texas, then split for Austin with a few bucks in his pocket. The place he rented several blocks west of campus had recently been moved from somewhere. It looked as though it had simply stalled, been left abandoned where it could go no further. It was a rough and rugged dwelling. Jim called it "a big ol' barn, but I c'n see potential." Potential was one of Jim's pets. He seldom took anything at face value.

During this time our relationship with Carter and Jimmy deepened, due in large part to Jim—due because I didn't devote to him the time I had before given. It had nothing to do with our relationship, Jim's and mine. We were embedded, solid rock. I was involved with doing my own thing It was easy falling into a trap, that of taking another for granted. Our relationship, the feeling we held for one another, didn't lessen. It didn't have the intimacy of daily and nightly contact we'd known living together.

The mood into which Jim and I had fallen seemed to have parallel with that of fall '64 moving into spring '65. That period was the advent of LBJ proper, its growing characteristic, frustration. Restless was no longer restless—it became agitation. Jim and I talked about it, our "hearts-to-heart," he called them. These were our serious conversations. Hearts-to-heart could be, and usually were, intense. "Things have gotten all screwed up," Jim said. "I thought I knew what I wanted, how to get it. The closer I come to it, the less I want it. It doesn't seem to be what's out there anymore. It's frustrating—I can't concentrate."

Discipline was one of our problems, lack of it. It's something JC had. He also had resolve to muster behind it. I guess that was a major difference between us and him. JC was going for the jugular; we, Jim and me, the balls.

My frustration was slightly off-center—according to many, off

———————— Σ ————————

course as well. Jim didn't see it that way. He said, "You can't go around all the time with your feelings hanging out to drip-dry on your sleeve. It's collision-course central. I'm afraid you're always going to get hurt because—well, Roomie, I don't know how to say this easy—because what you want is something I don't think exists in this world."

"Yeah," I nodded, "I've been accused of chasing rainbows, of being a leaf adrift on the breeze. Yeah, tossed about at the mercy of whimsical gusts and currents because I'm not in control. Control," I told him, "is what I haven't got. It's as though there's something else in charge, something more powerful, something I have no ability to change or alter. I can't seem to intercede. About all I can do is interact."

"Roomie," Jim said, "God's alive and well and he's living in Argentina. We all know that—what th' hell are *you* talking about?"

"Love, Jim, it's all I know. It's the only thing I've found that seems worthwhile. It's the only thing to which I seem able to anchor my life."

"But you don't *have* love," Jim reminded me, the tone in his voice part reprimand, part frustration. "You just keep *looking* for it."

"Yeah, ain't that the shits! I don't have it, but it seems I've got it!"

"What if you never find it?" Jim asked.

"Well, Jim, what if?" I shrugged. "If not, if I don't ever find it, the reason will never be, I didn't try."

Jim was pensive. "I hope you do find it," he said. "Most times I'm unsure whether it's your brain scrambled or mine fried. I don't know of anyone who sees love in the same way as you." Then he paused. "I do hope you find it. I just hope, when you find it, I hope it's not a punkin."

Jim believed, not necessarily as I believed, but he believed in me. I'm sure of that—he didn't knuckle his head. I knew he'd made a decision. His grades that spring had been lousy—Uncle Sam was looking his way. "I guess I'll stick it out to the end of the semester," he told me. "I may as well wait till grades are posted and get the bad news in person. I'm going to enlist in the Air Force. None of that ground-to-ground, hand-to-hand shit. If the Viet Cong get me, they'll have to knock my happy ass outta the sky!"

I tried to persuade Jim to check the box. "Nyah," he said, "I might as well rot there as rot here. Maybe I'll get lucky—find inspiration."

I was the coward. I *did* check the box. It wasn't at all simple. Uncle Sam didn't want me—he made not having me nothing like easy.

————— Σ —————

A couple of semesters later, I reached a point where I, too, needed to leave Austin. My decision was wrapped in a lot of things, mostly things lacking from my life—not least, motivation. More simply, on a larger clock, the time had come. It was the fall of '66, my fifth year at the University. I'd earned enough hours to graduate, none in concentrations that spelled diploma. I decided to withdraw as a student from UT—New York lay ahead.

I had a bear on my back. It wasn't exactly on my back, more in my hip pocket. My Selective Service Registration and Classification Card went everywhere I did. It had to—fine print clearly stated, "Under Penalty of Law you are required to have this card on your person at all times."

I wrestled fiercely with that bear, especially the night I sat at my desk staring at a blank sheet of paper weighted beneath a pen I wasn't sure I could lift. Finally, with nothing but raw courage, I slipped the card from my wallet and looked at it again. Nope, the words were there, no question about it. "You are required by Law to report to your Local Selective Service Board any change or additional information that could affect your Classification Standing." Nope, there was no question about it.

With a deep sigh I picked up the pen. "Dear SS: I'm gay. I'm homosexual. I'm suicidal. Sincerely yours." With a deeper sigh I dropped the envelope into a mailbox. Within a few days I received a reply. "Dear Sir: You are required by Law to provide substantiation evidencing information provided that might affect your Classification Standing prior to this Board's consideration of same. In your case, a letter from a psychiatrist should be provided. Sincerely yours."

I thought I was beginning to see how the whole thing worked. If the SS wanted a letter, a letter they'd surely get. At the Student Health Center I sat for sometime, palms sweaty, waiting to be called. For the life of me, I can't remember the man's face. It was hidden behind thick, tortoise-shell eyeglasses. His office was neat and tidy, bookcases a balanced arrangement of the right books coupled with the right accessories. He sat behind a large, scrupulous desk, on which I knew everything had its exact location—never mind a purpose. I was equally sure those exact locations, so strict and so rigid, were every bit as secure as was Fort Knox.

He sat expressionless, faceless behind tortoise-shells. "What can I do for you? You've listed as problem, homosexuality. Is that troubling you?"

I *loathed* the word *homosexuality*. It had about it a quality cold and clammy, like my sweating palms. What *was* troubling me was the sterile, clinical vacuum in which we played; he the spider, web professionally spun; me ,the tiny insect, escape for which was none. I was nervous as hell, but I determined to bite the bullet. "No, Sir," I said to his question.

He looked again at my admittance slip. "There's been a mistake?"

Doubtless he referred to possible error on the admittance slip. My thoughts were exploding with the wonder of being gay—that was about all I could muster to steel me through this unnerving interview. My reply did respond to his question. My answer had little to do with his slip of paper and all to do with my sexual preference. "No, Sir, I'm *sure* it's no mistake."

"Perhaps you believe you have *tendencies?*" His pronunciation made me shiver. It gave a sense of supreme indelicacy that screamed *affliction!*

Again, in my mind I re-framed the question before answering. "No, Sir, I don't believe so. I'm *sure* I don't have *tendencies."*

He laid aside the slip of paper and clasped his hands on the desk before him, placing them at rest in their exact location. "Then perhaps we'd do better if you just tell me in your own words."

It wasn't a concerted effort on my part to be evasive. I'd never been "treated" by a psychiatrist and I had no idea what was expected of me. Our initial set-to overstepped ridiculous. It seemed to me we were high and windy above absurd, well on our way to surreal. It occurred to me, what a foolish thing this is; while we sidestep semantics, fumble with phrases and tangle in terminology, he may be devising strategy whereby to cure my ill, to rid me of disorder, to take away that which came to me in brilliant light.

He asked for my own words. As I conceived those words I reflected on my true self. "I'm gay," I said, proudly.

"Good. Perhaps now we're getting somewhere. You're gay, as you seem to prefer that designation to the more clinical. You don't consider your being gay a problem?"

"No, not for me, it's no problem."

"You're comfortable being a homosexual?" He used *that* word again, sterile and impotent!

"Yes," I said. "I'm *proud* being *gay."*

"I take it, then," he resumed, "you're not here seeking my help to change your abnormality?"

It was apparent to me we operated from levels too deviant to expect

———————— Σ ————————

communication. "No," I told him. "I don't feel there's anything to change."

"If you're aware of your sexual proclivity and are content with it, then we would have no reason to proceed into analysis, is that correct?"

"I'd say so, yes."

He pushed aside my admittance slip and braced himself between chair and desk. "What, then, are you here for, what do you want?"

"A letter," I explained straightforwardly. "My Selective Service Board has requested a letter from a psychiatrist stating that I'm gay."

After he asked a few additional *perfunctory* questions, I gave him the necessary information. He told me he'd write the letter and send it to my local Board. Naturally, I thought the entire matter was over and done.

The last thing I did before leaving Austin was complete a form the SS provided to inform the Board I was no longer a student and no longer eligible for Student Deferment, Classification I-S. Before Thanksgiving I was once more on the coast, Bay Prairie environs—it was job-seeking time again.

I found one for the upcoming holiday season with the local Sears catalog-order store. It was my duty to receive early-morning shipments, correlate packages to pre-coded order sheets, match pre-codes to individual order forms, assign a bin location by number felt-tipped on both the package and the order form, alphabetize the order forms in alphabetical folders returned to alphabetical slots near the front desk, and make *certain* the package was in the bin, its *correct* bin. Pretty much a snap for a homo!

I admit, my self-esteem was wounded, suffering transition from liberalism in an intellectual community to confinement within a strictly conservative surrounding. I kept my sights on New York. I plunged into the job with complete abandon, eager to earn money needed for my trip.

I had a knot in my stomach. There remained the matter with Uncle Sam. After a few weeks with no word from the SS, I began to relax. I figured the letter must've confirmed to the Board's satisfaction I simply didn't measure up to its criteria, leaving no room for doubt I was merely a draft dodger. I expected re-classification IV-F. Daily, I looked for the card in the mail. When I still hadn't gotten it, I began to think I might've gotten lost in the shuffle, my inclination in that case one of maintaining a low profile. I didn't want needlessly to call attention to myself.

I soon discovered, though, I wasn't lost—I got a phone call. It came to me in the catalog-order store where I had to take it on a headset in the

—————— Σ ——————

telephone room with four proper ladies at cubicles taking Christmas orders.

The voice was that of the SS clerk, a matronly woman who *suggested* I drop by to have a chat with her. "When it's convenient," she told me. "Perhaps you might find time during the coming, say, week?" I didn't wait. I went gaily downtown, the entire two blocks downtown.

On one corner of the town square the SS occupied space in two stone rooms of a semi-basement area. It was located downstairs in the Post Office. Banks of steel filing cabinets painted regulation olive drab greeted me as I entered. The poster, *Uncle Sam Wants YOU!,* was of course there, as well as was the photo of LBJ himself.

The clerk at first said nothing, having hardly glanced at me—I was sure she identified me right away. She busied herself with the task of retrieving my file from one of her cabinets—I doubt the folder was hard to locate! She *suggested* we step into the other room, one used by the Board for meeting. In it was a single long table surrounded by chairs, one of which I slumped into at random. She walked ahead, going the entire length of the table to sit at its far end, placing my folder open before her. I sensed in her discomfort. She'd hardly spoken; she never looked at me, not once; still she kept her head down.

From elbow propped at either side of the folder, she shielded her eyes with hands clasped to forehead. Finally she addressed me. "Is there any additional information you want to add before the Board meets to consider re-classification?"

"Did you get *my* letter?" I asked anxiously. "Did you get the *psychiatrist's* letter?"

"Yes," she said, maintaining firmly her guarded position, "however, based on that information, the Board's alternative will be re-classification I-A, which means you'll get Pre-Induction Notice—."

"*I-A,*" I shouted, "*I-A! Din't you read my letter? Din't you read the psychiatrist's letter? I-A!*"

"Calm down," she muttered, pressing with thumbs at her temples. "That information was inconclusive—."

"*Inconclusive!* Whaddya want, *pictures?*"

"It won't be that bad," she insisted, "you'll go to Houston for Pre-Induction and have another opportunity—."

"*In a room filled with naked men?*"

—————— Σ ——————

"It won't be that bad," she said again, "no worse than undressing in gym class—."

"Undressing in gym class! I was never able even to do that!"

"Please calm down, it won't be that bad—."

"Won't be that bad! You can't do this, you cannot do this to me." I leaped from the chair where I was sitting and pounded the table with both fists. *"If you put me into a room filled with naked men, I can't!—I cannot!—I won't!—be responsible for what happens!"*

"I have no choice, based on your file—."

"What? What did he write in that letter?"

I grabbed for the open folder but she slammed fists hard atop it. "These files are confidential. I can't let you see it." All the while she never *looked* at me, not once. Then, with care and precision, she closed the folder. "However," she said quietly, more as though speaking to herself, "if I get up and go into the other room, neglecting to take this file with me, I can return later and pick it up."

That's what she did, walked out of the room, never having looked at me, not once—walked out, leaving me and leaving the file. I flipped open the folder, rifling through its contents. All that interested me was the fruitcake letter that jerk psychiatrist had written. "To Whom It May Concern: The subject in question was seen by me on only one occasion on matters allegedly relating to homosexuality, but sufficient time for analysis was not available and consequently no diagnosis was made. Respectfully."

"Respectfully," I spat. *"Respectfully, my ass!"*

I'd *thought* the matter all done; now, I realized it was far from over. Even for its size, Texas wasn't big enough for this story. I got Notice of Re-Classification, I-A, and Notice of Pre-Induction Orders, both in the same mail. I also got sick. A few days before I was to report for the dreaded Pre-Induction, I got another letter from the local SS. "Dear Sir: You are hereby served notice to disregard Notice of Pre-Induction Orders until advised otherwise by this Board. Sincerely."

"Well, by God, *sincerely* to you, too!" I shouted. Next day, in the local Tribune, I saw a news wire article. Its headline stated, "Texas Selective Service Out of Funds; Pre-Inductees Outside Metro Areas Canceled."

"Well, by God, *cancel* one for me, too!" I didn't bother phoning the local SS. I went down in person, to ask the Mrs. Clerk "what's it all about?"

——————— Σ ———————

and to tell her I had in my pocket a one-way ticket to New York City. I also wanted to *see* whether or not she could *look* at me.

"Guess that about shuts you down, huh?" I said flippantly. "How about my bus ticket?"

"Have a good trip," she said. "If we call you again, take your notice to the local Board nearest. They'll cancel it and re-schedule you from their call demands."

I turned to go and she called to me, "Dean." I turned round and faced her. "I hope it all works out for you. Good luck." She not only *looked* me in the eye, she *smiled.*

Several months later, my first summer in New York when I lived at Hotel Chelsea on West 23rd, I got the Notice. I reported it to Whitehall Street by phone and they canceled it. Then, within a matter of weeks, I got another. I did what most all of red-blooded American boys were doing the night before Pre-Induction—I got drunk, stinking drunk. The next morning I was a hung-over wreck when I reported to Whitehall Street, the army's induction center in lower Manhattan.

Referred to simply as Whitehall, the building was maybe five floors, open inside floor to ceiling, an atrium-like walkway around the perimeter of each floor. I'd never describe it as atrium, except for the flowers parading about on open parapets above. Yes, they were there—stripped to all but bare butt. I'm talking *production,* not just one piddling group. Assembly-line, mass production—it only needed conveyors. Alas, I was doomed later to discover they also had those.

Room One Hundred Something-Or-Other was arranged like a classroom, a large desk in front with flanks of smaller ones facing. Stacked on the front desk were files sealed in kraft envelopes, one for each individual of a group then being processed. Each envelope was stamped with a numerical designation, an inductee's new identity. Prior to getting one's file, there was first a lengthy questionnaire to be completed, personal history, family history, educational history, medical history—whatever else the U.S. Army deemed historically informational.

Finally, there it was, in a section headed "Do You Have Any Of The Following?" Grouped with Bed-wetting?, Suicidal Tendencies?, and several other less-than-desirable tendencies was *"Homosexual Tendencies? YES_ NO_."* The answer in my case was obvious. What until I was handed my file

————— Σ —————

hadn't been obvious became obvious. Rubber-stamped in red ink across my kraft envelope were capital letters three inches tall. *DO NOT ROUTE NOR-MALLY! ROUTE IMMEDIATELY TO ROOM 315!*

I'd like to know where Kinsey gets his stat figures. There were several hundreds of boys in Whitehall the morning I was there. When I opened the door to Room 315, Staff Psychiatrist, there was only *one* guy sitting in the waiting area. He was truly handsome, a clean-cut boy of the all-American variety, the sort whose wholesomeness conjures images of mom, apple pie and Sunday dinner. I'd *never* have pegged him for gay!

Paying the room's vacancy no mind, I walked over and sat in the chair nearest him—dragging it even closer. In another moment the door to 315 was flung open. Framed in its opening stood a slender Kookie, complete with comb. In dark sunglasses, form-fitting white shirt with cuffs rolled, white Levis displayed a trim body, narrow at waist and hip. He posed in a stance pure James Dean, black boots wide spread.

Oh, he was a vision! I think he figured the door opened directly to the Doc. When he discovered it didn't, he was disappointed, his only audience a nervous pair sitting huddled against the far wall. He did exactly as I'd done—bypassed every vacant chair to sit beside me. There we sat, three of us, One, Two, Three, side by side in a big, empty room, One, Two, Three.

Doc called us one at a time in order of appearance. I followed Wouldn't-Have-Thought-He-Was-Gay. Doc sat smoking a pipe at his desk. At a glance, he could've been the comedian Jonathon Winters. I took him to be a calm man by the unhurried way he reached for and opened my folder, by the casual manner he riffled haphazardly through its stack of pages, by the nonchalance with which he savored his pipe.

"You think you're homosexual?" he casually asked.

"Yes, I think so. I am homosexual," I immediately replied. I preferred the word of my choice, gay. This was no time for compromise. I was eager to get done with this interview.

"What makes you think so, like boys?" He tapped his pipe on the edge of a large ashtray that took prominence over a mild disarray of papers accumulated on the desk. It might've been viewed as clutter except for him; he gave no appearance of chagrin.

I, however, was bundled in anxiety. "Yes, I do like boys. I'm attracted to boys."

——————— Σ ———————

161

"Ever tried a woman?" He made it sound less a question.

I suppose the question should've been expected. I didn't anticipate it—I didn't think about women. "No, I've never done that," I said.

He paused, re-lighting his pipe. "These boys you like, ever do more than fantasize over them?"

"Sure," I said. "Yeah, sure."

"What?" he asked, teeth clenched to pipestem.

It was a direct question and I responded directly. "Suck and fuck, mostly suck."

My forthright reply may have astonished, my answer didn't shock; it wasn't intended for shock. He gripped his pipe by the bowl and I thought he may have chuckled. "You like that, do you?" he commented. For some reason my answer seemed to amuse him in a pleasant way.

"Oh, yes, I certainly do like it," I said, my exuberance largely reflexive. Enthusiasm for the meat of the matter seemed to be what was expected of me—I found nothing pleasant having to prove myself unacceptable.

"Would you call that having sex?"

It seemed to me a peculiar question, unless designed to trip me in a way I couldn't imagine. "That's what I call it, having sex. It is sex to me."

"Ever had sex with a female?" he asked again.

I suddenly found myself trying to envision this same interview played in reverse with a heterosexual—the mere thought was preposterous. "No, never!" I again declared.

"Ever think you would?"

"No," I told him, "I'm sure of it."

"Why not?" he asked, fiddling with his pipe.

I felt myself sitting naked and ashamed; shame, not because of my sexuality; shame of being stripped of dignity. "The anatomy's all wrong," I told him. "Just the thought is repulsive. Uuugh! I might get sick!"

His questions were simple yet indifferent, characterized by a manner not otherwise demeaning. Whatever may have been his personal viewpoint, I hadn't a further clue. What I did detect was his ability to approach me as a unique individual having distinct sexual identity. That, after all, was his function—clinical discernment rather than moral judgment.

"You understand that in the Army you'd be in close quarters with other men. Would that be a problem?"

—————— Σ ——————

"Yes," I said, nodding affirmative. His mode of expression seemed to need only brevity. I got the impression he'd formed his conclusion. He may have been giving *me* the opportunity for second thought.

"I take it by that you mean you'd have trouble controlling your sexual desires. Is that a fair assessment?"

Honestly, it was no fair assessment. I answered, "Yes."

"In other words, you'd have difficulty keeping your hands off the other boys?" He was getting to the meat of the matter.

There was only one answer for me to give and I gave it. "Yes," I said flatly. The word stung, hanging heavy with betrayal.

"Is there anything else you think I should know?"

I momentarily hesitated before answering and my hesitation surprised him. He suddenly studied my face intently. I was quick to reply, "No, nothing, Sir!" He scribbled on one of the sheets, re-sealed the envelope and handed it to me. "Thank you. That'll be all. Next!"

Fort Hood was the reason for my hesitation. All the while he was questioning I was thinking about the boys who came to Austin for weekends with me. Many of them could've been had sexually—it is shallow to suppose otherwise. The human psyche is a complex of variable factors. The sexual equation can't be reduced with such simplicity. In its superficiality I may have had difficulty controlling my desires, at times difficulty perhaps in keeping my hands off other soldiers. I also knew, among the boys themselves, others would've been little different regarding me.

On the lower floor, off to one side, was a room I call the bullpen. It was noisy and hot, and could've more easily accommodated half the number of bodies jammed inside. The three of us were stragglers. We were the last of our group to reach this destination, having been the only ones sidetracked to Room 315. The bullpen was entered from the rear, its first challenge that of getting my envelope to a long series of tables up front where the Chief Medical Examiner sat with his staff.

Guys were everywhere, all seats taken; walls of the room along both sides and rear, huddled masses of males. The narrow aisle way through the center was a sea of bodies, boys literally standing on boys. It was necessary to swim through bodies in order to reach the front. The three of us did so, One, Two, Three. We handed our envelope to a Receiving Clerk at the end of the first table, One, Two, Three. We swam back through the sea of bodies to the rear of the room, One, Two, Three, to await our turn at being called.

There were three things I noticed. First, *everyone* in the room followed with eyes as the three of us swam, One, Two, Three, up front; then they followed us, One, Two, Three, as we swam back.

Second, as the envelopes were received, each was passed in turn to the next officer who opened it and took a quick look before handing its contents to yet another staffer, a chain that led finally to the Chief Medical Examiner. Across the tables' entire length, as each packet of papers was handled but before it was passed on, that staff aide looked across the sea of faces and bodies to glare at each of us in turn, One, Two, Three, punctuating his disgust with a loud *TSCH!* It wasn't enough we had to writhe our slimy, queer bodies through a sweaty sea of straight ones, we also were singled out.

The third thing I noticed was order. If anything, I thought that's what Army is all about, precise numerical order—at the least, order based on first in, first out. Not so in the case of One, Two, Three.

Our packets had been placed on bottom in stacks with others. All activity then ground to an abrupt halt to assure we'd have time to make our slimy retreat to the room's rear. In the meantime, a dead silence fell across the room. The thump of my own heartbeat thundered at my ear. No sooner did we reach the room's rear, all three of us, than each of our packets was summarily retrieved and placed atop its stack. With great ceremony, the first of them was reopened, its contents again viewed, again with a loud expression of disgust, a hateful *TSCH!* The file was passed upward in rank across the table. Each succeeding officer seemed obliged to outrank the previous in his display of contempt—from each came an ever louder *TSCH!*

Finally the file was placed in the hands of the Assistant-to-the-Chief, who waved the folder in the air and announced, "Well, men, looks like we've got us one in the barrel!" Whereupon he *shouted* the boy's name—as though the three of us hadn't already commanded *complete* attention in that room.

Wouldn't-Have-Thought-He-Was-Gay was the first of us to set out again on that terrible trip, this time amid a clamor of nasty slurs from the crowd. I really hurt for him. That boy was an extremely shy guy. I think he entered the final stage of shock as he began his dreadful journey.

As he neared the front of the room, the second packet was treated to identical ceremony, with an added feature down rank, "Here's another, men. Number Two!" *TSCH! TSCH! TSCH!* I knew my name would be called.

———————— Σ ————————

As I heard it shouted, I thought, "What th' hell." Then, before I made a move, the room became quiet. In a space of deadly silence, a peculiar thing happened. The center aisle way of bodies, much like I suppose the Red Sea may have done, parted.

Hooting and jeering stopped. There was absolutely no sound. The moment, poised, hung as if suspended. I had a vague impression of tension riding the air, as though a stirring event were imminent. I got a sensation my body had risen. It seemed to float as I took the aisle, swept along on a surge of pride. Head held high, looking right to left, left to right, I passed the crowd of boys by. I looked them in the eye; looked in a way, not entirely conscious. I got a feeling of sorts, awareness in a sense, there was something about gay special. It seemed to be surrounding me. Then I saw, with other than vision, clear and brilliant light!

I was followed by "Number Three! Another one, Number Three!" It was Kookie, and *she* made *regal* use of the aisle! I guess that's what broke the spell; hoots and jeers redoubled. There was no humor to be found in the bullpen, not in all of what happened. There was maybe an irony. We came into the room last—yet, we came first.

We had to stand before the entire room, One, Two, Three, in front of the tables, while our files were being processed and their pages rubber-stamped. Meantime our military classifications were loudly announced, hatefully shouted. Stamp-Whonk! *"Four-Eff!"* Stamp-Whonk! *"Four-Eff!"* Stamp-Whonk! *"Four-Eff!"*

The Chief Medical Examiner stood from behind the table. He was a man of small stature, small indeed. His voice was one of magnitude as he addressed the crowd. "Men! Pay a'tention! Standin' up heah befoah you ah three pitiful creetchuhs, sick individuals, *puhvuhts!* Unfit foah suhvice in yoah United States Ahmy. Men! Take a good look so you'll recognize a puhvuht next time you encountah one. Fuhthamoah, ah'm awedring you men as recruits of this United States Ahmy not to have fuhtha dealin's with any of these puhvuhts. That means not so much as one single and not one solitree wuhd!"

I expected humiliation. I never imagined it to be accompanied by such degradation. I saw confusion on faces amid the crowd of recruits. I could see fear in many of the boys' eyes. I saw also in some of them, shame; in others, pain. What my thoughts then may have been, I can't now recall.

———————— Σ ————————

They've too long been buried too deeply to disturb. I think I was hurting; less for myself; more for some of those boys staring at me from the sea of bodies. My ordeal, and that of the two boys standing one at either side with me, I was certain must be over. We survived the outrage. Yet, even with that we still weren't done. Earlier, recall, I mentioned conveyors.

With the three of us still standing at the front of the room, the Chief Medical Examiner shouted, "Gawd!" A soldier efficiently appeared, an M-1 or whatever it was he carried slung at his shoulder. He snapped his heels and smartly saluted, "Sir!"

"Soldjah, I want uh cuntinjunt to escoat these three unfit *puhvuht creetchuhs* off govuhnmet propahtee."

"Sir! Yes, Sir!"

"And, Soldjah, I want these puhvuht creetchuhs escoated undah *ahmed* gawd, IS THAT CLEAH?"

"Sir! Yes, Sir!"

Suddenly we became the enemy, trapped in a narrowing ring, the three of us surrounded by *uh cuntinjunt* of M-1's loaded with bayonets.

"Fuhthamoah, Soldjah, I want it undahstood that th' propahtee of this United States Govuhnmet does not stop at th' doahs to this buildin'. The propahtee of this United States Govuhnmet extends out those doahs and down those steps and across that sidewalk to th' verre edge of th' cuhbstones whaya it encountahs th' propahtee of th' City of New Yoak City, and, Soldjah!, when I say escoat these *puhvuht creetchuhs* off United States Govuhnmet Propahtee, it is to th' verre edge of those cuhbstones at th' propahtee of th' City of New Yoak City that I am talking about, DO YOU UNDAHSTAND ME, SOLDJAH?"

"Sir! Yes, Sir!"

"Soldjah! That is an awedah!"

"Sir! Yes, Sir!"

"Fuhthamoah, ah'm awedring these puhvuhts not to make any effuht to re-entah these premises ah to make any effuht to make contact with any of owah recruits heah in this United States Ahmy. If any one of these puhvuhts makes any effuht to do so, if any one of them even so much as steps foot on th' sidewalk, it is to be construed an act of treason and aggression on the paht of all three. And, Soldjah!, you will use yoah weapon. Shoot to kill!"

——————— Σ ———————

"Sir! Yes, Sir!"

A sound of metal smooth to metal sharply clicked as rifle bolts were engaged. I wasn't at all sure a bullet wasn't yet forthcoming; it would've been no surprise, maybe even welcome. The other two boys must've felt much the same; all three of us, bodies rigid, stood stunned. Suddenly, I felt the stinging prick of bayonet points.

The *awedah* was carried out to the *lettah!* We were *escoated* out of Whitehall at rifle and bayonet point, down the steps and across the sidewalk to the *verre edge* of *New Yoak City.* We were thrust from the curb onto the street, literally at gunpoint. Kookie was sent sprawling, stretched prone on his belly face down on the asphalt. Suddenly he cried out, "We're free!" Then he kissed the pavement. It vaguely occurred to me to wonder how this scene was playing to civilian traffic and other passersby. I didn't give it a second thought. We all three were *proud* to be on plain American pavement.

We *stayed* on American pavement, soldiers standing guard, weapons ready. We were, as Kookie said, free. We milled about, skipping and dancing in the middle of the street, hugging one another over and again. I guess we were giddy. Come to think of it, I've no doubt we were dazed.

Kookie said, "Le's get a drink. There's got to be a bar someplace here." He looked to-and-fro. "Okay, wait. In this neighborhood, whaddya think—would it be a gay bar?"

We laughed uproariously, Kookie all but beside himself at his own humor. Finally we settled on food first, alcohol later. Wouldn't-Have-Thought-He-Was-Gay didn't want to make use of his U.S. Army meal ticket. Inductees were given one earlier that morning, good for lunch in the U.S. Cafeteria across Whitehall Street. "You guys go ahead," he said. "I don't think I'm hungry. I'm sure the food's lousy."

Kookie snatched him by the shirtfront using both hands. "The hell with that, Mary!" he screamed. "After what we've been through I'll drag your sweet ass in there across my shoulder and spoon feed you every bite of that army slop, if I have to sit on your head and shove it up your ass to do it." He stamped the pavement, first with one foot, then the other. "Don't think these cowboy heels are butch drag. This girl may be gay, but she ain't no shit and she ain't takin' no shit. Now," he smoothed at the other boy's shirt, "let's get in there and show 'em how queers eat!"

We camped at a table in the center of the dining hall and we

——————— Σ ———————

camped, as Kookie phrased it, like Sarah. We had the next thing to a private dining room—no one dared come near us. It wasn't merely that no one would use a table nearby, no one dared even skirt our table to gain access to others beyond. Our display didn't help promote a positive gay image. At that point it made little difference—image had been established across the street. Coward may be a word tacked onto me; another ought to be said—*balls*.

* * * * *

A sunny noon in early February '67, with a freight-damaged footlocker given me by co-workers at Sears and containing whatever I could stuff into it, I boarded a Trailways coach from the small station on State Highway 60 in Bay Prairie. Late that afternoon at the depot in Houston I presented my one-way ticket on the New York Express. The bus driver glanced at it, looking at me somewhat astonished. "Oh! You're the one!" he said. "Straight through, huh?" I didn't understand his reaction at the time.

Drivers changed every four hours, maybe eight. Passengers boarded and disembarked, freight loaded and unloaded. Through the Deep South, soldiers returning to base after furlough caught the bus. I almost referred to them as stray soldiers—the boys weren't stray. I had three of them different times during the trip. The boys each gravitated toward the vacant seat at the window beside me. Each boy did it the same way—slouched in the tall, cushiony seat, head resting on my shoulder, he slept like a baby. I certainly didn't mind. I rather liked it, a boy's shoulder against mine, the weight of him pressing, almost to my face. I thought, "It's a long road this, that began at land's end, past the highway beyond Sargent. It may yet be a long trip through this night. As we travel together on this one-way ferry, sleep, Pretty Boy, I'm near—I'd kiss you if I could."

Some sixty hours later, the Trailways coach with my footlocker and me arrived at Port Authority Bus Terminal in midtown Manhattan. Express comprised the three of us—only the three of us.

I'd like to say, after near six years had passed, I left New York much the same as I arrived. I'd like to say I left Manhattan with only a footlocker and what I crammed into it. I'd like to say I left with only a pocketful of ten's, some twenty's and spare change. I'd like to say I left with bright eyes, with hope and enthusiasm; with the prospect of a long bus trip and the sweet smell of pretty boys near my cheek.

I can't say these things. I drove from Manhattan in an E-Z Haul

——————— Σ ———————

loaded with an accumulation of things I've since carted place to place, often wondering why I bother with them. I left Manhattan burdened with guilt over leaving an alcoholic lover, crippled by doubt about my own feeling toward him. I left with a fat wallet and an equally fat parcel of bills coming due. I left New York in the late June of youth, with the prospect of pretty boys near my cheek moving from prospect to memory.

What had happened? The ad slogan said I could make it anywhere if I could make it in the Big Apple. I thought I made it. Mrs. Perl of the management office in London Terrace Gardens told me, "After signing these papers there's only one move left for you, all the way to the top. You began with us on the ground floor, went from there to the fourth, and, now, it's up to sixteen—I've added your name to the Penthouse list, Dean."

Yes, I made it in Manhattan. I made it with Danny Christian and with Eric David; with Jon-Jon, with Danny Nickel; with Jason and Fury, Ron and Moe, with Robert and with Doug. I made it with uncounted others, each now sensation without face or name. Once they all had faces, all had names. Once I was in love with each. Each of those times were ones I'd have said, "Yes, this is enough—this will do. I want off—stop the ferry!"

I want to trip on his briefs slung onto the floor, twisted with mine. I want his feet tangled in the sheets, teasing with mine. I want his hair in my face, his arm about me, cuddling. I want the weight of his body on mine, heat from his flesh searing mine. I want his sweat and his smell. I want his face first thing every morning, his eyes and his lips. I want a tomorrow and the day after and a calendar together we peel pages from. More than all these I want are three words—*I love you!*

None of it happened that way. Though each of my encounters was a time I thought it would, each a time it seemed it could, it never happened. I shouldn't complain. In my own way I'm lucky—as lucky as most, if not more lucky than many. Seldom was it I didn't go with a number I spotted and wanted. Surprising it may seem, times were few, honestly few, when it was altogether mere sex. My nights and my beds were for love, not romance. Touching another's body I touch deeper need, hunger no different from that of Slade, who offered himself to me. The complete giving of oneself I've discovered tantamount to love. I've come to think giving is more significant than getting. That seems to me the path of intimacy.

Intimacy is one word I'd choose to recapture those nights and their

————— Σ —————

moments of love. Though many of them were simply that, nights which evaporated with morning sun, the moments they held weren't bound by the ticking of a clock. Depth of sentiment must often be a lifetime measure. That none of my nights led to long-term commitment is a source of frustration and anguish. I guess I didn't turn the right trick. Even so, those moments gave me glimpse of finer capacity for love. One who's been there may know what I'm talking about—it's worth a swing around the block.

Touching another's body I touch something I can't hold; a sum seeming larger than its parts—maybe mystery. There may be a still deeper need, a need the body can't sustain—a thirst it's unable to quench.

* * * * *

Bernard and I lived at Hotel Chelsea the same summer. We each had a room on the east wing, first floor above street, one flight up. His was a smaller room overlooking West 23rd from the hotel's front. The end of a hallway had been walled to create a room. My room was toward the rear on the same hallway. I looked out from its only window into an air shaft rising ten stories. The air shaft once had purpose, updraft for ventilation. With AC, it became empty space, a nuisance to the hotel owner. Trash that accumulated clogged storm drains and with each rain had to be removed.

The ten-story shaft was totally enclosed, three-foot-thick outer walls of the hotel on three sides, the wall of an adjacent apartment building on the fourth. Troublesome trash had to be retrieved via the wide window in my room—the shaft's only access. That was the reason, I was told at the desk, I got the room for thirty dollars a week—air shaft access and no AC. I wasn't bothered by either prospect. Thirty dollars of my weekly pay, eighty-five gross, was all I could afford.

A deep window seat set into thick outer walls was the room's only distinction. It was in keeping with the hotel, Victorian, built in the late 1880s. By the late '60s when I was a resident, the hotel was a haven for artists, writers, and most any other creative genius who, while awaiting his bloom, couldn't find a spot elsewhere. That's not to say everyone at the Chelsea was still waiting. Charles James and Charlie Jackson, Shirley Clark, Larry Rivers and Jan Cramer, not failing to mention Jason Holliday, were among those claiming residence.

Less awesome than the Plaza, Hotel Chelsea was environment. I took special pride in a brass plaque affixed beside the hotel's plate-glass

—————— Σ ——————

entrance. It noted that Edgar Lee Masters once resided in the Chelsea. My first day at the hotel, the desk clerk, John, told me, "If you want to write, forget gay. Queer stuff'll never make it." He also took special delight in tapping the brass plaque teasingly with forefinger, "Dean, I'm keeping it highly polished so yours won't outshine his when we hang it underneath." Environment is a word I think suits the Chelsea.

Bernard was a tall boy, more sinewy than lanky, tough and strong. His appearance tended to fool—Bernard was as tender and as gentle, as sweet as any boy I've met. He had a wavy shock of summer-sand hair, baby-blue eyes and lips crying to be met—fully. I suppose he was atypical. Bernard was French, authentically so, from distant Paris. He was in the U.S. on a visiting visa, renewed and extended so far as bureaucracy could—or would—bend and extend. Bernard wanted to *stay* in the U.S. He and a Brooklyn girl he was dating were trying to finagle something, anything, to gain him more time.

Bernard's soon-to-be-revoked visa was one of our hallway topics. It could've been simply solved had she married him. The girl was already married—to another man. The married *he* wouldn't let the married *her* go. "You do not have such woman troubles," Bernard said, smiling, "your boy troubles, they are as bad as woman troubles, no?" Bernard was a nice guy to stand next. He didn't twitch or jerk; he didn't grind his heels and rear back. Those times arms and shoulders, even hands, came into contact, the little bumps and clips that occur man-to-man, he wasn't squeamish. He didn't squirm or recoil, didn't pull back suddenly. To Bernard, it was pink and blue. He preferred pink, I went for blue. There wasn't very much to it after all—Bernard was a nice guy to be standing next.

Across 23rd was a piano cocktail bar, the Nautilus. Why it was nautical must've been a whim—docks and wharves were blocks away. The Nautilus was nondescript, merely a non-gay neighborhood bar, drab and characterless. I occasionally went there for drinks, seeking piano and companionship when I was feeling too down for Greenwich Village gay bars and too mellow for sex. That was my mood the night I met a burly guy. He sent a beer across the bar, then came over to the stool beside me and bought more. Feeling down and too mellow for sex is a bad time for me to drink. I get drunk, *deep* drunk, as I did that night. The burly hulk wanted to come with me to the hotel. I didn't want sex with him. I thought, "What th' hell."

———— Σ ————

What I really wanted was someone I could sleep next. The guy was no ideal. He looked the part of a wharf rat and could've been a bum. He wasn't *my* ideal, no one I'd have chosen. Being deep drunk, I could close my eyes and pretend—I was going to pass out cold, regardless.

Bernard had gone up the stairs ahead of us. He was fumbling with his key at the door. He paused. I noticed him watching as we entered my room. The guy sat in an armchair, removed his boots, then began unbuttoning shirt to remove clothing. I sat on the edge of my bed. In harsher light, I realized deep drunk wasn't drunk enough—already I was in too deep.

The door suddenly opened. Bernard hadn't knocked. He came in and immediately sat on the bed—not near me but *next*. He put his arm around me, clutching with long fingers my shoulder. I melted against Bernard as he glared at the guy. "What's this?" Bernard demanded. "What's happening here?" The guy made an effort to mutter. Bernard said coldly to him, "You will have to pardon us while I take my lover out. We must talk." Bernard stood tall. Holding my hands high above my head, he pulled me from the bed. "Come, my love, come with me," he said tenderly.

Once in the hallway, Bernard shook me from the shoulder roughly. "My precious, you must tell me the meaning of this—*at once!*"

"Oh, Bernard, I am lonely—I am so lonely."

Bernard, still holding me at the shoulder, was stern. "You let a *monster* follow you home? Tell me at once, you do not want him!"

I shook my head, "No, Bernard, I don't want him."

"Oh, I knew it was not so!" Bernard said, clutching me at the shoulder. "I knew it could not be!" He folded me in his arms and hugged my body to his, squeezing hard. After a moment he held me at arm's length. "But now we must be rid of him. Let me think. Of course—it is simple. I shall say you are my lover. We had a silly lovers' quarrel. Now I have returned and he *shall* have to go—he *will* have to go!" Bernard still held me at arm's length, looking into my face, deeply into my eyes. "Can you do this, my love? Tell me *Yes!* and we *shall* do it!"

Bernard led me by the hand, fingers entwined. We sat on the bed, him holding me, pulling my body to his. A shock of summer-sand hair spilled across my eyes. I clung about his waist. Bernard kissed the top of my head as he told the man to go. Grudgingly, the man went, Bernard following to be certain. Bernard closed the door and sat again beside me.

————— Σ —————

"My precious, this frightens me, what might have happened—I *will* not think about it!" He hugged me tightly, then pulled away. "This is not good, my lamb. Boys, that's one matter—not an ugly monster! No, my precious, you must not do this—never!"

I told him again, "Bernard, I'm lonely, I don't want to be alone."

Bernard held me as he might have a child, "Yes, my pet. Yes, I do know your loneliness." He cradled my body, caressing with gentle fingers my head. "This is not the way of beautiful boys, as you must be, my love, for you also are one of the beautiful boys. It *must* be—it *shall* be!"

Bernard was kind. He didn't mind holding me, didn't mind my clinging to him. His body was strong, resilient. It had places my not-so-strong, not-so-resilient body sought in which to hide. When Bernard held me, hands and arms didn't merely reside. They found on my body places into which hands and fingers, arms and forearms fit, places needing held and places never held. Bernard was nice—so very, very nice to be next.

"Stay with me, Bernard. Sleep with me tonight," I pleaded. "Hold me, Bernard. Let me be near you tonight—I so need *closeness!*"

"My darling, I am not as you," Bernard said softly. "It cannot be, though I may wish it. I must go. I shall put you to bed. I *will* be near you. Ssh, ssh, sleep, my precious." He snuggled the covers about my shoulders, smoothing them tenderly beneath my chin. He leaned closely, his face near mine. He kissed me on the lips. "Sleep, my precious. Sleep, my lamb."

Later that summer, in afternoon sunlight, I was in Bernard's room. He was distressed, packing to leave. "What more is to be done?" he said. "Nothing, I think there is nothing. We've been every place to go. With every one we've talked—no longer does any one listen. It is tomorrow I *shall* have to go. Tomorrow I *will* have to go."

"Bernard," I said suddenly, "I can marry you and you can stay!"

"My darling, you know I am different from you!"

"Yeah. It wouldn't matter, Bernard. You can keep on doing as you want. I'll marry you and you can stay."

"But, this is something not done!"

"Yeah," I said, "it's something not done—I wonder, why. Bernard, we can do it anyway!"

"You will do this, marry me so I can stay?"

"Yeah," I told him, trying to think of the Chelsea without Bernard.

———————— Σ ————————

"But, I think, for you will not that be unfair? You know I cannot be with you, my love."

"Nyah," I said, "it won't matter so much—I know already you love me. Bernard, I wish we *could*—for real." It occurred to me to ask. I said brightly, "Bernard, *would* you marry me?"

He grabbed me into his arms and hugged, squeezing my body tightly to his. His shock of summer-sand hair fell about my face. "My precious, I do love you. I think, yes, I would marry you! You are my precious, my sweet, sweet lamb!" Bernard took my face between his hands, held my face within his hands. His eyes looked deeply into mine as he kissed me.

* * * * *

Living at Hotel Chelsea that summer I had another close encounter, this an experience of a different kind. There was nothing unusual beforehand, no event or occurrence out of the ordinary. I distinctly remember going to bed that night. Had it not been for what followed, I can't think of any reason such a simple routine would be so clearly recalled.

I kept the window raised, the room's only ventilation, hardly cause for concern—the ten-story air shaft had no other access; no fire escape, no door, no other window without bars. I determined all that first thing.

Unless window coverings are tightly drawn, it's never totally dark in Manhattan. Light from the hallway filtered through a frosted transom above my door. I switched off the light and got into bed. I rarely sleep on my back. That night I did, arms folded, hands lightly clasped at my chest. I fell asleep quickly. Had I been troubled and restless, I would've been aware tossing and turning—I've had too many worrisome nights.

My eyelids suddenly popped open, wide awake. *Suddenly* was instantaneous and startling, though only momentary. I couldn't hold my eyes open. They were being forced shut as I fought, fluttering eyelids rapidly blinking, so rapidly as to make vision impossible.

How long this may have occurred I've no way of knowing; it seemed a long while. During that *space* of time I was *something other than aware* of a presence outside the window; I was *something other than aware* of imminent threat. I *knew* the presence—*it*—was intent on entering my room, coming through the window. During that *space of time* it was my *desire* to get up from the bed and leave the room. I wasn't able to do so. I was unable to move any muscle *of* my body. How I could know such a staggering thing

———————— Σ ————————

isn't easy to tell. It was my *desire* to get up. When my body wouldn't respond to that *desire,* I channeled effort to what logically might be the first movement in a series necessary for getting up. I tried to lift the fingers of my hand. I couldn't. Even with a great effort of *will* and *desire,* I found *myself* unable to bring about muscle movement—not so much as to a little finger.

Yet, I *rose* from the bed. I *slipped* from the sheets and *rose* in a single, slow motion, moving toward the door. Movement was painful and difficult; painful, because I hurt at the center of my chest *from where* I'd risen; difficult, because I felt a force tugging at my shoulders, pulling against me in restraint. I was aware of *myself* held at an angle so acutely backward walking was impossible. I seemed to be swimming toward the door.

I no longer had sense of time. In its place, I had a feeling of immensity. Everything appeared gray haze. Above *me,* a long tube spiraled, twisting coil-like circles slightly overhead behind. The tube wasn't gray haze. It was silvery gray, glittery. As I neared the foot of the bed, several things simultaneously occurred. I turned partway round and *perceived* myself floating. My hand struck a cold object. I saw a silvery gray figure stepped through the window; I saw a body on the bed; I heard a hollow moan rage from the body on the bed; I recognized the body. Familiar, it was the body I had known.

The silvery gray figure stepped through the window. *He* crouched, one foot resting on the window seat, the other on the windowsill. *He* appeared from another time, *his* silvery gray attire coarse and homespun, *his* dark hat wide-brimmed. Where his *body* was uncovered, lower arms, hands and long fingers, face and neck, *it* was the same silvery gray glitter as the long spiraling tube circling above me—extending *into the space* between me and a body on the bed.

The body plainly visible was at rest on its back, arms folded, hands lightly clasped at its chest; head on the pillow, eyes closed in sleep—peaceful sleep. There was no movement to the body. The glittering silvery gray tube spiraling overhead extended from me into the center of its chest.

The body plainly visible was the body I'd known, the one I moved about and the one with which I moved about. It was the body I touched and the one others touched. It was inanimate—senseless, without feeling. It was not me. I was at the foot of the bed. Sense and sensation, assimilation and perception—*consciousness*—was with me, not with it. I was me; it wasn't. I existed—it didn't.

————— Σ —————

I could appreciate the beauty of a young, lovely body, its skin soft and lips cherry; a halo of fine hair framing its face, cascading down cheeks and flowing onto pillow. I could admire exciting contours firm limbs and torso presented. I could gaze on it, sensuous with eyes closed in peaceful sleep. I wasn't overcome. It was, after all, an animal thing, no greater or lesser value than a vegetable thing—no further significance than a turnip.

How it was possible I saw so much; rather, how long the occurrence, whether a long while or milliseconds, makes no difference. In that space, time, or what I'd known as time, either existed or didn't—it was irrelevant.

In a sharp split of silence beyond the hollow moan I heard rage from the body, my eyelids shot open. *From the bed,* I had a flash of instantaneous realization. I leaped from the bed, bounding toward the door. On a table at the foot of the bed, my hand struck a large, glass ashtray, its cold feeling to my touch immediately familiar.

I tore across the room, through the door; leaped steps downstairs to reach the lobby. No one was there, the night clerk gone, the lobby empty of all but chair and sofa. I paced, stood at the glass entrance looking onto West 23rd. I tried to sit; it wasn't possible to remain still. I couldn't think what to do, standing in the center of the lobby, suddenly aware of my body shivering. I was stark naked—nakedness seemed of no concern, more ironic. Alternately I stood and paced, unsure if I could return to the room. If not, where to go, what to do was blank. I knew I wouldn't sleep. I stepped to the desk to look at its clock. Four-forty-four clacked to four-forty-five. I felt from the bottoms of my feet, my steps on the stairs.

Later that morning at the Law Institute, a girl who shared work-space said, "Jesus! I'd get outta that spooky place—it's *haunted!*"

I discovered most people don't want to *hear* of such things, too bound up in fear and superstition, areas unknown—death. I was frightened, why lie about it? It wasn't death that disturbed me. After all, I had been as near—or as far into—the state called death as is possible without being in the state called dead. I may have entered that state—I won't argue. Fact is, into death or not, I didn't remain dead.

I heard any number of *explanations;* notable, Something Undead, Something Not At Rest, Something Not At Peace, Something Evil, Something Unclean, Something Searching, Something Lost, Something From A Time Warp, or simply Some Thing. I heard warnings not to sleep in the

————— Σ —————

176

room again—that *Some Thing* which attempted to drive me from my body, possibly to occupy it, might return to succeed. That warning sounds grim—it was delivered grimly! I hesitated to point it out, *attempt* that night *had* succeeded—I'd *been* out of my body.

There was the crux of the matter, as I discovered later when I found books at an occult bookshop. I also found out-of-body itself is rather cultish. Enthusiasts reportedly engage in out-of-body on a regular basis, for such purpose as communication, relaxation, pleasure, entertainment. Again I hesitated. Possibly those multiple experiences and my single experience weren't entirely related. I could not—*nor would I!*—class my experience within any stretch of such parlor trick. No one I talked with, no book I read, remotely touched an area I contemplated—spiritual holiness.

I may have misled. What little I've told took years of diligent search. I can't say I've got it figured out. Neither did I leave the Chelsea or my room in the Chelsea. Nor did I have trouble sleeping in the room afterward, the reason I can say confidently.

What I experienced and saw that night I reason to be anima, in Latin, soul. Carl Jung made it jargon in his analytic psychology dictionary. I'd like not to strip it entirely of Jung's elaborate definition. I would like to strip it entirely of psychoanalytic implication to have left a more eloquent simplification—an individual's pure inner self, encompassing an inner part feminine in the male. I think of it being essence—*vital* essence.

Why I've not called it spirit or soul is because these are words I call trade. They've been so hard sucked they no longer turn the trick. They're dried-up, wizened, shriveled; trite, hackneyed; better suited for Gothic and Romance. Were I to use the word *soul,* the covers of this book could snap quickly shut. Soul shares with death—no one wants to hear about it.

Anima, essence, what I saw that night—the body a shroud, used for only a moment. Anima, essence—these aren't body. Anima, essence—these extend. I recall a line of poetry from *Thanatopsis,* "approach thy grave like one who wraps the drapery of his couch about him and lies down to pleasant dreams." I shout, *"No!"* I'd rather say, "like one who *disrobes* and *rises* from his bed." Anima, essence; it's what's *in* bodies we touch—*vital* essence.

* * * * *

The world moved apace, mine with it. I was spontaneous and eager, careless in my abandon—heedless of time's passing. That can be charged to

——————— Σ ———————

youthful folly. I'm often surprised at autumn suddenly swirling summer leaves about my feet. Summer days are long; they lull me to languor. Easily I forget, year to year, their passing—summer is to me a season of mind.

After I left the hotel, I lived on West 73rd, near Central Park West. June 5, 1968, I was sleeping with James, a man I was seeing. We had make-do on the living room floor of Fury's Murray Hill apartment, he and Fury onetime lovers. Late in the night, Fury called loudly, RFK murdered in California. The three of us, huddled on Fury's bed, watched in black-and-white and darkness. Stillness hovered above silence. Martin Luther King, Jr., a short time earlier was murdered in Tennessee. Now, there was no voice.

By spring 1969 I moved from my ground-floor efficiency in the London Terrace Gardens to a fourth-floor alcove apartment overlooking West 23rd. Soon after, I met Danny Nickel, a boy as striking as any I've seen.

I met Danny a Saturday evening, invited to an apartment across the garden for pre-bar drinks, Danny, one of the guests. I was given a tiny white tablet called Strawberry Sunshine, a tab of LSD—Timothy Leary LSD. Hi-fi speakers blasted a new rock opera by The Who—*Tommy* swallowed me!

Listening to you...Gazing at you...Following you...I get excitement at your feet. Danny Nickel, beautiful boy; Tommy, purple, yellow, plum tumbleweeds. I get the music, I get the heat, I get excitement at your feet. Danny Nickel, beautiful boy. Gazing at you, following you, I climb the mountain. High in the sky over Lexington Avenue. Danny Nickel's apartment, fifty, sixty floors. Danny Nickel. Gives me African dashiki. Ceremonial robe. Beautiful boy. I strip. Cotton, soft, feels, good. Lights on Lex, Red Yellow Green, Red Yellow Green, Never out of sequence, Red Yellow Green. He likes me. Beautiful boy, Danny Nickel. He whispers. Beautiful boy. To me. See me...Feel me...Touch me...Heal me. He whispers. See me—Feel me—Touch me—Heal me. He whispers. I want to...make love to...you, too. Beautiful boy, yes, love, Danny Nickel, me. Make love. To me. Beautiful boy. Beautiful body. Beautiful love. Beautiful boy. In my body. Beautiful love. In me. Danny Nickel. Yes—I love—Danny Nickel!

Danny moved in with me—Strawberry Sunshine, *The Doors to Perception, Heaven and Hell.* I became psychedelic, elektrik. I fell in love with Danny Nickel. Our love was good for awhile, acid a mind-expander. We dropped LSD often, tripping with friends. I saw things; others grooved. I saw a wall expand into atoms, molecules; become like the universe, space of

—————— Σ ——————

matter through which I could see, maybe walk; stars, the planets and suns a table too big to see. Danny would whisper, "Let's go home. I want to...make love to...you, too." I was swallowed in his words.

Hallucination or reality, I was high on love. "Danny Nickel! I love you, Danny Nickel!" I said it often. As I did so, I saw in his eyes a look restless. Tune in, turn on, drop out was the catch phrase. Others grooved, didn't see what I saw. Something ancient in Egypt, not yet found, pulls me, magnetic. I can find it! Temples. Priests. Worship. "Danny Nickel! I love you, Danny Nickel!" It is the last thing I said to him. I saw in his mind, our last night together, while he lay sleeping beside me, I knew he'd be gone. Next day, I came home from Time; time had been taken, Danny gone.

I got a rush. I saw from the east marching legions too dark to clearly make out. I saw again the figure robed in white, left hand extended holding a crystal globe; right palm raised. He was floating, standing in a desolate place, entrance into a rugged valley steep with treacherous outcrop and craggy wall, everything gray-green. He looked at me as he spoke, "Death beyond this point, death to all who enter."

I saw acid turn to gray-green the sky and air, my skin and sense. I seemed to understand. No more—turn from the desolate valley. Flush the tabs. I sobbed, "Remember me! Remember Danny!"

I loved Danny Nickel. Later, he came back to me. I had to say *No!* He was a beautiful boy, as striking as any I've seen. I still love Danny Nickel.

Through spring into summer, I wasn't seeing anyone in particular, had no one special. June 27, 1969, I walked with a friend, Wayne, down 9th Avenue to Greenwich Village. We spent the evening in Danny's, a gay bar on Christopher Street at Houston. It was my favorite of Village bars. My first night in New York I was in this bar. Then, it was non-gay and derelict, a waterfront bar run-down and dying. I sat in a plywood booth drinking Chivas and soda; sat in the near-empty bar looking out plate glass windows onto Christopher. Now, it was alive with excitement, gay energy at night; the bar bright with light and laughter, its large windows open, looking onto Christopher. I consider Danny's the first among what I call *new* gay bars.

Wayne and I left Danny's at 12:30. We walked up Christopher to Sheridan Square. A boisterous crowd was gathered outside the Stonewall Inn. It was the last of the *old* gay bars, dark and confining under Mafia and Syndicate control. I had a ticket for a 7:30 flight JFK to Intercontinental in

—————— Σ ——————

Houston, a week's vacation. We didn't stop in at the Stonewall. We veered from Sheridan Square, walked 14th Street to 9th Avenue walking to Chelsea.

Near Bay Prairie, from my parents' home, I saw network TV news. There was an uprising at The Stonewall Inn, a gay bar in New York's Greenwich Village. Homosexuals and transvestites, patrons of the bar protesting a police raid, staged a riot. They fought with bricks and whatever was at hand, holding New York's finest at bay, forcing cops to send for reinforcement. Unrest in Greenwich Village centering on the gay population continued several more days, events collectively called The Stonewall Riots.

I got an odd feeling, watching news film accompanying the report. I was on Sheridan Square less than twenty-four hours earlier, the locale shown in footage altogether familiar. I was glad Wayne and I had not stopped at the bar. Yet, this was my fight as well. I had a sensation, here in Bay Prairie my life was suspended, "take five." I belonged to a world far removed, one I could not share in Bay Prairie and could not acknowledge—a world lying at such distance it could intrude only in fleeting image.

By Thanksgiving 1969 Jim and Cozby were living with me in my fourth-floor alcove apartment. They came to New York a month earlier, at my urging. Jim, in north Texas after the Air Force, found himself miserable with the prospect he faced—one he had admitted to me years before in Austin. Cozby, in west Texas after Vietnam, reestablished contact with Jim, having sought him out—typical Cozby. Jim confided in letters to me, Cozby seemed to him changed.

I gave the two of them my bed in the alcove. It was more spacious, more comfortable for two. I took the sofa hide-a-bed. I was sleeping with Frank, a new-found fling—I wanted less space between the two of us . This was the period of the White Wings.

I agreed to cook Thanksgiving Dinner and Jim bought a 28-pound turkey. We were the four of us, Jim, Cozby, Jimmy and me; there was Frank; and from my office at Time Inc., Howard and Lorenzo, swell guys. It didn't matter they were not gay; they weren't troubled that myself and others were. They had no place else to go for Thanksgiving Dinner.

There was coffee all morning—I had open-bar from 4:30 am. Dinner was late. The big bird barely fit into the oven—it refused to bake. We drank rosé with the traditional dinner, served on Wedgewood with crystal from Tiffany's. I got smashed. So did everyone else. We piled on the queen-size

——————— Σ ———————

bed in the alcove, dog-pile, a bunch of cub bears. We curled up, cuddled up and slept. It was the last time the four of us, Jim, Cozby, Jimmy and me, had a holiday together, the last time we shared dinner together—the last time the four of us, all four, were together.

* * * * *

The world moved apace, my life with it— I'd hardly taken notice. I was so absorbed in the rush to arrive, I wasn't aware of getting there. Life can be that way—the exhilaration expected, too much.

Too much, that is to say, in the sense of excessive—more like my totally *absorbent* jack off. I didn't finish it—the story, I mean. I *did* finish the jack off, it *was* absorbing. I didn't finish the story about Barbara. I've waited to finish in Austin, suitable as having been a place of beginning. There may be another gay adage, the place last written about is the place of return.

Body of Christ. That's where Barbara came from, Corpus Christi. It's about all I can determine we shared in common, the coast and the Gulf of Mexico. Barbara was a lovely girl. I should say *woman*—she was no child. I think of us as children, not kids or juvenile—more, the children we are. In the same way boys are to me boys, Barbara is to me girl. She was a *very* lovely girl. Tall, not big; fresh features with shiny black hair; large, hazel-green eyes—Barbara was feminine. Delicate and dainty are words that come to mind. I don't apply those words to her—feminine says more. Barbara was an actress, damned good. Her Medea gave me goose bumps. Medea says a lot about Barbara—passion and rage, compassion and love, the woman.

It would be my last summer in Austin, the summer of '66. It's lost to me exactly how we became close that summer, except we both were in summer school with class together. Even being the large university it was, UT could nonetheless be a small world.

I've wasted a lot of hours at this keyboard if by now it isn't clear, I make of it no secret which way I swing. Barbara wasn't gay. I don't want to imply she was straight, hetero or anything else—designations are all labels. Barbara was in a way similar to Bernard, pink and blue, except in the case with her, we both liked blue.

I'm sure Barbara was acquainted with other gay males—she had to take drama courses by correspondence in order to miss us. I was her first *close* encounter of the *third* kind—the *gay* kind.

I don't mean sex. Mine was a fresh point of view—refreshing, her

—————— Σ ——————

181

exact word. Mine was the viewpoint of a guy hot for guys in the same way she was hot for them—that's what she found refreshing. Barbara was not hung up on the notion of gay guys as threat. She didn't take it personally. She didn't consider me a menace to her competitive edge, teamwork better for sizing up potential. "See that guy over there, sort of blond, the one with the *really* cute ass? Whaddya think, Dean, would ya' make it with him?"

"In a minute, sweetheart!"

"Ha-ha! I *knew* he was your type!" She'd flash a big grin and taunt me, "Fight ya' for him!"

"Barb, you won't be fighting over that guy when you see the little number standing over there," I'd tell her, "he's *your* type!"

I admit, Barbara's viewpoint was also refreshing. Physical attraction as complement to sexual attraction can't be ignored. It wasn't only the physical at which we looked, bodies and extraordinary body parts. It never was merely sex to Barbara. She, like me, had to have more, had to have intimacy. "Whaddya think about him," she'd ask, "good lover or not?"

"Nyah," I'd tell her, "probably hot sex but no love."

Our conversations that summer became dialog. Barbara wasn't simply curious about mating habits she'd hitherto not known, as though I were a species onto which she suddenly stumbled. She was no tourist gawking at sights on a seamier side of life. A lot of what fascinated her was motivation, what made it tick. That may have been the actress in her—it's probably what made her the actress. I think she discovered in an alternate complexity, richness that gave her vista variety and new meaning.

We found ourselves in the midst of sexual revolution promising love in the guise of sex—love as free as the air. The water was as much uncharted for her as for me, though for me it may have seemed less unsteady. My being gay divorced me from traditional attitudes surrounding sex, leaving a sense of vacancy I had to reconstruct—absence of morality is chaos. I had the advantage of a two-way mirror, two sides of one coin. Barbara's first steps into the chaos of sexual freedom were tender—she was somewhat shaky.

She once asked, "When a guy is saying love, how d'ya know if he means it?" Saying love was Barbara's invention—woo pitched from the bed.

"Depends on the guy—how he hops into bed," I told her. "With a gay guy, I'd say *if* by the third date he still wants to do dinner *first,* and *if* he still likes to cuddle in bed and talk *afterward,* he's probably saying love."

————— Σ —————

"Dean, you're making that up. Your affairs don't get to third date."

"Yeah, Barb," I said flatly, "I *know* they're not saying love."

"Oh, Dean, I didn't mean to be cruel. It's pretty hard, isn't it, trying to find a guy whose feelings are more than sticky goo on the end of his dick. At least for me, if a guy's willing to shell out bucks for a ring, I've got a little more, maybe not much—something at least to hold onto."

"Sure, Barb," I said, "I'd do better dating straight guys. Most straight guys are schmerks—all they know to do is lay there and grunt."

"How d'ya come up with that, Dean?"

"It's image, Barb. A straight guy's got more to lose. I don't mean his straightness, more to lose like his butchness. Sure, a straight guy'll let his body be touched—only so long as the touching doesn't soil his image. Aah, straight guys—they're schmerks."

"You don't think gay guys have *schmerk* syndrone?"

"Darling, we're over all that—we can't be bothered!" I said.

She grinned teasingly. "You'd be sexy as hell in bed with a woman."

"Barb," I intoned, "*no one* can be sexy with a woman."

"I'll kill you! I swear, I'll kill you, you friggin' little queer!"

Barbara had a sensational laugh, sensational and stupendous. I *loved* making her laugh. Once, there was a time when we had no laughter.

The morning after my jack off on the sunroof, Barbara was making tuna salad at the apartment—lunch always a midday date. She invited her fiancé, Barry—the one guy we couldn't agree on. Barbara was in love with him, *madly.* I said, "He's a schnook—you asked, Barb!" We *had* that conversation weeks earlier. Barbara said to me, "So I asked—you didn't *have* to tell me. At least, I know my boyfriend is *safe* from your queer little hands!"

Our topic the day of tuna salad was a *moving,* absorbent jack off. I told Barbara I'd been *absorbed* in my naughtiness until Stanley's untimely intrusion—resulting in my being thrown from the apartment onto the street. "Dean, I hope you didn't lose the urge," she mused. "Heck, no, Barb," I told her, "I was *absorbed*—buck-naked hot and got hotter!" "Absorbed in an *absorbent* jack off," she dramatized, "now a *moving,* absorbent jack off!"

Barbara finished the hard-boil eggs and discovered we had no milk. "Dammit, Barry likes milk," she fussed. I went out for milk, meeting Barry coming upstairs as I was going down. "Hi, Barry, Barb's upstairs. Go on up."

I returned to find Barbara standing lost in the center of the kitchen,

——————— Σ ———————

hands outstretched. In one palm she held a hard-boil egg; in the other, her engagement ring. "Where's Barry?" I asked.

"That goddamned *schnook!* He's gone!"

"Gone, as in not coming back?" I asked.

"He's *gone!* I should've listened to you, that goddamned *schnook!* He bopped in and asked for his ring back—*I want my ring back!"*

She was holding the egg in one hand and the ring in her other. "Oh, Barb, what did you tell him?" I asked pitifully.

"I said, take the goddamned ring! I pulled it off my finger. Then he told me he wanted to give it to some bitch he's been seeing. The *schnook!"*

Tears welled in her eyes and rolled onto cheeks; she didn't cry. She made whimpering sounds, alternating between sob and laugh. "I wouldn't give him the goddamned ring. I won't wear it now in hell, Dean—he'll never get a chance to give it again. I told him, 'take this goddamned egg to the bitch—it's the *hardest* thing she'll ever get from *you!'"*

"Oh, Barb," I said, once more pitifully.

"Is that all you can say *'Uuh, Bahrb?'* I'm holding a goddamned egg and a goddamned ring, my whole goddamned life messed up, and this friggin', little queer can't say anything but *'Uuh, Bahrb!'"*

I knew she was hurting. "Oh, Dean," she suddenly broke, "I didn't mean that." She threw the ring and the egg on the floor. She threw her arms around me and she cried.

"I *never* should call you queer. You've been in love—you know what I'm feeling. I thought I knew—I'm glad you're here."

"Barb, it doesn't matter, you can call me queer anytime you want."

"You jerk! You let me stand here and make a fool of myself, bawling my eyes out calling you queer—you didn't give a rat's-ass shit?"

"Queer's one thing, Barb—don't call me *jerk!"*

"Know what?" she said, "I wish like hell I was a friggin' guy right now. You wouldn't get a chance to jack off—I'd eat you up!"

——————— Σ ———————

These are my boys, the boys who've loved me, and the boys whom I have loved. Watch over them. Hold them close, keep them near.

——————— Σ ———————

——————— Σ ———————

A gathering of angels

Shane was my cowboy. I met him in Houston on a weekend escape from Bay Prairie—the place where I returned after leaving New York. Houston was a regular haunt, especially its gay mecca Montrose near downtown. Life in Bay Prairie by any comparison was humdrum. In little more than an hour, I could emerge from my chrysalis amid the pulse of gay bustle.

Discontent wasn't altogether disliking for Bay Prairie. The change was what I needed. Open fields reaching beyond sight under blistering Texas sun had a soothing effect, its calm healing in mind and spirit. I hadn't been aware what wounds I carried. I stretched languidly once more in the sun's embrace, seeking in its warmth to regain inner sanctum I seemed to have lost. I don't imply indolence. Hard labor on the Texas range gave muscles of my body tone, its long hours tanning my skin deeply, bleaching my hair golden, as strands of honey—it was streaked, shimmering in sunlight.

I met Shane one afternoon at Dirty Sally's, a gay bar off Montrose Boulevard. A prominent feature of the bar was a large expanse of bay window fronting the alley between Westheimer and Lovett. A feeling of openness attended what otherwise may have seemed crowded and confining. I'm unsure exactly how we met—I am sure of immediate attraction. I sensed in Shane desire for me. I doubt in me desire was hidden from him—it blazed.

At times passion can be consumed in the heat of its own fire; at others, it smolders into obscurity. This was one time passion flamed with brilliance. It may seem I've not been circumspect, I've been overindulgent. Without the trappings of social convention, impulse is the drum's beat. I learned to seize opportunity, living life on its cutting edge. For as long as memory serves, it's been a matter of survival. It would be erroneous of me to say I inherited the trait. In one sense it is true—I came by it honestly.

Whatever the many reasons, none of which I intend to thrash, Shane and I fell in love with each other. Barbara might well ask how I could be sure he was saying love. I likely can give no better answer now than I was able

———————— Σ ————————

then, except to say I believed with sufficient heart to bare my most tender feeling and stand before him naked—vulnerable.

Chemistry between two people at times connects—merely wanting stubborn wrinkles removed. That's how it was with Shane and me. As we exchanged rings, I thought for certain we'd finally made it. Life for me in Bay Prairie became tedious. I filled lackluster days with thoughts of Shane, thoughts of his body, his eyes, his love. Endless nights were filled with the promise of him. A lifetime seemed to pass before the week, my every weekend devoted to Shane. We were ironing out details for my move to Houston, planning to share life together. It was for me a dream come true—I suppose I should've said a little prayer.

Shane was no slouch. He had a keen way about him, bending into me. The movement came first from the knee, then involved hip and back in a smooth flex of body coordination. Most often it was at Dirty Sally's he'd bend to me, Sally's having become *our* bar. That was hardly surprising—Sally's was a favorite among Montrose clubs.

Sally's occupied a place midway between cruise-bar and strictly-for-sex pickup. Sally's was fresh, one of the new bars Gay Liberation sprung. Light and open, sunny, airy and breezy—it held a decidedly *gay* atmosphere. That was before airy and breezy meant no clothes, before light and open meant sex with anyone, anywhere, anytime. Sunny didn't fit *post*-gay. Hardly two blocks down Westheimer and barely half a decade from The Stonewall Inn, another bar, Mary's, announced the end of Gay Liberation, announced it *loudly* rather than *proudly*—sleaze.

Sally's wasn't sleazy. It was a place two guys could go as a couple, spend the evening as a couple, then later leave as a couple—still together as a couple. Even at Sally's it wasn't a sexual thing Shane did, his bending to me the way he did. It always had with it his deep brown eyes, sometimes—often—tongue tipped against upper lip, moist and glistening. His eyes spoke to me heavily. *It's thrilling—should I believe it? It's thrilling!* Then, from alongside thighs, he'd slip his hands into mine. In one way it was a private message communicated, thoughts and ideas to be explored later at the Fran-Jeni, Shane's apartment on Alabama at Yupon. Shane's bending had its public address as well—*Take note, no rutting here!*

Ruggles on Westheimer inspired a variation of the bend. We went to Ruggles often for dinner, sometimes again late to share escargot and

———————— Σ ————————

drink White Russians. Being an upscale gay restaurant in the heart of Houston's Gay Montrose didn't lessen Ruggles' popularity—the food was worth the wait for a table. It was an in place broadly discovered, out for the cushiony who wouldn't stand for the wait. In the queue at Ruggles, Shane from behind would bend his knees into the backs of mine, just enough for me to feel his touch. I'd sneak a quick look over my shoulder into his big, brown eyes glinting above a moist, tongue-tipped lip. Shane found it easy to grasp hands in the crush of crowded wait, sandwiched with Houston's non-gay nouveau—bubble and beehive, bucket-butt and balding. To this crowd, Gay not only found its place, it kept to it—waiting tables.

Shane's bending to me wasn't an act of daring, teasing at Ruggles. It wasn't altogether he was in love with me—certainly he was. That was part of it—love *adores* fingers and hands. It wasn't a need he felt to be territorial, *Hey, no rutting here!* His playing was Shane's way of grasping community, sense of belonging. What he reached for stretched beyond immediate confines; beyond common characteristic and likeness of activity; beyond boundary of cultural bonding; was greater even than sense of gay subculture. Shane reached to a larger community—the community of man. I think in the absence of inclusion within that community he felt estranged, more so than a matter of sexual preference alone can warrant.

I guess what it amounts to is the worth and value placed by the totality of human beings on an individual's most basic and fundamental, his finest sense of self. Where appreciable worth is lacking, has been sufficiently downgraded, one is rendered nonessential, dispensable—the inescapable finality begging mankind's darkest question. Nowhere in a society can be found esteem more revered than in customs adhering to conventional love. I think more than anything it was that to which Shane aimed. Probably it was so, what he whispered to me one night waiting in line at Ruggles, "D'ya think *I* love *you* as much as *they* love *them?*"

"Sure," I whispered back.

"Unh-unh," he lip-tipped, "I love you *more!*"

It might have worked out for us had there been community to which we could belong, community other than gay. I liked our nights together. Shane was narrow at the hip, sloping shoulders broad—both, snug places into which I fit, burrowing deeply. He stood tall, was equally tall without cowboy boots. Between hip and heel he was precision honed. There was no

——————— Σ ———————

coarseness about Shane. He had the quality of gloved buckskin—supple even in making love. He wasn't rushed, not hurried. He'd close the door and stand with his back against it, gazing at me. His eyes did the talking. Those deep brown eyes knew the words. *Come to me, bend to me.* No command, that kiss; no command, that lithe body. *Come, surround me. Come to me, bend with me—come.*

I like to think we could have made it had there been a scrap of paper other than Shane's notebook kept day-to-day, his thoughts about us read to me on Friday nights. I like to think a scrap of paper as caring as letters and notes he wrote, as pretty as cards he sent, would've made a difference. I like to think we would have made it, had we been given the chance. It's what Shane wanted, to go with the rings we wore, a scrap of paper sanctifying our love—a scrap of paper we couldn't get from Hallmark.

Shane could've been the cowboy he dreamed. He rode tall in the saddle. He also rode the range. The last night I slept at Fran-Jeni I did so without Shane. He left me a note that Friday evening, was gone when I arrived. "Going to Gilley's with birthday bunch from office. Be home later— *you, too!* Love." Later, I was—Shane wasn't. Next day I went to his office, thinking we could have lunch. He had already grabbed a sandwich, "so I can get outta here early," he said, "see y'at home." I guess it was more than the community of man we needed. We didn't have the community of God.

I waited for Shane at the Fran-Jeni. He never came. My hunger passed—not the pain. I didn't want to go to Ruggles alone. I went to Dirty Sally's. After sometime I had to leave—the bar was too lonely without Shane. I walked down Montrose to The Midnight Sun, a bar recently open. I only intended to stop for a drink, check out the new club. I found Shane, in another boy's arms. I took his ring from my finger and placed it before him on the table. He pushed the ring across the table, sliding it back to me. "No, Dean. Put it back on your finger. *Please!* We can't *let* us be this way!"

"We can't help it, Shane." That was all I said. I could say no more— Shane's eyes were melting. I picked up the ring and placed it in his palm, closing fingers over it.

"Please, Dean, *please* don't do this," Shane begged. "I don't want the ring, I want you—I *love* you. *Please!*"

I could see—in his beautiful brown eyes—love. I couldn't see clearly —mine were misty.

———————— Σ ————————

"Shane, some words are not easy," I said, *"these* words—*I love you."* I had to say it choppy—my voice was choked. I had to leave quickly—I couldn't bear to see Shane cry.

I went back to Sally's, alone, where I remained until the bar closed. I walked again down Montrose. Two young men stood on the sidewalk out front at The Midnight Sun. They were handing out Jesus and God leaflets to sinners and sodomites, to the damned and the wretched, to blasphemers and those plain drunk. I was one of the latter—I should've been. I guess alcohol at times can't pickle—that night was such a time.

The younger of the two, age nineteen or thereabouts, called himself Bobby. He had dark hair and bright eyes, eyes the blue of iridescent lapis lazuli. Bobby handed me a leaflet along with his speech. "Jesus is waiting. He'll forgive your sins to God the Father if you repent."

"Tell me about this god," I asked haltingly, "what's he all about?" It wasn't mockery or jest prompting me. I was suffused with pain, numb. I would've begged for word of comfort.

"He's the God of Mercy," Bobby repeated by rote. "He'll save your soul from damnation through Christ Jesus who died for your sins!"

"My sins?" I asked with redundancy. As I did so, I truly couldn't think what *my* sins may be. Yet, the suffering I felt surely must be deserving of some large, unpardonable act.

"Yes," Bobby said, *"your* sins!" He swung his arm in a wide arc taking in all the gay bars and, I suppose, all the homos as well. *"These* sins— *homosexuality!"*

I hurt more deeply than I ever imagined possible; my hurt, one of love. I couldn't conceive anything more human. "Bobby," I asked him, "is *that* in the Bible? Is it *said* in the Bible, being gay's a sin?"

Bobby quoted verses, *several* verses. They seemed to satisfy him—a *well-versed* young man. I was stunned.

I had come to accept some aspects of life being cruel—Jim often called it a shit sandwich. I recognized a cruelty with which people oftentimes respond. Even religion I had long since abandoned—it had no room for me. To confront the Galilean as *hateful* is a thought even I found untenable.

"Jesus said all that?" I asked.

"No," Bobby said flatly. "Jesus didn't say any of it. It was all said before Jesus."

———————— Σ ————————

"Well, then," I wanted to know, "what *did* Jesus say?"

"Jesus didn't *have* to say anything," Bobby announced perfunctorily, *"God* said it. It's *in* the Bible—God *said* it."

I got an odd feeling, one that had about it a sense of calm—more, tranquillity. My body seemed to blend with a larger space. "Bobby," I said slowly, "I think I know this Jesus. I think this Jesus loves me. I *know* he must love me. When I'm in love I *feel* him near. I seem to *touch* him when I'm *making* love."

A mist of rain began falling—honest, it was raining! Bobby's friend said, "Pay no attention to him, Bobby. Can't you see he's drunk? Queer, too."

"Yeah, I am," I said. "I'm not *too* drunk and I'm not too *queer* to know Jesus. I know, if he were with us now, standing *here,* on this spot, he'd tell you so himself—*he loves me!"*

Bobby's friend was horrified. "That's saying Jesus is queer!"

"I didn't say *queer,"* I told him. "I said Jesus *loves* me. If loving *me* makes *him* a little bit *gay*—I guess Jesus *is* a little bit *gay!"*

"Bobby!" his friend shrieked, "Don't listen to that drunk queer!"

Bobby *was* listening. Bobby said, "No, let me hear this guy. I feel—something—what he says—he *believes!"*

I wasn't *too* drunk and I wasn't too *queer* to know *why* Bobby said that. I saw, surrounding me, clear and brilliant light!

"Come on, Bobby, le's get outta here. Don't listen to no drunk queer saying Jesus Christ is *one* of 'em. Besides, it's rainin' harder, we'll get wet."

I was left alone on Montrose, the street cleared, the rain unsteady. It didn't pelt, it didn't puddle—it shimmered on the street kaleidoscopic through my uneasy eyes. On Montrose I thought of Shane. In the rain I called his name. "Shane! Bend with me, Shane! Bend in the rain—*Shane!"*

Through that night I slept so very much alone at the Fran-Jeni. I thought Shane might return. I thought he might be there, he might come. I thought there may yet be words still needed. In Shane's bed, had he come, I know we would've said them. I know we'd have tried. I know—on the sheets I gathered round me was the smell of him. From the pillow where I laid my head a thought was tearing at me—I may not know *how* to love him.

That night, from Shane's bed, I saw the White Wings again. They came as before, sailed through the wall, a dove hovering above me; hovering with the words, *I'm leaving you awhile, I'll return*—then, swiftly, flew.

———————— Σ ————————

I thought the experience had to do with Shane and me. I was convinced of it when Shane phoned five months later. He left Houston for Austin where he was staying with his sister and new brother-in-law. During August he wrote, then we phoned one another. On Labor Day weekend 1975, I went to Austin. The apartment was in an area new to me, far out on North Lamar. Shane and I had makeshift on the living room floor. Next morning, early, the four of us, two couples together, drove out west in the newlyweds' compact car. Its rear seat and Shane's legs struggled all the way. We drove to Junction, then to Mountain Home, finally, Sonora. From the hot Texas sun we cooled in the damp Caverns of Sonora.

Shane was my cowboy again, bending to me along the tour path, slipping his hand into mine, stealing kisses amid fragile soda straws, embracing in the silent shadow of crystalline angel's wings. This was a time we didn't need to make statements, a time we just needed to be in love.

We drove from Sonora, scraggy butte and mesa burning fiery beneath a blazing red ball hanging low in an endless Texas sky. It had been a long day. Shane slept against me on the return drive to Austin. There, on North Lamar, words we needed to say were said. His brown eyes surrounded as he bent to me and whispered, "Come to me, come—I love you."

* * * * *

Shane was the last of my boys, the last of my loves. Of them all, it is Shane I yet love most dearly. It is Shane who loved me most dearly.

I'd like to tell what happened. I'd like to tell why our letters and phone calls couldn't bridge the miles that lay between us on the road from Bay Prairie to Austin—a road I know all too well. I'd like to tell why I've not seen Shane again. I'd like to tell why those words we said, words that held us bent together, weren't able to hold us together. I'd like to tell these things —if I could tell them, I, too, would know.

I reached a point where reason failed. What Shane and I found together was complete. I don't think we'd have needed that scrap of paper in Austin. Had we had it in Houston, there would never have been need in Austin. I like to think—I *believe*—we'd have made it, Shane and me.

I reached a further point at which reason foundered. What began in Austin, stretched on an endless highway, ended in Austin, stretched on the same highway. It had taken more than a decade—still it wasn't finished.

On a tiny patch of Houston's inner city, isolated from oil town's pace

———————— Σ ————————

and fury, I discovered a place giving me a feeling of sanctity and peace. Rothko Chapel at the University of St. Thomas was two blocks behind the Fran-Jeni. Philip Johnson created the Chapel's octagonal space to contain five large panels and three enormous triptychs painted by Mark Rothko, the Chapel's small space watched over in great detail by Rothko until he took his own life in early 1970. Exactly one year later the Chapel was dedicated. Placement of the panels today reflects Mark's arrangement of them then.

Rothko Chapel reflects Mark, too. Outside, it appears rather small and unimposing, having no windows and only a single pair of large entrance doors. That's its second juxtaposition. Once inside, space soars gigantically, out of proportion, out of human scale; soars out of physical capability; out of reach—beyond sensory ability.

Light enters the Chapel from a skylight dome. I was there when the dome was unrestricted, light harsh. I was there when heavy kraft paper taped together at seams hung suspended beneath it, an experimental scrim to soften Houston's sunlight, to meld Houston's sunlight into the softness of the panels it strikes.

The paintings themselves, the panels, overwhelm. At first glance, they seem massive slabs of black, hardly out of scale with their space. One forgets the limitation size arbitrarily placed on the exterior walls. Then one sees the panels are the windows—from the inside out, from without within, from within, beyond. One recognizes the dark, the unknown as truly being limitation. One recognizes in the solace of Rothko Chapel, in the solace of darkness, darkness itself is the window.

Each time I returned to the Chapel I got a sense of serenity, much like the feeling I'd known at my lagoon on Sargent Beach. I needed to know, tried to understand what force of circumstance kept Shane and me apart. The feeling that came was inner awareness I can only describe as placid; complacent, only to the extent it had with it a sort of assurance I can't explain. More than that I was unable to grasp—I'd been put into a sleep.

It happened sometime after I returned to Bay Prairie from my Austin weekend with Shane. Asleep in bed one night, I became aware of a stranger. He seemed to be at my side, near me or next. That's the place from where he rose, beckoning, "Follow." I felt the familiarity leaving my bed at the Chelsea as I followed him. He led me to a wilderness place, up the side of a gently sloping hill, weedy and brushy. He was cast in shadow before me.

——————— Σ ———————

A stark and hurtful light beamed against me, seeming to emanate somewhere in front of him. Near the top of the low hill he called out to me, "Turn and don't look at me until I've told you—you'll be blinded."

I did as he said. Before I heard him call to me again, I once more became aware of light about me. "Look now," he said.

He was at the top of the hill, not standing on the ground—near it. I stood before him, both our feet uncovered. They didn't touch earth. He was tall, his hair brilliant. It shimmered in waves, cascading his shoulders. The garment he wore seemed made of finely loomed cloth. Neither gauzy nor gossamer, it gathered in soft pleats about his waist, flowing delicately to his feet. From waist to neck and about the shoulder, the garment was tightly gathered in pleats, girded with a thin belting I thought shone like gold. Particles of light, like gold, flecked his hair and garment, swirled in brilliant light surrounding him—light so clear it had no characteristic other than brilliancy. Within its radiance, I felt a sense of deep warmth. The light didn't appear to shine onto him, it seemed to surround him.

He stretched forth his hand, "Come." I wasn't afraid. I stood above the ground before him, surrounded by light. The light didn't come from above. He was the light—it shined from him. I felt, within the light, love.

He said, "I've come, and you'll know." Before he spoke again, he put me into a sleep, that I'd hear but not understand, I'd know but not comprehend. He breathed into my mouth. Then, what he told me, I knew not.

After he'd spoken, he said to me again, "I've come, and you'll know. The love given is mine. Surrounding you I've placed a sign. Those who see will enter; others, pass. I've come, and you'll know. I am, I am."

I wasn't able to understand why these things happened or how they happened or the manner in which they happened. I knew the experience was extraordinary. Sporadically throughout the previous thirty years I had other experiences also more than ordinary. It became part of my life, one I accepted, though a part I seldom shared with others. Like the White Wings on West 23rd or the spirit-soul-death I experienced at Hotel Chelsea, such things seemed to be involved in matters others found uncomfortable. I found keeping silent easier than attempting explanation I couldn't give.

I tried to fashion from my experience on the hill a story. I couldn't hear what had been said, and I couldn't penetrate deeply enough the vision remaining within my mind to grasp answer to the question, I am *who?*

———————— Σ ————————

I'd been put into a sleep. Comprehension and understanding were denied. For these, I searched philosophies and religions of the East, Buddhism and Tibetan Yoga. It was necessary, in a way not explainable, to find in them answers that weren't there. That, indeed, is what I found. The great Tibetan Yogi Milarepa said, "The Divine Truth of thine own mind thou shalt see; and seeing That, thou shalt have seen the All—The Vision Infinite, the Round of Death and Birth and State of Freedom." Seen or merely glimpsed, I was convinced a speck of essence, though not readily accessible, could be touched if a quester determined the quest worth his effort. What ultimately left me unsatisfied was "the vision infinite, the round of death, birth and state of freedom." It was cold and empty, seemingly senseless. It held for me no promise and no reason. It held no warmth—no love.

I'd been put into a sleep. Logic failed. Within the systematic sphere of my own knowledge, I *knew* I was capable of love, capable of *giving* and *receiving* love; capable of *sharing* love. I *knew* there were times love lay at the tip of my finger. I also *knew* those times I reached out to grasp it, love seemingly was snatched from me. A thought crept surreptitiously through my mind—I'd been denied. My power of intellect became frail indeed. Love is the only thing in which I've been able to believe, the only thing for which I've lived, for which I would fight—the one thing for which I would die.

I'd been put into a sleep. I wasn't able to understand *why* and couldn't determine *how*. I was crushed, my rationale of life extinguished. From that point, I wanted to change my surroundings, escape Bay Prairie altogether. I felt there was little else available to me other than my being simply a gay person—Bay Prairie offered no access to my gay self. Twice during the next ten years I tried to escape. Twice I did leave, both times successfully. Circumstance each time intervened. In 1983, I once again returned to Bay Prairie, this time resigned to its environs. I came to accept within the phenomenon of some higher rationale it was the place determined I should be. I no longer thought of Slade, who was Pacer's buddy. I no longer thought of any other among my boys. I had no buddy. I had my Bud. I'd been put into a sleep. I acquiesced to a point of staying brain-dead on Budweiser. I tended my father's fields and his herd. The land was fertile and his stock grew fat. That's as close to Bible as I got. My Bud and I kept company—we slept together.

* * Σ * *

——————— Σ ———————

I knew Izzy most of his life. We became friends as he began the process coming out. That's the rite of passage, coming out. Ours wasn't a sexual relationship. That attraction wasn't there, not for Izzy or me. Intimacy of a different sort sprang between us, friendship. I have to say it was more than friendship—it was gay friendship. That's an important and special thing, particularly in a small town, especially for one who's gay.

His name was Arnold. He'd always been called Izzy, the reason seeming lost in obscurity. Izzy was native Bay Prairie. He never ventured forth. He commuted to nearby Junior College while working to buy his dream house. The old Victorian number needed lots of TLC, having escaped the wrecking ball of emerging modern Bay Prairie. The house had been moved to make way for a new supermarket. Izzy bought it—on Elm Street.

Elm Street says more about Izzy than ever I can—solid, old-fashioned values and ideals; a genuine homespun boy who caters to tradition and heritage. While Bay Prairie modernized, Elm Street revitalized, urban renewal with a contemporary kink—gay. Izzy snatched a closet from the middle bedroom, opened it onto the sun porch and slit its gut to create a bar. He had his name scripted in neon to hang overhead—*Izzy's!*

I'm tempted to say *Izzy's* was the *very* last of the Gay Liberation bars. That's not entirely true—it was never open to the public for business. The bar was always open and a lot of local talent passed through. It fast became a gathering place for the young and the restless, the bold and the beautiful, those searching for tomorrow with no guiding light. At *Izzy's,* one's business, no matter how private, was always public.

Early on, I urged Izzy to share with his folks his lifestyle. I'm glad I did and I'm glad Izzy listened. I knew he'd have a better life—he'd still have his folks. I knew *that* was important on Elm Street. Afterward, along with Izzy and lover of different times, I frequently was in company with Izzy's Mom and Dad, and Gran and Babba. It should be that way—on Elm Street.

I've heard it said, "Home is where, when you have to go, they have to take you in." Gay blood's that thick. That's the blood we shared, Izzy and me. I was there for him, from his first lover on, after he and his childhood sweetheart split. They were together for years—it's worth the saying they're still together as friends, his sweetheart's wife and their daughter included. A guy needs his gay friends to help absorb some of love's initial enthusiasm, needs them to help him balance it through summers and winters, to spread

———————— Σ ————————

the excitement on holidays and special occasions. He needs his gay friends to help hold him together when love falls apart and all his world with it. That's the blood we had, Izzy and me.

A bond of friendship can often be as strong as one of deeper love. I came to depend on my relationship with Izzy. It was unwavering and steady, had about it a sense of stability otherwise absent in my life. Partly I think stability came from intimacy of communication we shared. I didn't look on it as substitute for the intimacy of a lover, something for which I seemed not destined. Surely it somewhat filled a need for closeness to another human being. Perhaps it was that on which I placed too much confidence.

Toward mid-autumn 1985, Jimmy phoned from New York. After a few silent moments, he said hesitantly, "Jim's sick. He has AIDS."

I was dumbfounded. "Oh?" I gasped.

Between us on the line there was silence for a time. Then I asked quietly, "How is Jim?"

Jimmy said, "He's doing maybe pretty good—not real good, Dean. He looks pretty good—his skin, I mean."

I wasn't yet able to react, and I gasped again, "Oh?"

Jimmy thought I'd not heard clearly. "Well, to me, Jim looks good," he repeated. Then he asked, "Dean, do you know what I mean?"

I said, "Yes, Jimmy, I do. I know what you mean." I hadn't any idea beyond the terminal fact. That's really what Jimmy had asked, to determine if I was aware of AIDS confronting Jim with finality.

Jimmy told me cautiously, "Don't say anything about it—to Jim, I mean. Don't mention it. It seems to upset him—it's better if you don't."

I didn't know what to do—I'd never had anything like that to do. I could've written Jim. Instead, I phoned. Our conversation was warm though somewhat distant. Jim told me he had been ill—now feeling better. I didn't pursue the matter. I felt, in not doing so, I betrayed Jim and all we had become. Yet, neither could I be disrespectful—Jim was my brother. I intended to talk with him again. This conversation was our last. Much sooner than I thought possible, Jimmy called me again. "Dean, Jim is dead."

"Oh!" I tried—I couldn't grasp reality from words. Something inside I felt fly from me, gone. I couldn't talk. I replaced the phone in its cradle. Later, when there was sound still without words, I dialed Jimmy's number.

We talked awhile. Toward the end of our conversation, Jimmy said,

——————— Σ ———————

"It was quick, Dean. I don't think Jim suffered, at least he didn't suffer long."

I don't know if those words were ones I groped to hear. I don't know if they offered comfort. I thought of much together Jim and I shared. One thought left me numb, the thought of my own silence—knowing I hadn't shared with Jim during his final of life's events.

Death is not a matter I dealt with profoundly, not my own. It was too far removed. Death itself is remote. In youth it's heroic or tragic; by middle age, pushed aside—no one has time for it. In later years it looms an inevitability—unwelcome. Death isn't American, not the business of death. It's death the business that's American, a routine widely touted, putting one's affairs into order—the business viewpoint. The business itself—*death* —is mostly untouched, touched only by standard phrases, words learned by rote. Religion with its supposed faith and belief has become Americanized— not so much a way of life as an excuse by which to justify one's life and to excuse his death. That's hardly a way of preparation—commitment as a concept is more often the chink of coins tossed into a collection plate.

I wasn't able to understand how things happened, why they happened, the manner in which they happened. Jim may have been partly right, "What you want is something I don't think exists in this world."

Love, I've begun to think, doesn't exist in this world—rather, it doesn't *belong* in this world. Love has no part of the earth because love is not of the earth. It's ethereal, as are angels. Love belongs to regions beyond the earth. It is here for only a moment—it gets trampled, here in this dust.

Love is the only reality I've found, the only thing that doesn't pass away, isn't consumed or interred. Love doesn't enter the box. It departs, long before ash and dust settle ash and dust—*it is here for only a moment.*

Izzy didn't like it when I talked about *those things*. He preferred my gay Indians on Peyton Creek—delighted in telling about them. It began innocently enough, a time we camped at the creek. I looked across tall, green reeds lining the banks of Peyton. "Izzy, how wonderful if Indians suddenly stepped from those reeds!"

"Wonderful!" he exclaimed, "I'd run like hell!"

"So would I," I told him. "Straight into waiting arms!"

Izzy wasn't with me a later time when a canoe, paddled by two blond numbers—both near-naked—slipped up the creek. I told him about it. "Izzy, I saw Indians on the creek, two of them in a canoe—they were *blond!*"

——————— Σ ———————

"Unh-unh!" he reprimanded. "There's not any Indians on Peyton Creek—*certainly* not any *blond* Indians!"

They *might* not have been Indians. They *were* in a canoe and they *were* blond. Izzy kept telling the story, especially those times I arrived late to one of his parties. "There's Dean," he'd announce, *"finally!* It's those gay Indians, *blond* Indians he found on Peyton Creek. They waylaid him, stopped him in the middle of the highway—*with their canoes!"*

Izzy said it often enough it became almost believable—more real than the event from which it was created. Izzy didn't believe everything I said. Before he met his present companion but after breaking with his previous lover, we had one of our last afternoons together on Peyton Creek. It was breathing fresh air and letting the pain out, healing the wound. Izzy said, "Look at you, Dean, you've got everything, your own house, money, someday this land. It's all there, in the palm of your hand. I know you've worked for it, but you've got it all."

"No," I told him, *"things* are all I've got. What I've most wanted I've never had. I'd trade it all, Izzy, every stick and twig, down to the very last nickel, I'd trade it all for what I want—love."

I said to him, "Izzy, I don't know why or how—I can't explain. Here on Peyton Creek, I get a special feeling—gay is the way."

"Have you lost your mind?" he stammered. "Have you gone plumb crazy? Dean Hamilton, did you *listen* to what you just said? Do you think the whole world could be gay? Who'd be fuckin' and makin' babies so there'd be new queers? That's *plumb* insane—I don't want to hear no more about it!"

The final year of the '80s and the first of the '90s were the bleakest I'd known. It was frustrating when friends of years with whom I'd felt close abandoned me. It *hurt* when Izzy pushed me away. "Get your own life—stop botherin' me!" he said. "I'm sick of givin', givin', givin'—ever'body takin', takin', takin'. Startin' now, I'm livin' for myself!" It was harsh. I never parted even from a dispassionate lover with words that cold.

I couldn't understand why our friendship of so many years suddenly was being discarded. I searched within, groping for an answer. At different times we'd spilled our guts to one another. That's a part of living, a part of loving and a part of hurting. It's especially a part of being gay. I thought he understood that, our gay blood, as much as he'd understood my blond Indians. We each had our own Indians of one sort or another. It's what kept

——————— Σ ———————

us going—a private gay place where, at anytime, the reeds may suddenly part to let step through, toward us, love.

I'd always been a fifth wheel. It wasn't easy for me, being so near and yet so far from love. We'd each been there, one time or another. There had been many times Izzy heard me quote the first verse of what he called my Gay Gospel, *Hey! A lover's sacred!*

I was left with nothing. I had never felt so rejected and despised. On the banks of Peyton Creek I tried to sort through the rubble. An image came to mind—the living dictionary created by George and Joe, computer programmers for the IBM system at Time Inc. when I worked there. The IBM was their baby. They were especially proud of the living dictionary, once giving me a personal tour.

The entire IBM system was enclosed behind glass in a controlled environment—row upon row of gleaming cabinets with lights, buttons and switches. The living dictionary stood apart from the computer banks. At first glance, all I saw was a low pedestal holding a shiny metal dish. It resembled a large salad bowl, some sort of electronic finger standing in its center, the entire dish covered by a sealed glass dome.

There was nothing in the dish—it appeared empty. George and Joe assured me the dictionary was there, electronically swirling at some incredible speed. "Actually," one of them said, "it isn't there. It'll never be there. It's perpetually in an input state. If ever it were to be input, it would be static, dead. Every word from the IBM banks travels through it—a gigantic salad continually tossed but never eaten."

That's as near as I'm able to describe the state in which I found myself—a giant bowl with everything there, none of which could be grasped and none of which it seemed could ever have determination.

A sound I heard coming from within my body that afternoon was the same sound I heard coming from the body on the bed at Hotel Chelsea —a hollow, empty moan raging from inner depths. I felt I had nothing. I felt I was nothing. I felt surrounding me, nothing. I would've cried, had there been tears. I would've screamed, had there been reason. In such desolation, seeming without hope, there's only one action. I turned my back on that. Jim once made me promise. I refused to be a casualty confirming the helplessness and the hopelessness society dumps on gay.

I turned my face upward to heaven and I shouted, "I have love! *I*

——————— Σ ———————

have love! I'll *never* let it go. *Never* let it be taken from me—*it's all I have!"*

I may have known I was sick. By early spring '91 I could deny it no longer. I refused to see a doctor until unable to walk, massive blood clotting within my right leg. The night before my appointment, I downed several six-packs of Bud. "To hell with the shakes," I thought. "I'll worry with that later."

I remained in bed the next three months. It struck me oddly, I had no desire for beer; more oddly, I didn't get the shakes or DT's. During this time, I found a calm. I can't describe it as peace—certainly it had somewhat that quality. It was more a feeling of stillness, much like stillness described within the eye of great storms. The calm was healing, not of muscle and tissue, healing of spirit; healing in such a way my mind, my psyche was cleansed, made ready to attune itself to a different vibration; made ready to receive and to accept—free from the clutter of routine—an incoming signal. There was no sense of immediacy, no anticipation, as in a casual way one doesn't arbitrarily reach for the phone with predetermined knowledge it is at that moment going to ring. Insofar as can be related, that was my frame of reference as I lay in bed on one particular day. I'd been put into a sleep. Now, the time had come for me to awake.

From my bed I saw a book. It simply appeared, suspended somewhere outside my window within what seemed a bright cloud iridescent before the pale blue of clear firmament. The cloud wasn't of single whiteness. It ranged counterclockwise from soft white on its right to a darker gray, black like angry storm on its left. Within the stormy area I saw shafts of bright light and flashes like lightning.

The book was suspended open, every page leafed separately, though none randomly displayed and none discernible. It was suspended vertically, motionless, its covers a white so white light reflected in hue. The book neither sparkled nor glittered and neither did it glow; rather, it had about it a radiance that was more iridescent.

Somewhat in front of the book, in a space somewhere between me and it, I saw displayed a sequence of events I experienced *through* my life. The situation wasn't one in which my life ostensibly passed before my eyes. Those events which I saw had been especially culled, rid of any superficial clutter. They were events spaced over a wide period of years, events I'd not before seen as correlated beyond their being distinct experiences belonging to a single individual, myself. They flowed in startling detail, not separate or

———————— Σ ————————

separated, one folded into the next and that into the following.

I saw the events a continuum precisely focused *at* the instant of that moment. I saw they hadn't occurred randomly, accidentally or haphazardly. They'd been prefigured. Then I heard, coming from the cloud, coming from somewhere near the book, "Tell this as it happened. Tell this story of love."

Before I'd written the final sections of *Naked in the grace of heaven*, the open book appeared again. As before, its contents couldn't be distinguished. I now saw the book as something greater than at first I was aware. Initially, I presumed it to be symbolic of a book I'd write. At this second appearance, I realized otherwise—it was far more than that.

The words didn't come from the book. They came from somewhere near around it. The words came softly and gently, with clarity and assurance. They may have come with no voice at all—come they surely did.

"As you've written, you'll know. In an instant you were given light; those you've touched, chosen. That you go not alone through dark night are these given. It can't be comprehended; though shown, not seen. For what is promised was never at your hand; yet it waits.

"Say these things—

"Love's not despised. It's the way, the only. Those who love as you love will be shown; they themselves are loved, counted first among the first. The light is love, boundless, beginning, end. These things are written, no word pass from them; the mark, placed and sealed. Those who see and understand will come forth into light; others, fall to darkness.

"Say these things—

"Say, that I am."

* * * * *

I try to understand my vision. I think it was seen before. John said, "At first there came word; it was near, around god; god was near, within it."

We may travel different paths, our road long, the journey short. Still, it is a long night on the ferry—we are each alone. The human soul rails against darkness. What creature thus, however low or humble, does not cry out for comfort and assurance. Yet, in our frailty, we engage in tawdry commerce proffered as love. Love is of all one ether. The dwelling it makes within the human breast is more a matter of choice than circumstance. Love does not grow from within. Love is nourished and sustained from without. The wayfarer who opens forth his heart, freely, with no expectation, may one

——————— Σ ———————

———— Σ ————

day, in the still early hour before dawn, stand in the light of an angel.

What few words I'm able to utter may seem no more than spit on the wind. I have little doubt—God has not forsaken his angels.

*   *   *   *   *

Love's not for long being trampled, here in this dust. There's been a harvest; now, there is a gathering of angels.

——————— Σ ———————

Finally, I weep

I had not grieved for Jim until I marched with ACT-UP in Houston. At what would've been a rally at the end of a long march, I suddenly found myself surrounded within a narrowing ring—this, no schoolboy scuffle. I saw faces of hatred, heard voices of abomination. I witnessed wrath of the righteous. The spirit commanding me is as different from that as I am different from them. I can't now think spirit moves within hollow tombs, such as ones I once knew on Church Row in Austin.

Houston, we have a problem. We take our first steps onto the Free Speech area across from Houston's Astrodome. Inside, the Roll-Call by State will begin shortly, nominating George Bush for a second term in the White House. It is late afternoon, the sun hot. Pat walks beside me. He is twenty-nine and stocky, a coarse sort of boy but gentle. I am glad to feel him near me. We are hunted. Mounted troops march, single-file, within spitting distance. Behind them, foot squadrons approach, riot gear in hand.

The grassy area becomes quiet. People sense a situation in the making. Ahead, before I see them, I hear drums, NOW's signal corps. They expect us. The signal leader's head snaps alert. I read her lips, *They're here!* Three sharp cracks on the rim of her drum draw stillness. The drums explode—a different cadence, faster, louder. A large group of curious onlookers is forced to move away. Space quickly fills with queers and dykes, inheritors of the Pink Triangle.

Pat squeezes my hand. We stop. He looks suddenly into my face, eyes calm, searching. Neither of us speak. Pat smiles at me. *I'm holding your hand—I won't let go.* The corners of his mouth twitch. He squeezes my hand again, holding hard. The muscles of his jaw tighten. He presses me forward.

I met Pat three days earlier at Red Square, a gay club near downtown Houston—the club reserved as a place for gays to meet after the long march. Three days—a lot of silence; a lot of tears; mostly, fear. We were funneled into a concrete-and-wire canyon—trapped in ambush. And Death.

——————— Σ ———————

Pat and I connected at Red Square. He took me to the hotel where he lodged—ACT-UP had five floors. We slept together for comfort, flesh quivering. We huddled in darkness, trusting each other's body. Pat cried out in sleep. His body jerked in spasm. He sobbed in fits. I held him tightly. At last his body relaxed, his breath steady against my throat. I knew his unrest. I shared his dream—a nightmare too dark to face.

The drums roll a steady cadence—distant thunder before approaching storm. Daylight fades. The Death-Toll by State rises in oppressive air. A die-in begins. Bodies fall. Some boys are sick, others weak, all pressed by urgency—approaching death. More bodies fall. Beside me, on trampled ground, Pat's body is motionless.

I share his unrest. A warrior mounted atop steed towers before me. His hand grips a nightstick. His arm begins to move. The blunt end of his stick traces an arc, sweeps from the rear, soars like an eagle—high above the warrior's head. *Charge!*

I share his dream. This work is for men. They dress in splatter-proof rubber aprons, thick leather boots. They wear heavy gloves, wield stout sticks. Screams pierce the night. Dark thuds. Bodies bruise, break. After this night's work is done, these men go to their women. They lie with them and whimper. *Mama, I killed again!*

The Death-Toll continues. More people die. A young married couple join hands and fall. A single mother with two children beside her, drops. An old woman, her body stiff, struggles to the ground. Her shoulders heave. *This is what it's about.* Finally, I weep.

———— Σ ————

It is finished

He came during the evening a day I've not expected. I know him—he told me I would. I remember the time, one when our feet didn't touch the earth.

I remember what he told me. "Your work is over, your task done. It is finished. Let go of the earth. You can't hold it longer than it holds you."

He took me to a room. It doesn't seem spacious, though for only a simple table I suppose it was adequate. The others all had been there, now are gone, low stools and benches left scattered. Near the table, he has me lean against him, as I remember once having done.

He led me into what seems a garden. In a far corner he lays aside his staff. I know later he'll be waiting.

In another place, one I don't yet know, he showed me three moments. The first, the moment I'll leave with him, as I remember once having done.

The second, the way I'll follow him, as I remember on the hill in the wilderness having done.

The third, the place I await him, a place of sorrow I remember once having known. He'll be here—he promised to return.

Others standing nearby are looking on. He stands before me, his mantle worn loosely at the shoulder. He speaks, and I see light surround us, *This is my beloved—I'm pleased with him!*